TEACHERS AND PARENTS: THE ANTI BULLY

*Alleviating Childrens'
Danger Inside The Internet*

L. Wayne Reid, Ph.D.

authorHOUSE®

AuthorHouse™
1663 Liberty Drive, Suite 200
Bloomington, IN 47403
www.authorhouse.com
Phone: 1-800-839-8640

First published by AuthorHouse 9/28/2009

ISBN: 978-1-4389-5594-0 (sc)

Printed in the United States of America
Bloomington, Indiana

This book is printed on acid-free paper.

CONTENTS

(Pictured are Leslie and Margaret Reid (center) along
with the author and his children Kim, Lori, Tammy, & Michele)

ACKNOWLEDGEMENTS

This book is dedicated to my mom (Margaret Ellen Jones Reid) and dad (Frank Leslie Reid). They raised two boys and six beautiful grandchildren with the guidance and example of being friendly and helpful to everyone they encountered. Along with the Lord, they were the solid rock under my feet. They helped my brother (Frank Lynn Reid) and myself, Wayne Reid, learn positive ways of supporting our children, to stand up for them when necessary.

To My Tormentor

Have you walked through your own soul lately?
I'd be fearful if I were you.
You'll find the beginnings of scars,
Too small, now, to cause alarm.

One is called callousness, another ridicule.
They spawn hatred, mockery-
These metastasize into sadistic cruelty
Requiring victims to devour.

As you apply your poison with a keyboard,
The light from the monitor screen
Reflects in your eyes your spirit's decay.
Each anonymous attack robs you, not me, of humanity.

Oh, little cyberking, so magnificent in your own mind,
Won't you awaken and cast off the spell that binds you?
You can stop the evaporation of your soul.
Come back; kindness and joy can heal your wounds.
Join the living.

Carole Karber Reid

PART I:
Guidance For Children, Parents, And Teachers

Chapter 1:
Background of Study

The first personal computer built in 1976 is now in the Smithsonian. Tim Berners-Lee had an incredible vision for the Internet when he began development of the World Wide Web in 1989. It became a new standard for generations to come.

A 2003 survey by Pew Research discovered that more than 53 million American adults or 44 percent of adult Internet users had used the Internet to publish their thoughts, respond to others, post pictures, share files and otherwise contribute to the explosion of content available online. Today, creating content of all shapes and sizes is getting easier and easier. It is universally acclaimed for it's contribution to rapid communication, wider distribution of information, and enhanced commerce. High bandwidth Internet access and expanded computer memory and storage continue to grow. Children, exposed to the quickness of electronics have also become collaborators in the creation of a large storehouse of personal information.

What do our K-12 children want? Tech, tech, and more tech. From the latest cell phone to a new Apple i-something, technology increasingly defines the lifestyles of our children. Our children are the first generation to come of age on the Internet. As such, they have created their own virtual society. It is a world largely hidden from most adults. It has remained essentially invisible to teachers and parents. It is not a passing fad. Nobody is in charge. Society has never known a generation of children that were more social than this group. The Internet has created the greatest generation gap since Rock and Roll. Technology is starting to define what's cool in a way that fashion used to define what's cool. For most children, as long as it's technology, it's what's hot. In our youth's world, technology is power. Those who have access to this knowledge have a great advantage.

The difference between kids is maximized in America's 46,000 high schools. There are 1.8 million high schoolers in California alone. Thanks to the Internet, even the smallest high schools can offer classes tailored to a student's individual interests. Schools have used online learning to offer courses that would not otherwise be economically feasible. With online learning, students gain opportunities to explore interests while increasingly assuring charge of their own learning. They can use technological skills that will benefit them for years to come. Our children can go beyond the barriers of the school building and access a vast sea of knowledge. The Internet gives students access to types of resources that would be unavailable to them if they were learning from only a textbook.

The National Center for Education Statistics reported that 99 percent of American public schools have computers connected to the Internet. Add to this picture the omnipresence of Internet access at home and the near-ubiquity of mobile phones, many with text-messaging options, and parents can be guaranteed that our children are charging down the information superhighway at full speed. These characteristics also have introduced cyberbullying.

One 17 year old student said: "Every day, on a daily basis, I see people getting made fun of for whatever reason-their clothing, their smell, their intelligence level, whether they be extremely intelligent or unintelligent. It can be overwhelming, sometimes, how much bullying goes on."

National University's David Karell and Wayne Reid recently surveyed the bullying tendencies in four of Sacramento's major high schools and four middle schools. Forty-six percent of those surveyed in both high school and middle school indicated that they witnessed or experienced bullying at their schools. For those who were cyberbullied, the largest contributor was MySpace followed closely by use of the cell phone. Fifty-six per cent of the high school students and eighty-one per cent of the middle school students felt that bullying and cyberbullying was a significant problem at their school.

The Internet changed many things. Computer technology is now a conduit to the world-wide-web with access to every imaginable source of information. With the Internet, what semblance of control humanity may have had over technology, disappeared into the nether world of machines with artificial intelligence. (Saltinski, Ronald, 2008). The Internet has opened up marvelous opportunities for education and for the home. Most people who go online have mainly positive experiences. There is a vast array of services available online. Reference information such as airline fares, encyclopedias, movie reviews, news, sports, stock quotes, and weather are readily available. Users can conduct transactions such as banking, making travel reservations, shopping and trading stocks online. You can find information about your school, government, vital health matters, or read an out-of-town newspaper or watch television and listen to radio from thousands of online stations around the globe.

The Internet can be a wonderful resource for kids. It is a gateway to information throughout the world. They can use it to research school reports, communicate with teachers and other kids, and play interactive games. A child who is old enough to punch in a few letters on the keyboard can literally access the world.

The need to utilize the computer network has spiraled down to even younger children. Twenty-five percent of two year olds have their own television sets. It jumps up to 51 percent by the age of five. Twenty-four percent of grade four students access the Internet through their own personal computer. Twenty-two percent have their own Webcam. In grade eleven the number is thirty one percent. Twenty-three percent of students have their own cell phone with forty-four percent of phones having Internet capability. Fifty-six percent of student cell phones have text messaging and seventeen percent have built in cameras. According to the U.S. Department of Education, twenty-three percent of nursery school children in the United States use the Internet, 32 percent of kindergartners go online and by high school eighty percent of children use the internet. (U.S. Department of Education, 2003)

Educators and parents have showered children with technological equipment. No wonder that these children are more technologically advanced than most parents and teachers. Children today are more technologically savvy than any other generation. Today's homes and schools are faced with a difficult dilemma that pits a child that has grown up immersed in technology against an adult generation that is less facile with the tools of the trade. This is one of the first times in recorded history when the young people are leading the technology challenge ahead of the adults in their lives. Today's children, of almost any age, are far ahead of their parents and teachers in computer literacy. These students are literally "Digital Natives" who are well versed in the uses, superb performances, and capabilities of computers, digital cameras, cell phones, text messaging, and Weblogs. Technology has turned computer and software companies upside down, with each scrambling to adapt to Internet video, digital video recorders, mobile media devices and online social networking. It's a tech-heavy world that children take for granted.

Our youth are receptive to new technology in ways that adults find hard to understand. They are the early explorers in mobile technology. Some have adopted text messaging as a second language. The American Academy of Pediatrics notes that this technology reverberation can create craters of violence unheard of previously.

> ➤ **85 %**. Over 1,000 studies confirm the link between media violence and aggressive behavior in children. It is a classic confrontation between good and evil.
> ➤ **93%**. Today's 18 year olds will likely have viewed 200,000 acts of television violence within their lifetimes. It is a nightmare of world intrigue and deceit thrust on our children's emotions.

> ➤ **25%.** Saturday morning programming for children has more violent acts per hour than normal prime time- up to 25 acts per hour on Saturday as compared to up to 5 acts per hour during prime time. In 2001, television shows averaged 40 acts of violence per hour.
> ➤ **37%.** Students do not feel safe at school; 50 percent know someone who switched schools to feel better; 63 percent said they would learn more if they felt safer.
> ➤ **43%.** Teenagers avoid the school's restroom.
> ➤ **79%.** Student say violence is over stupid things like bumping into someone or the spreading of rumors; 55 percent of teenagers have seen weapons on campus.
> ➤ **15%.** In grades one through eight, 6 percent admit to bullying others at least twice a week; 15 percent report being victimized.
> ➤ **90%.** Students do not like to see someone bullied; yet 33 percent say they would join in.
> ➤ **4%.** Adults are aware of only 4 percent of the bullying and cyberbullying that goes on in and around campus. Someone is bullied every seven minutes. Students are using social networking sites more than many school officials may realize. Children ages 9 to 17 spend as much time using the Internet for social activities as they spend watching television-about 9 hours a week according to a 2007 study by the Alexandria, Virginia-based NSBA.
> ➤ **96%.** A NSBA study of more than 1,200 students found that 96 percent of those with online access had used social networking technology-including text messaging- and 81 percent said they had visited a social networking Web site at least once within the three months before the study was conducted.
> ➤ **60%.** By age 24, of identified bullies, 60 percent have a criminal record, 45 percent are alcoholics, and 55 percent have a personality disorder and seek mental health experts.
> ➤ **85%.** Studies reveal a cyberspace consistency where bullies strike fear in the hearts of opponents. They have become practitioners of the snub supreme;. trippingly written and

verbal insults come off their tongues.

➢ **65%.** "BuzzSpotters" indicates that 65 percent of teens plan to purchase one or two tech items this summer before heading back to school. More than half say they will buy tech items when they can afford them.

➢ **10%.** Only one in ten children is happy with the tech gadgets they have. 69 percent of teens prefer magazines to blogs. Magazines remain especially important to teen girls, who see them as a social, hands-on experience.

➢ **93%.** A recent study polled 680 United States participants; 93 percent say they prefer the Internet to television. Many say that they can watch television shows on the Internet so what's the point?

➢ **57%.** Wells' research found that 57 percent of teens prefer Facebook over MySpace; 71 percent choose text messages over instant messaging; 65 percent would rather use a Mac computer instead of a PC.

➢ **48%.** In the important civil rights agenda, another problem has materialized. The Public Policy Institute of California surveyed Internet users. Only 48 percent of California's Latinos use the Internet while 40 percent have Internet connections at home. That compares with the 80 percent to 82 percent of blacks, whites and Asians who use the Web- and 70 percent to 77 percent have access at their homes. Knowledge is power and particularly in the Information Age of a postindustrial society like we have today.

➢ **37%.** Researchers interviewed more than 2,500 people in five languages and found that income is a major factor in understanding Internet use. Those with incomes of less than $40,000 a year had similarly poor usage rates as Latino; 37 percent of respondents cited the cost of a computer as the main reason they didn't have a computer at home. The gap between the wired and unwired is growing. The airwaves bombard us with Web sites and email addresses we should use, and the assumption is that the consumer has access to a computer. And unfortunately, many of our families don't.

The fastest growing age group for using the Internet is two to five year olds. For the tots of Generation X and Y, parents' encouragement of computer use has created children who may think differently than their parents. YouTube videos have been a learning tool on everything from potty training to "Wheels on the Bus" videos for two year olds. Some parents jump through time, inserting a healthy dose of what they once learned from or at least laughed at. Together with their parents, two to six year old children watch cartoon episodes like "Droopy" or "Tom and Jerry" or watch old Judy Garland and Fred Astaire clips. One mom has her youngsters tune in to Spanish language videos of children's songs thereby turning to the computer for their musical education. If a youngster is talking about skiing, parents will YouTube the videos of skiing or for being an astronaut, to YouTubing footage of the first moon landing. Others YouTube the U.K. episodes of "Thomas the Train" that Ringo Starr narrates. Still others can YouTube across the world for the Korean egg song or Korean and Chinese adoptions.

As these children learn to surf the Net, sometimes the art of insult permeates their culture. Whereas children are trained to multitask well, parents and teachers are unable to do so and the gap is widening. It has become a period of total eclipse from the shelter of parents on the home front.

A national poll by Cox Communications and the National Center for Missing and Exploited Children of "tweens", kids ages 8 to 12 revealed additional information about Web sites. One in 10 of these pre-teenagers have responded and chatted online with people they don't know. The poll described a child's cyberspace world where 90 percent of American kids have used the Internet by the age of 9 and more than a third of the 11 and 12 year olds have their own profile on social network sites such as MySpace and Facebook. Of the tweens with social network profiles, 6 percent post personal photos online, 48 percent admit to posting a fake age online and 51 percent have received messages from people they didn't know.

The survey showed tweens online presence doubles or even triples in the age range of 8 to 10 and 11 to 12. The 42 percent of 8 to 10 years olds with personal email accounts increases to 71 percent for 11 and 12 year olds and 41 percent of 11 and 12 year olds have an instant Messaging screen name compared with 15 percent of 8 to 10 year olds. Half of the 11 and 12 year olds have their own cell phones-used for text messaging and taking and transmitting digital photos as well as for traditional calling; 19 percent of the 8 to 10 year olds have their own cell phones. The study also showed that tween girls are much more socially active online than are boys. The girls were more apt to have emailed, chatted over IM, posted photos of themselves and friends and updated their social network profiles than were boys.

Life without the Internet is virtually unimaginable from elementary school to college. As involved as our youth are, many older adults are simply not plugged in to the Internet. A recent study by the Pew Research Center reported 85 percent of adults in the 45 age bracket generally are finding good use of the Internet. However, only 35 percent of Americans over age 65 are online. They might be classified as those in "digital denial." But when you account for factors like race, wealth and education, the picture changes dramatically. About three-quarters of white, college-educated men age over 65 use the Internet. What keeps some American seniors unwired? Some lack immediate access to a computer. But intimidation is the greatest problem. One has to be compassionate with a person who hasn't gotten onto the information highway early, because the cumulative vocabulary is so intimidating.

Unfortunately, the huge scale of grand and grandeur advances in computer and telecommunications technology that allow our children to reach out to new sources of knowledge and cultural experiences are also leaving them vulnerable to exploitation and harm by cyberbullies and computer sex offenders. Like any endeavor, there are some risks and annoyances. Most people are decent and respectful, but some may be rude, obnoxious, insulting or even mean and exploitative. Children get a lot of benefit from being online, but they can also be targets of crime, exploitation, and harassment. Trusting, curious and anxious to explore this new world and the relationships it brings, children need parental supervision and common-sense advice on how to be sure that their experiences in cyberspace are happy, healthy and productive.

Adults have undergone bullying for many years as well. Studies of adults reveal that 37 percent of United States workers have experienced bullying and abusive conduct. The largest scientific survey of bullying in the United States was completed by WBI-Zogby International and sponsored by WAITT Institute for Violence Prevention. In 2007, the survey conducted 7,740 interviews. Among their more significant findings was that 37 percent of workers have been bullied (54 million Americans). An additional 12 percent witnessed the bullying. Most of the targets were women (57 percent); 62 percent of employers ignore the problem; 45 percent of the targets suffer stress-related health problems. Additional research found that the victims suffered debilitating anxiety, panic attacks, clinical depression and even post-traumatic stress. Once targeted, a person has a 64 percent chance of losing their job for no apparent reason; 40 percent of the bullied individuals never tell their employers. Only 3 percent of bullied people file lawsuits whereas 49 percent of workers report neither experiencing nor witnessing bullying. Hence, there is a "silent epidemic."

Research reveals that there are 3 children seriously bullied in every classroom across the United States. Bullying affects 5 million students every year. The United States Department of Justice estimates that 160,000 children stay home from school every day because of bullying. Yet, parents do not always observe it, thus they may not understand how extreme bullying can become. The Kaiser Foundation found that of those students interviewed, three fourths said bullying is a regular occurrence; 86 percent of children between the ages of 12 and 15 said they get teased or bullied at school.

This book is a call to understanding and action. It is not diatribe, nor a manuscript of long-winded aspirations. It is an attempt to assist parents and other adults to avoid an impending disaster. "Teachers and Parents: The Anti-Bully" peers inside the world of this cyber-savvy generation through the eyes of parents, educators, researchers, technology wizards, and children who often find themselves on opposite sides of a new digital divide. Teachers and parents are asked to picture grass growing in the streets, planets in collision, a conspiracy so immense, a time so black, as to dwarf any children's problems in the history of man. This is a generation with radically different notion of privacy and personal space where today's children are grappling with issues adults never had to deal with: from cyberbullying to instant Internet fame, to the specter of online sexual predators.

The contents of this book are designed to assist teachers and parents in helping their children to effectively deal with bullying and cyberbullying. Although children are much more familiar with modern technology than adults, just being facile with the devices, just being operationally skilled with the machinery, doesn't mean you know how to use it. If a child does a Web search and comes up with 5 million hits, anyone can do that very easily. It is what the child does with those 5 million hits, how they narrow it down and look for bias and other things. It is a skill that parents and teachers in large measure have more expertise than young people. It is recognizing that students have something to learn from adults about information management and knowledge creation and bias and perspective and literacy and a whole range of topics that the technology can enable.

The book will help teachers and parents know "What is the Internet? What is Cyberspace? What is YouTube?" They will be taught how to go online and learn, for instance, vocabulary at: http://about-the-web.com/shtml/glossary.shytml.

Teachers and parents must put a proverbial noose around the bully's and cyberbully's neck' to save the remainder of our children. It is to put an end to the original 'Evil Empires' reign of dominance. That empire is one composed of bullies and cyberbullies.

Look at the comment by the early anti-bully advocate, Dan Olweus.

> *"Every child should have the right to be spared oppression and repeated, intentional humiliation, in school as in society at large. No student should be afraid of going to school for fear of being harassed or degraded, and no parent should need to worry about such things happening to his or her child."*

Every child has the right to be treated with dignity. Every child has the right to go to school, concentrate on their schoolwork, and not fear for their safety. Almost every state constitution guarantees a child's rights. Article 1, section 28(c) of the California Constitution guarantees the right to safe schools. All students and staff of public, primary, elementary, junior high and senior high school have the right to attend campuses which are safe, secure, and peaceful. The California Student Safety and Violence Prevention Act (Education Code 220) states that "no person shall be subjected to discrimination on the basis of sex, ethnic group identification, race, national origin, religion, color, mental or physical disability, sexual orientation, gender identity; or any basis that is contained in the prohibition of hate crimes." Federally, 18 U.S.C. Section 241 prohibits conspiracies to injure, oppress, threaten or intimidate a person who is exercising rights protected by the constitution or laws of the United States. Such rights include the right to attend school and the right to occupy a home free of violence.

Let us understand from the outset, there is a form of violence in our society today that is chronic, pervasive and harmful to a large number of our children. The greatest problem young people are experiencing in our schools today is bullying and cyberbullying. It is the new "wild west" where nobody seems to be in charge. With it's proliferation of pictures and videos, some 15 percent of children state they have been bullied regularly or are themselves bullies. This translates to approximately 5 million elementary and middle school students. Direct bullying seems to increase through elementary school, peak during middle school and decline during high school. While physical assaults decrease with age, verbal abuse appears to remain constant. Cruelty may be far removed from some people's experience, but it is a daily reality to others.

Children become like their environment and our environment becomes like them. While many generations have viewed the phenomenon of social cruelty as a childhood rite of passage, research has shown the early isolation some children experience can follow them throughout their academic careers, sometimes leading to depression, low self-esteem, thoughts of suicide, and violence. Today, our American culture views hazing as fun and exciting. In an environment where bullying has created a climate of fear and anxiety students pay a terrible price physically, emotionally, and academically. America's obsession with fun apparently gives children and adults alike license to justify almost any type of behavior, no mater how abusive. The parents of those who have taken their own lives wonder why it is considered fun and exciting to demean another human being.

Cyberbullying and bullying acts against our children are looked at differently when directed at our children rather than at other adults. Adults have legal guarantees to help them in civil rights violations, but our children simply do not. When similar bullying acts are directed against adults they are called theft, extortion, stalking, threats, assault and battery. In our weird technological society, adults can stop them, but children cannot. Societal and school loopholes may allow cyberbullying and bullying to occur without benefit of policy to specifically address these behaviors.

Parents and teachers are starting to realize that they too are joining other victims in appearing as guest performers on YouTube or MySpace complete with unflattering comments. Change does not come with one Parent Teacher Meeting or by simply instituting an antibullying policy. Change takes place on a larger scale and requires significant amounts of time and effort. As importantly, this violation of human rights is occurring worldwide.

The term globalization has taken on many meanings, but one fact is indisputable- we now live in an interconnected and interdependent world. Internationally, most parents truly care about their children. The Japanese word for bullying is "Ljime"; in South Korea it is "Wang-ta." Another expression is "Tae-wum/Tae-wugi which means to burn something. Regardless of which continent a parent or educator lives, our obligation is to teach our children what is acceptable and safe and what isn't. Most teachers and parents appear to be doing the best they can, yet they need to ask themselves, "Can I do better?" Adults need to challenge themselves to do better. One of the most difficult roads to navigate in the technological world is how to balance the safety of the child with the benefits that come with students taking ownership of the work they do. Globally, cyberbullying may be grounds for legal action.

Unfortunately, in the United States we foster, warrant and accept aggression. When this happens, it affects the entire family unit. It can even become an explosive family. This family is in a fragile state. Whenever their children are being bullied or cyberbullied, parents do not have to manufacture a sign and march down the street with banners to demand social justice. They simply must speak out and act. This type of courage is speaking out when you want to be silent.

Like the school, the home is responsible. Kids who live with yelling, name-calling, put-downs, harsh criticism or physical anger from a sibling or a parent may similarly act out either on the schoolyard or online. They are driven to prove their superiority by the very actions played out in their homes. Teachers and parents are the real role models. Around their children, teachers and parents need to learn how to keep their own behavior in check.

It is our sacred responsibility to our children. While children need a certain amount of privacy, they also need parental involvement and supervision in their daily lives. The same general parenting skills that apply to the real world also apply while online. Educators and parents need to help children learn effective methods of stopping the cycles of violence that plague them. Cyberbullying and bullying behaviors, left unchecked, are some of the seeds of our violent society. Unchecked aggression in childhood becomes a life-long pattern.

Each teacher and parent has a God-given responsibility to protect the child. You have a major responsibility to get involved. You must become the sentries. Begin a dialogue with your kids about Internet use. Help them understand what to do if they are being victimized.

"Life affords no greater responsibility, no greater privilege, than the raising of the next generation." (C. Everett Koop) Adding to this statement Alvin Price said, "Parents need to fill child's bucket of self-esteem so high that the rest of the world can't poke enough holes to drain it dry." Parents and teachers need to help their child fully understand that despite how terrible they feel or what others do to them. There is a divine purpose for their life!

As parents we are the first and perhaps most important block in building a child's self-images. In this technological society inundated with cultural misinformation, negative messages and stereotypes, doing so can seem more of an uphill journey than Jack and Jill and the water pail. But while we cannot keep our kids from falling down, we can certainly become more vigilant in making sure their self-images don't.

James Dobson has always placed a great emphasis on quality parenting. He admonishes parents and teachers to protect that self worth, that soul of a child. The child's life has been exacerbated by the culture today. Hollywood, MTV, and other such things are doing immeasurable harm. Kids are being bombarded by these lingering messages. Adults are finding problems protecting their kids. This culture is all consuming. It is like a river. We are all in the river being swept along by the current. It is very hard not to get wet.

From Norway to Japan to England to Australia to Canada to Lithuania to the United States, bullying and cyberbullying problems of youth exist for teachers and parents around the globe. The Internet has forced our children's world into close proximity with each other. In each country, youth are battling with issues their parents never had to deal with. They are virtually trying to be someone they are not. As the following poem maintains, children are wearing different masks, one for their friends, one for their parents, one for the classroom, and one for themselves.

Don't be fooled by me!
Don't be fooled by the face I wear.
For I wear a mask!
I wear a thousand masks!
Masks that I'm afraid to take off.
And none of them are me.
Pretending is an art.
That is second nature to me.
But don't be fooled, please.
Don't be fooled!
Who am I, you may wonder?
I am someone that you know very well.
For I am every man and every woman
That you will ever meet.

CHAPTER 2:
INTRODUCTION

Our children are our Nation's most valuable asset. They represent the bright future of our country and hold our hopes for a better Nation. Theirs can be a story full of soul and spirit. Yet, our children are also the most vulnerable members of society. As humanity's heart grows cold, parents must protect their children against fear of harassment and crime and from becoming victims of bullying and cyberbulling. It must become a national priority.

The most important task as for adults is to raise children who will be decent, responsible and caring individuals devoted to making this world a more just and compassionate place. Neil Kursham in "Raising Your Child to Be a Mensch" feels that parents and teachers can fashion for themselves and their children a warmer, kinder world that will dispel the darkness of the isolation.

The North Star for parental and teacher upbringing of children is the heart. It is the ability to let your child know that you love and trust them. It is to enhance the child's self-confidence.

➤Behavior patterns begin at the home. A child's self-esteem is built into people from early childhood and is associated with what has been termed "positive parenting." This includes showing love and respect for each child through verbal and nonverbal demonstrations of appropriate affection and encouragement and ensuring that a sense of securing for the young person is provided in the home.

SCHOOL SHOOTINGS
violence, hot temper,
panic, aggressiveness, terror
BULLYCIDE
hopelessness, exclusion,
degrees of nastiness, ostracism,

frustration, humiliation, ignored feelings,
fear, peer conflict, low self-esteem, isolation
CYBERBULLYING
Internet, cell phones, anonymous,
harassment, discrimination, social exclusion,
student conspiracy, 24/7, low morality, defamation,
Little adult supervision,
PREJUDICE
taunting, scape-goating, name calling, epithets, fighting,
ridicule, social avoidance, de-humanization, assault
ACTS OF BIAS
stereotyping, bad jokes, rumors, acceptance of negative,
insensitive remarks, threats, lack of empathy, teasing, profanity

Hate & Harassment Triangle

Today's youthful society can become a real scary place to live. Acts of violence may be directed at individuals, institutions, or entire communities. This violence has a direct impact on individuals and violence directed at individuals. Youth under twenty-one years old constitute less than a third of the population, but they commit half the known bias crimes. In about two-thirds of the school shootings that the United States Secret Service reviewed, the attackers had felt persecuted, bullied, threatened, attacked or injured by others. The agency found that a number of the children had suffered sustained, severe bullying and harassment. The experience appeared to play a major role in motivating the ensuing violence. In his work on ostracism, John Steinbeck found that thirteen out of fifteen shooters were precipitated by ostracism. His quote for the victims was: "If I can't be liked, at least let me have an impact!" Whenever a child's brain is affected by serious bullying, it is like that portion of the brain is hit hard with a hammer or one burns his hand on an open flame. It shifts a child's view of his/her life to be even more meaningless.

In this society, when school lets out, kids flock en masse to their favorite social networking site. It is a continuation of their existence. This generation is more comfortable with being less private without realizing once they are on the net, it is open to everyone. Another person can always find everything on the Net. A child's bad judgment may make a child pay for it forever. They seem to take things much less seriously. The Internet marketplace breaks into "tribes" said Tina Wells, CEO of Buzz Marketing Group. She said two of them are Preppies, the popular kids, and Techies, who "five or six years ago were called nerds and geeks." As times have changed, these are really cool kids. They are the ones that know about an iPhone eighteen months before an iPhone comes out and they teach a Preppie how to use it.

The magnitude of the challenge is strengthened whenever a teacher or parent wants the child to be a good reader. Being a good reader of literature is disappearing in the age of the Internet. Books are not our children's things any more. For instance, Natasha Vogel is fifteen years old living in Lewisville Texas. Her mother wants to entice her to read by bringing home volumes of reading material from the library. Instead, Natasha is addicted to the Internet. She regularly spends about six hours a day in front of the family's computer. Natasha checks her email and peruses myyearbook. com, a social networking site, reading messages or posting updates on her mood. She searches for music videos on YouTube and logs onto Gaia Online, a role-playing site where members fashion alternate identities as cutesy cartoon characters. But she spends most of her time on quizilla. com or fanfiction.net, reading and commenting on stories written by other users. She is still an "A" student at school.

This type of child lies at the heart of a passionate debate about just what it means to read in the digital age. The discussion is playing out among education policymakers and reading experts around the world. As teenagers' scores on standardized reading tests have declined or stagnated, some argue that the hours spent prowling the Internet are the enemy of reading. But others say the Internet has created a new kind of reading, one that schools and society should not discount. A child's involvement with the Internet entails some engagement with text. Many think it is unrealistic to expect all children to read "To Kill a Mockingbird" or "Pride and Prejudice" for fun. Some literary experts say online reading skills will help children fare better when they begin looking for digital age jobs.

Some Web evangelists say children should be evaluated for their proficiency on the Internet just as they are tested on their print reading comprehension. Starting next year, some countries will participate in new international assessments of digital literacy, but the United States, for now, will not. Next year, the Organization for Economic Cooperation and Developing, which administers reading, math and science tests to a sample of fifteen year old students in more than fifty countries, will add an electronic reading component. It is important to realize that most of our young people are not as troubled as some of we parents are by reading that doesn't go in a line. Actually, this may be a good thing because the world doesn't go in a line, and the world isn't organized into separate compartments or chapters. Web proponents believe that strong readers on the Web may eventually surpass those who rely on books. Reading five Web sites, an op-ed article and a blog post, experts say, can be more enriching than reading one book.

Yet, many traditionalists warn that digital reading is the intellectual equivalent of empty calories. They argue that writers on the Internet employ a cryptic argot that vexes teachers and parents. Zigzagging through a cornucopia of words, pictures, video and sounds, they say, distracts more than strengthens readers. And many youths spend most of their time on the Internet playing games or sending messages, activities that involve minimal reading at best.

"It takes a long time to read a four hundred page book," said Rand J. Spiro, professor of educational psychology at Michigan State University. "In a tenth of the time, the Internet allows a reader to cover a lot more of the topic from different points of view." Kids are using sound images so they have a world of ideas to put together that aren't necessarily language oriented. Books are not out of the picture, but they are only one way of experiencing information in the world today. Still, Web readers are persistently weak at judging whether information is trustworthy.

In one study, Donald J. Leu, who researches literacy and technology at the University of Connecticut, asked forty-eight students to look at a spoof Web site (http://zapatopi.net/treeoctopus/) about a mythical species known as the "Pacific Northwest tree octopus." Nearly 90 percent of them missed the joke and deemed the site a reliable source. Reading and comprehending are not the same.

Six independent studies help both teachers and parents conceptualize the magnitude of the challenge before them.

- o (1).American Association of University Women (AAUW) Educational Foundation. 2,064 students, ages 8 to 11 were surveyed. 83 percent of girls and 79 percent of boys experienced some harassment in their schools. Locker rooms and rest rooms were pointed out to be the worst areas.
- o (2).Kaiser Family Foundation and Nickelodeon Television. Survey of 823 children and adolescents. 55 percent of 8 to 11 years olds and 68 percent of 12 to 15 year olds said that bullying was a "big problem" for people their age. 74 percent and 86 percent said children were bullied in their schools.
- o (3).The Journal of American Medical Association (JAMA). Close to 30 percent of students said that they were somehow involved in the bully-victim relationships either as a bully, victim or both. The report concluded that the prevalence of bullying among United States youth is substantial.
- o (4).According to Parents Resource Institute for Drug Education (PRIDE), 40 percent of youngsters in grade six through twelve have threatened to hurt another student at school. Some in the field estimate that 75 percent of

adolescents nationally have been bullied at some time in school. Other estimates claim that 10 percent to 15 percent of kids are bullied on a regular basis.

- o (5).The 1999 United States Department of Justice survey reported that 13 percent of students ages 12 through 18 reported that someone at school had used hate-related words against them. That is, in the prior six months someone at school called them a derogatory word having to do with race/ethnicity, religion, disability, gender or sexual orientation.
- o (6).The National Resource Center for Safe Schools (NRCSS) explained bullies identified by the age eight are six times more likely than non-bullies to be convicted of a crime by the time they reach age 24 and five times more likely to end up with serious criminal records by age 30. Children who are chronic bullies seem to remain bullies as adults. (NRCSS, 1999).

Former director of the Federal Bureau of Investigation, Louis J. Freeh, said the same advances in computer and telecommunication technology that allow our children to reach out to new sources of knowledge and cultural experiences are also leaving them vulnerable to exploitation and harm by cyberbullies and computer-sex offenders.

Today's children have an entertainment system at their fingertips. Kids can read stories, tour museums, visit other countries, play games, look at photographs, shop and do research to help in their homework. The services are world-wide. Twenty-four percent of grade four kids have access to the Internet through their own personal computer. That number climbs to fifty-one percent by grade eleven. twelve percent of our children report having their own cell phone and 44 percent of these have Internet capability with fifty-six percent having text messaging. seventeen percent of these have cameras. 22 percent have their own Webcam.

As these percentages indicate humankind has allowed themselves, and will continue to allow themselves, to drift into a state of umbilical dependence upon machines. In a world of their own making, youth will find it easier and expedient to allow machines to make more and more decisions independent of human intervention. (Weizenbaum,) Thomas

M. Georges echo's these comments by explaining that "in time, especially as machines are designed to run faster and self-program, humans will be incapable of understanding the manner in which the machines manage and control all those essential functions critical to human survival and well being." (Georges,) Is it possible that this time is upon us today?

It could be as adults and children use email to communicate rapidly and cost-effectively with people all over the world. Email transmits messages, documents and photos to others in a matter of seconds or minutes. Social networking sites allow kids to express themselves and keep in touch with friends exchanging messages or comments and posting personal profiles describing who they are and their interest, blogs or online diaries, photos, creative writing, artwork, videos, and music. Webcams, microphones, and digital cameras allow kids to post videos, photos, and audio files online and engage in video conversations. Kids often use this equipment to see each other as they IM and chat. P2P allows kids to exchange files without having to go through a web site or other centralized system. Here kids can exchange music, videos, movies, photographs, documents and software.

As the younger generation shifts to texting and instant messaging, some think the "old-fashioned" way to communicate is dying. One senior suggested he uses email really sparingly. To him email is reserved for communicating with teachers or-oh, the irony- getting MySpace and Facebook notifications. Another senior says email offer less at your fingertips convenience. He says that he is attached to his cell phone. He really only uses email for sending attachment or keeping up with school assignments.

Microblogging sites such as Twitter and programs such as Skype, which allow users to make phone calls using the Internet, are popular. A pair of 2007 studies conducted by the Pew Internet and American Life Project showed that teens are steadily drifting away from the old-fashioned medium. While ninety-two percent of surveyed adults said they regularly use email, only sixteen percent of teens made it a part of daily life while text messaging (thirty-six percent), instant messaging (twenty-nine percent) and social network site messaging (twenty three percent) gained in popularity.

Our children's generation cannot remember life without the Internet, and most teens think they are pretty savvy about Internet safety. Yet, our youthful society is a hamlet of violence. Bullying is the name of the game. This includes fighting, threatening, name-calling, teasing, excluding someone repeatedly and over time. There is an imbalance of power, such as size or popularity. There is always physical or emotional harm to the victim. The bully will keep bullying as long as it works. A recent British survey revealed that one in four youths, ages eleven to ninteen has been threatened via their computers or cell phones.

Adults have welcomed the computer and the Internet for all of its' amazing academic abilities. But the flip side of the coin is that the misuse of technology has caught both parents and educators off guard. Overseeing our children in cyberspace is a terrific logistical problem especially when any child may access it just about anywhere, anytime, day or night. The sender is often anonymous or disguised as someone else.

This misuse of technology has caught most adults off-guard. Cyberbullies are an inflammatory bunch. They send mean, vulgar, or threatening messages or images quickly and to a wide audience. Animosity is a given. Cyberbullies can post sensitive and private information about another person, pretend to be someone else in order to flame their victim, or intentionally exclude someone from the group. They can cyberbully each other through emails, instant messaging, text or digital messages sent on cell phones, web pages, web logs (blogs), chat room or discussion groups and other information communication technologies. Cyberbullying runs the gamut from minor incidents to major concerns, all of which should be addressed by adults. At the major concerns level, the students who are victimized can become very depressed. They are likely unable to study or focus in class and may avoid school leading to school failure. At the worst end, some are committing suicide. Others are engaging in school violence.

To these children the Internet has become a place where hidden agendas and false information can trip up both youth new to a topic and adults searching for credible sources of historical data. Children do not know how to discriminate when doing research online. They do not know how to evaluate a Web site. They do a "Google" search and whatever comes up for them is reality. Even a child working on a school homework project can become disillusioned. While sitting at the home computer, a child can be browsing collections such as the photographer Mathew Brady's classic pictures from the Civil War or watch Thomas Edison's early films through the Library of Congress' site. But elsewhere on the Web, they may stumble across sites that deny the Holocaust took place or that propound other wild and inaccurate claims. A child can type in certain words to do a search and Holocaust denial sites jump to the top of the list. That is kind of scary for parents and teachers.

A child who is working on the civil rights movement will begin to surf for information. They lock in on the Rev. Martin Luther King, Jr. They expect that a site bearing his name-and one of the top matches in a Google search-would contain accurate historical data about the most famous leader of the American civil rights movement. Instead, www.martinlutherking.org is a site hosted by a white-supremacist organization calling for the repeal of the holiday named for King and disparaging his achievements. The site bills itself as a valuable resource for students and teachers alike. To this end the Library of Congress provides about ninety teacher training session a year and part of that training includes strategies for helping students examine Web sites to determine if information is authentic. The training is free for the half-day to daylong professional develop sessions.

Parents unintentionally can play into the Internet's hands. One parent unfortunately noticed a photo she had posted of her daughter coming out of a bathtub. She uploaded it to a photo-sharing site. It received hundreds of hits while a photo of her daughter fully clothed got only a handful. In an instant the mother was made aware of the "creeps" one might attract by innocently sharing baby photos.

An example of premeditated bullying can be obese children. Science Daily (2006, April 2) suggested that bullying keeps overweight kids off the field. Overweight children will avoid situations where they have been bullied before, such as gym class and sports, making it even harder for them to get in shape. Bullying can happen in sports. Some coaches seem to enjoy certain aspects of bullying. It is their own right of passage into the team.

Another article, (2007, May 4) suggests that psychological bullying hits just as hard. School bullying doesn't have to leave physical bumps and bruises to contribute to a hostile and potentially dangerous school environment. Kids with obsessive-compulsive disorder are bullied more often. More than one quarter of the children with OCD who researchers studied reported chronic bullying as a problem.

Many conscientious teachers and parents are well aware of the importance of fostering respect for every other child's race, class or religion. But size difference is often overlooked. There are many ways educators and parents can help combat media images, build their personal self-esteem, and tone-down the bullying that occurs among children. They should be cognizant of what they say and do in front of their children. Do not make negative comments about large people. Don't laugh at others' fat jokes. They should encourage children to take care of their own bodies. Do not obsess over your own weight. Eat healthy and avoid displaying negative or guilty response about food. In the home evenings, discuss why car commercials have skinny women beside expensive automobiles. Pay attention to the celebrities your kids emulate. Know the magazines your child reads, and the shows they watch on television. Talk to your kids about the images their favorite characters portray and point out that these images don't necessarily equal happiness. Teach children that there are happy people in the world who do not look like supermodels and bodybuilders. Encourage your children to have real-life, everyday role models. Finally, respect each other. Don't make jokes about mom or dad's "thunder thighs" or "beer gut." Give each spouse explicit admiration for your accomplishments. Teach children that it is desirable and that they are desirable and greatly respected for who they are and what they do, rather than what they look like.

For youth with physical disabilities bullying becomes aggressive behavior that is intentional and involves an imbalance of power or strength. Usually it is repeated over time. Bullying is relentless. Traditionally, bullying has involved actions such as: hitting or punching (physical bullying), teasing or name-calling (verbal bullying), or intimidation through gestures or social exclusions. In recent years, cyber technology has given children a new means of bullying each other. Spreading rumors and gossiping may not cause bruises or black eyes, but the psychological consequences of this social type of bullying can linger into early adulthood. Rather than threatening a child with physical violence, these bullies target a child's social status and relationships by shunning them, excluding them from social activities or spreading rumors. Even though youth graduate from high school, the memories of these bullying experiences continue to be associated with depression and social anxiety.

FAMILY

No adult supervision
Inconsistent punishment
EMOTIONAL
A relationship disappointment
Peer ridicule children
PEERS:
Few close friends
Low self-esteem
FAMILY:
No positive role model
No family values
EMOTIONAL:
unfair treatment from an adult
SOCIAL:
Poverty
High crime
Few activities available

PEERS:
Makes prejudicial comments
Profanity
FAMILY
Inconsistent punishment
Breaks parents rules
EMTIONAL
Trouble at home
Teased disability

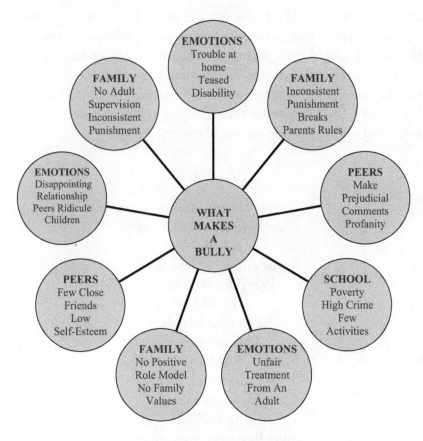

(What Makes a Bully?)

According to Bill Belsey (www.cyberbullying.ca) *"cyberbullying involves the use of information and communication technologies such as email, cell phone and pager text messages, instant messaging, defamatory personal Web sites and online personal polling Web sites, to support deliberate, repeated and hostile behavior by an individual or group that is intended to harm others. The power and speed of technology has made it nearly impossible to contain a regrettable action or keep it confidential."*

The phenomenon of cyberbullying is also called "cyber bullying," "electronic bullying," "e-bullying," "SMS bullying," "mobile bullying," "digital bullying," or "Internet bullying." But regardless how you term it, cyberbullying involves cyberthreats. Cyberthreats are either direct threats or "distressing material"-general statements that make it sound like the writer is emotionally upset and may be considering harming someone else, harming himself, or committing suicide. Before the cyberthreats begin, it is important to point out that Cyberbullying can take different forms:

Flaming: Online fights using electronic messages with angry and vulgar language. For instance: "Joyce and Alice's online exchange got angrier and angrier. Insults were flying. Joyce warned Alice to watch her back in school the next day."

Harassment: Repeatedly sending nasty, mean, and insulting messages. For instance: "Stan reported to the principal that Kevin was bullying another student. When Stan got home, he had 45 angry messages in his email box. The anonymous cruel messages kept coming-some from complete strangers."

Denigration: "Dissing" someone online. Sending or posting gossip or rumors about a person to damage his or her reputation or friendships. For instance: "Some girls created a "We Hate Jenny" Webb site where they posted jokes, cartoons, gossip, and rumors, all dissing Jenny."

Impersonation: Pretending to be someone else and sending or posting material to get that person in trouble or danger or to damage that person's reputation or friendships. For instance: "Leslie watched closely as Becky Sue logged on to her account and discovered her password. Later, Leslie logged on to Becky Sue's account and sent a hurtful message to Becky Sue's boyfriend, Marlin."

Outing: Sharing someone's secrets or embarrassing information or images online. For instance: "Gary, an obese high school student, was changing in the locker room after gym class. Robert took a picture of him with his cell phone camera. Within seconds, the picture was flying around the phones at school."

Trickery: Talking to someone into revealing secrets or embarrassing information, and then sharing it online. For instance: "Krista sent a message to Melanie pretending to be her friend and asking lots of questions. Melanie responded, sharing really personal information. Krista forwarded the message to lots of other people with her own comment, "Jessica is a loser."

Exclusion: Intentionally and cruelly excluding someone from an online group. For instance: "Jane tries hard to fit in with a group of girls at school.

She recently got on the "outs" with a leader in this clique. Now Jane has been blocked from the friendship links of all of the girls."

Cyberstalking: Repeated, intense harassment and denigration that includes threats or creates significant fear. For instance: "When April broke up with John, he sent her many angry, threatening, pleading messages. He spread nasty rumors about her to her friends and posted a sexually suggestive picture she had given him in a sex-oriented discussion group, along with her email address and cell phone number."

Cyberbullying text or images may be posted on personal Web sites or blogs or transmitted via email, discussion groups, message boards, chat, IM, or cell phones. A cyberbully may be a person whom the victim knows or an online stranger. Or the cyberbully may be anonymous, so it is not possible to tell. A cyberbully may solicit involvement of other people who do not know the victim- cyberbullying by proxy. For instance: "Penny convinced Patsy to post anonymous comments on a discussion board slamming Arlene, a student she had gotten into a fight with. Patsy was eager to win Penny's approval and fit into her group of friends, so she did as Penny requested." Some teens may think that cyberbullying is entertaining-a game to hurt other people. For instance: "Sitting around the computer with her friends, Sally asked, "Who can we mess with?" Sally started IM-ing with Brandy, asking her many personal questions. The next day, the girls were passing around Brandy's IM at school."

There are certain characteristics inherent in online technologies which increase the likelihood that children will be exploited for deviant purposes. **First**, electronic bullies can remain virtually anonymous using temporary email accounts, pseudonyms in chat rooms, instant messaging programs, cell-phone text messaging, and other Internet venues to mask their identity. Research suggests that this perhaps frees the cyberbully from normative and social constraints on their behavior. Furthermore, cyberbullies might be emboldened when using electronic means to carry out their antagonistic agenda because it takes less energy and courage to express hurtful comments using a keypad or a keyboard than with one's voice.

Second, electronic forums can often lack supervision. While chat hosts regularly observe the dialog in some chat rooms in an effort to police conversations and evict offensive individuals, personal messages sent between users (such as electronic mail or text messages) are viewable only by the sender and the recipient and therefore outside the regulatory reach of such authorities. In addition, teenagers often know more about computers and cellular phones than adults and are therefore able to operate the technologies without worry or concern that a probing parent or teacher will discover their experience with bullying.

Third, the inseparability of a cellular phone from its owner makes that child a perpetual target for victimization. Users often need to keep their phone turned on for legitimate purposes, which provides the opportunity for those with malicious intentions to engage in persistent unwelcome behavior such as harassing telephone calls or threatening and insulting statements via the cellular phone's text messaging capabilities. Cyberbullying thus penetrates the walls of a home, traditionally a place where victims could seek refuge from other forms of bullying.

All kids act out fantasies online, pretending to be someone or something they're not. They try on different identities in a dramatic and succinct way. But sometimes they act out violent fantasies online, too. Cyberbullying involves the use of information and communication technologies to support deliberate, repeated, and hostile behavior by an individual or a group that is intended to harm others.

One such young lady was fourteen year old Jessica Hunter who complained daily that she was humiliated by her peers, both at school and online. She didn't fit the mold. She told the few friends she had that she felt like an "alien." But online she was reborn. Her new online name became the sexy "Autumn Meadows." Consistently lying to her parents, they were not aware of who she had become. She applied considerable makeup, took scantily clad photos in provocative lingerie, and began her climb to fame. Posting her profile online as being eighteen years old, she felt like someone completely different. She would spend all day online answering inquiries and responding to requests. Finally, the principal of her school became aware and called her parents. It was a big surprise. Jessica was exposed to her classmates and many took it out on her. They called her many names, including a whore. She felt terrible. The parents went into her computer files and deleted everything. She said having her computer taken away was her worst nightmare. Parents sometimes give in despite the odds of success. Seeing Jessica slump into depression, her father restored all the privileges and even allowed Autumn Meadows to be reinvented.

Cyberbullying, online social cruelty or electronic bullying, can involve:

- Sending mean, vulgar, or threatening email and instant messages or images.
- Sending email to someone who has said they want no further contact with the sender
- Posting sensitive, private information about another person. Some may post victims' photos or victims' edited photos like defaming captions or pasting victims' faces on nude bodies.
- Threats, sexual remarks.
- Pretending to be someone else in order to make that person look bad
- Intentionally excluding someone from an online group (Willard, 2008).
- Pejorative labels (hate speech) Word can and do hurt. Words can become either the inspiration to overcome the challenges one faces or the nails in the coffin of self-loathing. Putdowns drill themselves deep into the psyche of a child and fester during times alone. The world does not appear to be such a nice place to live.
- Disclose a victim's personal data (e.g., real name or school) at websites or forums or may attempt to assume the identity of a victim for the purpose of publishing material in their name that defames or ridicules them.
- Use of rumors and misinformation is used as a primary mode of attack. Rumors often focus on the sexual reputation of a target. "She's a ho or slut" or having sex with multiple partners. Labeling one as a lesbian is a favorite. It's most common form comes under the ruse of "Did you hear what she said about you?"
- Ostracism (shunning) This is another form of aggression practiced to an art form by especially females. It is part of a

formation of cliques. The feeling of ostracism is the feeling of irritability, an object of inattention. Nobody sees, nobody cares! It is a non-behavior, hard to detect. It is deniable. This becomes the kiss of death amongst teens. No one talks to the target, sits by her at lunch, agrees to willingly partner with her in school day assignments, or invites her to information after school social activities. It includes such terms as excluding, ignoring, freezing out, use of the silent treatment, cold shoulder, This type of shunning is usually instigated by a strong in-group cyberbully leader who exerts tremendous power over her domain. She is the queen bee in this "Girl's World."

Worldwide, the Amish call ostracism "meidung". The Germans "wieluftbehandein"(means to look at as air). The Dutch called it "doodzooigen" (silence someone to death). In Japan, they merely move the person to the window (without any others) and he becomes what is called a "window gazer."

Cyberbullying, like other forms of bullying, is about human relationships, power and control. Those who bully others are trying to establish power and control over others that they perceive to be "weaker" than them. Those who bully want to make victims feel that there is something wrong with them. Cyberbullying is particularly cowardly. Cyberbullies can more easily hide behind the anonymity that the Internet can provide. They can also communicate their hurtful messages to a very wide audience with remarkable speed. Cyberbullies do not have to own their actions, as it is usually very difficult to identify cyberbullies, so they do not fear being punished for their actions. What is extremely troublesome is that cyberbullying is often outside the legal reach of schools and school boards as their behavior often happens outside of school on home computers or via mobile phones.

And why shouldn't cyberbullies do what they do? They have learned from an adult generation engulfed in put-downs and political graffiti. While political graffiti on buildings can be idealistic, the stuff adults use online is coldly calculated. For instance, a recent mayor's race found cyberbullies utilizing slick and clandestine emails and Web sites where each side tried to take the other people down with knife-like missiles. The most divisive messages came from messengers seemingly independent of either challenger. But the average voter does not know for certain that they are independent. The voter doesn't even know the identity of the author of the most scathing Internet smears. We only know that smears are being penned by someone posing as "Joe Sacramento" of www.joesacramento. com. To click on this page is to find sensationalized generalizations of half-truths. But who cares about facts when the cyberbully can package fact with fiction and present it as gospel. Most charges are not fair, accurate or proven in any court of law. With the use of the Internet the mayor's race quickly descended into the sewers. Both sides want to keep these stories, however inaccurate, before the media. Why fight the other candidate on the facts when you can smear him, right? It brings to mind the old joke where the guy was asked: "How goes the rat race"? And he replied: "The rats are winning."

As technology doubles every six months, the worst may yet be on the horizon. Appearing in our homes and schools is the arrival of the new line of camera phones that can instantly access the Web. As America becomes more technologically advanced, online bullying has replaced old-fashioned schoolyard name calling and brawls. The consequences of bullying are tremendous. In the traditional definition of school bullying, bullying affects some 5 million students every year. The U.S. Department of Justice estimates that 160,000 K-12 students stay home from school every day from fear of being bullied at school. Nationwide, three children in every classroom is bullied.

- **32 %**- According to Pew Research(2006), about one third (thirty-two percent) of all teenagers who use the Internet say they have been targets of some cyberbullying that ranged from receiving threatening messages and having their private emails or text messages forwarded to having an embarrassing picture posted or rumors about them spread online.
- **75%**- Seventy five percent have visited a Web site bashing another student.
- **18%**- Eighteen percent of students in grades six to eight said

they had been cyberbullied at least once in the last couple of months and six percent said it happened to them two or more times (Kowalski , 2005).

- **19%**- Nineteen percent of regular Internet users between the ages of ten and seventeen reported being involved in online aggression; fifteen percent had been aggressors and seven percent had been targets (three percent were both aggressors and targets). (Ybarra & Mitchell, 2004).
- **17%**- Seventeen percent of six to eleven year-olds and thirty-six percent of twelve to seventeen year-olds reported that someone said threatening or embarrassing things about them through email, instant messages, web sites, chat room or text messages (Fight Crime: Invest in Kids, 2006).
- **40%**- Forty percent have had their password stolen and changed by a cyberbully who then locked them out of their own account or sent communication to others passing as the victim
- **33%**- One in three teens and one in six preteens has been a victim of cyberbullying according to a recent poll from Fight Crime: Invest in Kids.
- **18%**- More than thirteen million children ages six to seventeen were victims of cyberbullying. More than 2 million of those victims told no one about the attacks. Only fifteen percent of parents polled knew what the term "cyberbully" meant.
- **10%**- Ten percent of teens and four percent of younger children were threatened online. sixteen percent told no one about it. Only fifty percent of younger children tell their parents while thirty percent of older teens tell their parents.
- **45%**- Research indicates that preteens were as likely to receive harmful messages at school (forty-five percent) as at home (forty-four percent). Older children received thirty percent of harmful messages at school and seventy percent at home.
- **25%**- Globally one in four in the United Kingdom was the victim of online bullying. And in the United States a popular site, www.schoolromors.com, had to be closed down for technical reasons after receiving 70,000 visits in just a few

weeks. Visitors to this site could "click on a particular high school and post their own insults of real students using a false name." (NetSmartz, 2008).

- **50%**- Cyberbullying has increased in recent year. In nationally representative surveys of 10-17 year-olds, twice as many children and youth indicated that they had been victims and perpetrators of online harassment in 2005 compared with 1999/2000. (Wolak, Mitchell, and Finkelhor, 2006).

- **200%**- Girls were about twice as likely as boys to be victims and perpetrators of cyberbullying.

- **45%**- In a recent telephone survey of preteens six to eleven year olds and teens twelve to seventeen year olds, it was found that forty-five percent of preteens and thirty percent of teens who had been cyberbullied received the messages while at school. Forty-four percent of preteens and seventy percent of teens who had been cyberbullied received the messages at home and thirty-four percent of preteens and twenty-five percent of teens who had been cyberbullied received the messages while at a friend's house. (Fight Crime: Invest in Kids, 2006).

- **42%**- In September 2006, ABC News produced a survey done by I-Safe.Org. The data was based on a 2004 survey of 1,500 students between grades four to eight. The results showed:

(1) **42%**- Forty-two percent of kids have been bullied while online. One in four have had it happen more than once.

(2) **35%**- Thirty five percent of kids have been threatened online. Nearly one in five had had it happen more than once.

(3) **21%**- Twenty-one percent of kids have received mean or threatening emails or other messages.

(4) **58%**- Fifty-eight percent of kids admit someone has said mean or hurtful things to them online. More than four out of ten say it has happened more than once.

(5) **58%**- Fifty-eight percent have not told their parents or an adult about something mean or hurtful that happened to them online.

In 2007, Debbie Heimowitz, a Stanford University Master's student created Adina's Deck, a film based upon accredited research through Stanford. She worked in focus groups for ten weeks in three different schools to learn about the problem of cyberbullying in Northern California. She found that over sixty percent of students had been cyber bullied or victims of cyberbullying. Adiona's Deck is now being used in classrooms nationwide as it was designed around learning goals pertaining to problems students had understanding the topic. (Heimowitz, 2007)

The Youth Internet Safety Survey, conducted by the Crimes Against Children Research Center at the University of New Hampshire in 2005 found that nine percent of young people in the survey had experienced some form of harassment. This survey was a nationally representative telephone survey of 1500 youth ten to seventeen years old. One third reported feeling distressed by the incident. (Wolak, 2006).

Hinduja and Patchin completed a study in the summer of 2005 of approximately 1500 Internet-using adolescents and found that over one-third of youth reported being victimized online and over sixteen percent of respondents admitted to cyberbullying others. While most of the instances of cyberbullying involved relatively minor behavior (forty-one percent were disrespected, nineteen percent were called names), over twelve percent were physically threatened and about five percent were scared for their safety. Notably, less than fifteen percent of victims told an adult about the incident. Additional research by Hinduja and Patchin found that youth who reported being victims of cyberbullying also experience stress or strain that is related to offline problem behaviors such as running away from home, cheating on a school test, skipping school, or using alcohol or marijuana. (Hinduja 2005).

According to another 2005 survey by the National Children's Home Charity and Tesco Mobile of 770 youth between the ages of eleven and nineteen, twenty percent of respondents revealed that they had been bullied via electronic means. Seventy-three percent stated that they knew the bully, while twenty-six percent stated that the offender was a stranger ten percent indicated that another person has taken a picture and/or video of them via a cellular phone camera, consequently making them feel uncomfortable, embarrassed, or threatened. Many youth are not comfortable telling an authority figure about their cyberbullying victimization for fear their access to technology will be taken from them; while twenty-four percent told a parent and fourteen percent told a teacher. Twenty-eight percent did not tell anyone while forty-one percent told a friend. (National Children's Survey, 2005).

A survey by the Crimes Against Children Research Center at the University of New Hampshire in 2000 found that six percent of the young people in the survey had experienced some form of harassment including threats and negative rumors and two percent had suffered distressing harassment.

Therefore, for many children, the Internet isn't simply a convenient way to research or a fun after-school activity- it's a big part of their social life. Emailing and chatting with friends are children's most common online activity after studying and playing games. But like many other social situations, some kids bully other kids online. Both boys and girls sometimes bully online. Just as in face-to-face bullying, they tend to do so in different ways.

PART II
Statement Of The Problem:
The Serious Consequences

CHAPTER 3:
THE SERIOUS CONSEQUENCES

When ninety percent of teenagers are online, a child's peaceful existence can take a tumultuous turn. They become a cyberspace target for the awesome destructive power of a cyberbully. According to one victim, the difference between being bullied at school and being bullied on the Internet is that you cannot get away from cyberbullying as easily. In this drastic confrontation, cyberbullying follows the victim even after they get home from school. Cyberbullying may be influenced by gripping, gut-wrenching videos that are uploaded to video sharing websites online which contain offensive content or examples of acts of bullying.

These are extremely dangerous Websites that currently do not filter such videos. YouTube and Metacafe, have been asked to take legal action against videos of people being attacked, harassed or ridiculed, in order to reduce cyberbullying. Some jurisdictions are currently using the videos posted on YouTube as evidence in later convictions and as a way of monitoring youth.

Similarly, a few Websites are created by expectant mothers. Pre-baby photographs are interesting phenomenon on today's cyberspace. Many mothers-to-be are posting ultrasound photos in an easy way to announce an exciting piece of information to lots of people all at once. Sharing fetal pictures could be over-sharing-like posting drunken make-out photos-and fret about what happens if the pregnancy goes wrong. Moms-to-be post the prenatal shots with adoring comments like "Here you can see the spine and little riblets" and "cute little foot!" Many believe their blog, Facebook and MySpace pages are meant for family and friends scattered around the country. Pregnant bloggers can join conversation groups based on their due date and compare their experiences with others going through the same thing.

Networking sites for new parents abound, bursting with message boards, baby-shower registries, expert advice and other information about what to expect. TheCradle.com, which caters to an audience of women from pre-pregnancy through their baby's first year, offers the chance for users to create their own pages, read celebrity interviews with pregnant stars and chat with other expectant moms. With technology and social networking in general, it's just creating this venue for things that everyone kind of thought was more private than it should be or than moms want it to be.

But there are dangers! With ultrasound photos, there is usually personal information written on the scan. Also, when posting such a photo or other personal images onto a social networking site, you can forget who will see the photo and accidentally make your news known to the wrong people, such as an ex-boyfriend who didn't know you were pregnant. Many expectant mothers say they have taken advantage of privacy filters and other measures to make sure only designated readers can view the photos.

Kids go much further than the expectant moms. They are more sophisticated than their parents in computer technology. Many kids point out the fact that their parent cannot even work a printer or know how to effectively use email. It is an outlet for self expression where youth complain about parents, about other children, and other negative forms of socializing.

Today's children, of almost any age, are far ahead of their parents and teachers in computer literacy. According to Will Richardson, "these students are "Digital Natives" who are well versed in the uses and etiquette of computers, digital cameras, cell phones, text messaging, Weblogs, and the like." (Richardson, 2008). A child engaged in using the Net can have five windows up and talking to three people all at the same time. In fact, they can be talking to twenty-five people all at once. Many do not even take the summer off or have private time to take a vacation with the family. Instead they are constantly texting friends. It seems they cannot be without their cell phones or computers for even ten minutes at a time.

But this over indulgence can cause problems. Let's look at Sally as an example. She is a ninth grader and has just signed onto her computer. She begins to browse the blogs of familiar faces. Suddenly, she notices that someone has written hateful and derogatory remarks about her. Embarrassed and overwhelmed, several questions race through her mind. "What should I do?" "Why would someone write such damaging remarks about me?" "Will people believe what they read?" Sally's entire body becomes numb and her mind becomes a blur. She has fallen prey to a cyberbully.

In another scenario, Brandy has just signed onto her computer. Her favorite blog site is called MySpace. She is excited. She eagerly smiles as she begins to browse the blogs of familiar faces. Suddenly, out of nowhere, someone has written something about her. The message is terribly hateful. Cursing and profanities fill the screen. She shudders as the cyberbully is zeroing in on her. Brandy feels embarrassed and overwhelmed as a number of questions permeate her mind. "What should I do? Why would someone write such damaging remarks about me? Will my friends and other acquaintances believe what they read? " Brandy's entire body becomes numb. Her mind becomes a blur. The cyberbully has found her, somehow. She might have even been able to handle regular physical harassment of the typical bully, but this type of assault makes it emotionally difficult to go on. Harassment like this is capable of creating even deeper wounds than tangible wounds. Brandy's feelings are hurt. She is shocked and confused and it helps to destroy her self-esteem. She is not certain she wants to go to school...ever!

This type of cyberbullying can work its' way into any school. Principal Alan Goodwin from Maryland's Walt Whitman High School was faced with handling two separate incidents in which taunting and name-calling on Facebook resulted in physical fights at school. Two of the combatants were boys and two were girls. Consequently, Goodwin put out an email to all parents asking them to more closely monitor what their children were writing on Facebook and to consider calling the police and other legal authorities if a child of theirs was being bullied online. As a consequence, it propelled the signing of a new Maryland law adding "cyberbullying" to the legal definition of bullying in the state. It also required all school boards in the state to write anti-bullying policies by the next school year.

At Sacramento's McClatchy High School in 2007 the administration ran into a difficult cyber problem. Two female friends had been fighting with two others. They were trash-talking online. The situation increased with intensity. Extremely bad things were posted. This led to some minor physical altercations and ongoing threats. Eventually it was transformed into repeated verbal vitriol on MySpace. Next the two girls got two boys to come to their aid. At school, the ongoing cyber dispute almost turned deadly when a fifteen year old boy, whose worst crime had been skipping school for forty-five days, was caught with a loaded gun and ammunition near the campus. The boy, a runaway who is a friend of the girls, planned to bring the gun into the school and shoot the other two female students. Interestingly, the police and school administration did not consider him a serious troublemaker.

The gunman had been living with a fourteen year old boy from Martin Luther King, Jr. High who was involved in the simmering dispute. The boy was carrying photographs of the two alleged targets. A fourteen year old girl from McClatchy and a thirteen year old boy who attended John H. Still Middle School provided the firearm. Now the students face a variety of charges including conspiracy to commit assault with a deadly weapon. The fifteen year old also faces a weapons possession charge. All four appeared in juvenile court. Principal Cynthia Clark said the six girls, three on each side, are for the most part pretty likable young ladies.

As a result, the Sacramento City School District said it will consider using metal detectors, gun-sniffing dogs and other safety measures to prevent the kind of tragedy which nearly struck C. K. McClatchy High School.

Board President Manny Hernandez said, "If there is a threat out there, we must adapt." One problem was that the principal knew about the threat at 8:30 a.m. but did not alert the parents until 5:00 p.m. Superintendent Maggie Mejia did not learn about the incident until 1:00 p.m. Parents want to know why they were not informed earlier. District policy states that schools are to be locked down when there is an imminent threat. But the policy does not define what constitutes an imminent threat when the threat is off campus.

Most kids aren't intentionally vicious. But many youthful bystanders simply get roped in by the bullies. Other kids get involved because it seems fun and they don't really understand the effect of what they are doing until it snowballs. Still, the victim is the loser. Students, like adults, establish a pecking order that is clearly delineated and honored. Physical prowess is honored above intellectual ability. There is a "pile on" mentality that can quickly escalate so that the victim feels the whole school is against them. This is why experts agree that addressing the bystander is the best way to curb cyberbullying. By encouraging the bystander to have the courage to intervene rather than take part, most incidents of cyberbullying would fizzle before catching fire online. Peers have the ability to support the bully-directly or by their silence- or to challenge the bully by refusing to take part.

Bullies are basically a small scale terrorist with similar aims as a mainstream terrorist in today's interwoven world society. Vindictive individuals realize that they can easily spread gossip and rumors to a much wider audience through such technology as MySpace and Facebook.

As such a continuum of cyberbullying and bullying behaviors is generated:

> - **MILD** harassment includes dirty looks, name-calling, taunting, gossiping, spiting, humiliation, graffiti, pushing, shoving, threats to reveal secrets, and public embarrassment.
> - **MODERATE** harassment includes public exclusion (shunning), demeaning acts (public and private), vandalism, intimidating phone calls, ethnic, racial and religious slurs,

regular petty thefts, verbal or proximity intimidation, threats of harm to or coercion of family or friends, blatant extortion, clearly intentional physical violence.

➢ **SEVERE** harassment includes inflicting total isolation from peer groups, regular and routine intimidating behaviors, regular and routine extortion, vandalism, destruction of property, mobbing, ganging up on victim, threats with weapons, inflicting major bodily harm.

Depending on the emotional makeup of the target or victim, any of the types of harassment may lead to one of two serious violent reactions: implosion or explosion.

REACTION ONE: Implosion: This involves bullycide or suicide committed by the target of the bully. There has been no playfulness in the attack. Victims first begin to cry. A child's tear is pure and innocent. Looking deep into his/her eyes, one can see that a child's soul is written in the eyes. Words are powerful tools and can break the spirit of any child.

Children are reacting to the verbal and physical torment of their attackers. They decide to end it all. The tormentors may even say they are sorry, but you cannot unring a bell. Sticks and stones is a lie. Words do hurt immeasurably. In this type of bullying, as devastating as physical beatings, there are no visible scars. The hurt is much more damaging. They may also have been rejected due to bullying from their circle of former friends. This is most devastating when kids are in most need of their social connections.

A story called "Nails in the Fence" helps to explain:

> *"There once was a little boy who had a bad temper. His father gave him a bag of nails and told him that every time he lost his temper, he must hammer a nail into the back of the fence. The first day the boy had driven 37 nails into the fence. Over the next few weeks, as he learned to control his anger, the number of nails hammered daily gradually dwindled down. He discovered it was easier to hold his temper than to drive*

those nails into the fence. Finally the day came when the boy didn't lose his temper at all. He told his father about it and the father suggested that the boy now pull out one nail for each day that he was able to hold his temper. The days passed and the young boy was finally able to tell his father that all the nails were gone. The father took his son by the hand and led him to the fence. He said, "You have done well, my son, but look at the hole in the fence. The fence will never be the same. When you say things in anger, they leave a scar just like this one. You can put a knife in a man and draw it out. But it won't matter how many times you say I'm sorry, the wound will still be there. A verbal wound is as bad as a physical one. Remember that friends are very rare jewels, indeed. They make you smile and encourage you to succeed. They lend an ear; they share words of praise and they always want to open their hearts to us."

It is believed that depression causes most teenage suicides. Suicide is the third leading cause of teenager death. But this creates a new question-what causes the depression? A person just doesn't wake up one morning with depression.

Victims become very depressed. Federal health officials (Food and Drug Administration) suggest a surprising new interpretation of suicidal fantasies and depression. Sadness, anxiety and self-destructive thoughts are not symptoms but side effects. Federal regulators have warned that a surprising barrage of drugs could play a role in spurring thoughts of self-destruction. Medicines that treat epilepsy, asthma and influenza are under suspicion, as is one that helps smokers kick the tobacco habit. Prompted by reports that suggested children taking antidepressants were more likely to commit suicide, the agency in 2004 warned that antidepressants might increase the risk of suicidal fantasies and behaviors among children. That link is now in doubt, after recent studies showed a rise in youth suicide even as antidepressant use in that population has plummeted. 30% of bullied brought weapons to school for defense. (Investigative Reports, 2000). Three out of ten students are either victims, bullies or both. There are 3.2 million victims and 3.7 perpetrators. (Brunner, 2005).

One victim, we will call Ginger, was only eleven years old. She was a computer "geek." She received straight "A's" in school. Many kids were intimidated and a few showed how cruel they could be. Typically, they called her "Teacher's Pet, Geek, weird," and many other names. Consequently she did not have many friends at school or in her neighborhood. The kids found her "too smart" and "geeky" to play with. For her the Internet came along at the right time. She loved it that she was so smart and could fix things. Her favorite place to chat online was a room that was meant for teenage computer geeks. She was as smart at they were and didn't have to worry about being picked on. One day a new girl, Jane, joined, who was the same age as Ginger. She welcomed Jane. Ginger shared her deep feelings and items with Jane.

The next day Ginger went to school. There was a note taped to her locker. She shoved it into her jeans. In math class she heard some of the snobby girls behind her laughing. They were laughing and pointing at her. During lunch, sitting all alone under a tree, because no one would eat with her, she pulled out the note. It said," Dear Ginger: I know you have been talking about me and if you know what is good for you then you will stop before I have to make you stop." Signed "Math class beauty." She couldn't even finish her sandwich. Her stomach was in knots thinking that someone she didn't know was threatening her.

That night she logged onto her favorite chat room. She privately messaged Jane. Another person told Ginger that with her computer knowledge she could hack this person's computer and teach them a lesson. Her email began flashing and there were some fifty messages from the same address all saying," Watch you back at school Geek. You are going to pay for talking about me." Ginger checked the headers of the email and knew that she could, with a little work trace this email and perhaps fight back. She was small for her age. She would end up losing in a physical fight. She thought about the online organization called "Wiredsafety" that helps stalking and stuff like that. She couldn't go to sleep. Which option should she take? What would you tell your kids to do if they were her?

Conine Wilson developed depression from bullying and assaults at school. Parents said she was the most beautiful baby with big blue eyes and blonde curly hair. Her family found her to be an amazing child with a lot of personality and intelligence. At a new school, players on the softball team teased her relentlessly. She cried after every practice. Then some young men began to notice her, but her beauty and popularity was condemned by a number of girls. They started an online campaign against her which was played out with ruthless delight. They called her fat, ugly, her hair was frizzy. They called her a whore and began writing horrible notes to her all day. Later one day, parents found her dead from a single gunshot to her forehead. Instead of listening to their daughter perform at the rodeo, the parents buried her. The pain of losing their daughter is immeasurable.

Brandon Swartwood developed Post Traumatic Stress Disorder and depression after being harassed, tormented, isolated, assaulted and brutally beaten. Parents watched their son die a slow and painful death. The sparkling light of joy, love and hope in his big beautiful brown eyes-were slowly replaced with the darkness of pain, devastation and hopelessness. He told others that he felt dead inside. The parents tried to act. They took a protective order against one of the bullies. But the bully counteracted by sending a friend to the principal's office saying Brandon had made a bomb threat. Brandon put a loaded gun to his head, pulled the trigger and ended his pain. Some of the bullies said, through their crocodile tears, that they didn't realize what they were doing-that they were just having fun. Brandon and all of the people who loved him were not having fun. Where was there any justice for Brandon? Now, the parents feel dead inside. Brandon's mother, Cathy Swartwood Mitchell, is now serving as the Director of Bully Police-Oklahoma, a watch-dog group that advocates for children who are bullied and works with lawmakers to get anti-bullying laws enacted.

A bully's gang or a mob can be considered a group of individuals who have bonded together for certain negative purposes. They become agents of terror seeking targets to mob. Their strength is both real and imagined by their victims. They have the advantage of numbers and strength. To insult one member is to insult them all. Gangs make life miserable for others.

Another twelve year old middle school girl chose to end her life after years of taunting. She was the odd girl out of the in-group. She was quiet and shy. She dressed in dark clothes and identified with the Goth community. She read about Wicca, a religion identified with witchcraft. In retaliation, her peers would sing Christian hymns to embarrass her. Her private journal revealed much of the pain she felt during her time at school. Desperate, she was driven by these bullies to action. She hanged herself in her bedroom closet. Over one hundred classmates went to her funeral stating: "I'm sorry I said mean things to her!"

Freshman Emmet Fralick from Halifax, Nova Scotia shot and killed himself in his bedroom. He left behind a suicide note saying he could no longer take the bullying from his peers. It was reported that Emmet faced extortion, threats and beatings from other teenagers.

April Himes enjoyed a good joke. She had a wonderful sense of humor and was very active in painting, skiing and roller skating. Animals were her specialty and she talked about becoming an animal groomer. Bullies teased as if she were fat. Having minor acne was another flaw harassers hurt her with. She was told to go to school this Valentine's Day at her Carmichael Middle School. Go to school where she had been teased, harassed and taunted by classmates or appear before a truancy board and maybe go to juvenile hall. April made another choice. She hung herself in her bedroom, leaving a devastated stricken family behind. Depression caused by bullies can kill! George, her pet bird, loved her, but died soon after April's death from a broken heart.

The father of thirteen year old Ryan Halligan admitted that he made a terrible mistake in putting a personal computer in Ryan's room. His father told others that the computer in Ryan's room exacerbated a very unhealthy situation that started with schoolyard bullying. The computer in his room provided an environment that reinforced his bad feelings. Starting in the seventh grade, Ryan was bullied so relentlessly at school he finally learned kickboxing in his basement to defend himself from the physical assaults. He was a happy-go-lucky kid. Relatives knew him as a sweet, gentle and very sensitive soul. He had a way of bringing a smile to everyone. Yet thee were early concerns about his speech, language and motor skills development. He was a special education student. During the fifth grade, the attacks began.

With the Internet the attacks moved online, he had no way to fight back, and any refuge day or night. He received emails and instant messages from classmates ridiculing him and calling him a loser. They picked on his academic weaknesses and poor physical coordination. They found they could make him cry at will. Parents found him crying openly at the kitchen table. He tried to take his problem to the principal, but found this was also useless. He was treated very abrasively by one of his teachers. She would humiliate him in front of the class for being slow to answer or for missing an assignment. When a pretty girl at school pretended to like him online through IM and chat but later revealed she was only joking, the taunting emails and instant messages increased, only with even more venom. Ryan had shared a rectal exam with one he felt was his friend. She had succeeded in embarrassing and humiliating him. A few weeks later, in October 2003, Ryan hanged himself in his family's bathroom. He was found dangling from a noose by his sister. His father asked "why?" He turned to his son's computer looking for answers. Many began to talk to him online. On his son's computer were such things as: "sexually you are a loser," " suck u fag." There was a serious campaign against Ryan by a group at school which surfaced on the Internet. One boy in Ryan's special file told his father that they had talked about suicide and death regularly. The computer allowed Ryan the opportunity to explore the option of suicide. One Web site taught him how to hang himself. Nothing will ever heal the family's broken hearts. Ryan emailed another boy: "My son: tonight is the night. You are going to read about in the paper tomorrow." The boy emailed back: "It's about time." Nothing will bring him back. Now Ryan's father travels to schools around the country as part of I-Safe America programs to share the events that led up to his son's suicide and to warn everyone about the evils of cyberbullying.

" I shall remember forever and will never forget
Monday: my money was taken
Tuesday: names called
Wednesday: my shirt was torn
Thursday: my body pouring with blood
Friday: it's ended
Saturday: freedom"

> The final diary pages of fourteen year old Vijay Singh. He was found hanging from his banister rail at home on Sunday.

In Pasco, Washington middle schooler Jared High telephoned his father just to say "goodbye!" The father sat disbelieving as the shot rang through the receiver. This beautiful, quiet gentle soul was loved greatly by his family. He died instantly. The cause was simple. The cause was bullying! Jared was enrolled in special education classes to assist with his hearing development. He also displayed a genuine desire to be included by becoming the manager of the eighth grade baseball team. He took the abuse from a well-known bully who was a member of the team who had a history of violent and hurtful actions. The bully had the propensity for hitting, punching, kicking and harassing Jared. Fear and humiliation began to pile up. Jared was suspended after one of the confrontations even though he was the one attacked.

In the months that followed Jared became clinically depressed. Jared's loss filled his family with grief and sorrow. As a healing project, Jared's mother Brenda began to write his story which attracted over a million visitors looking for information on bullying. She became a passionate crusader. She claims "It is believed that depression causes most teenage suicides, but this creates a new question- what causes the depression? A person just doesn't wake up one morning with depression."

The family of Julian Houts said that their family loves each other very much. They were happy together until Julian was bullied. Kids said he always got picked on and teased at school. Parents asked for help from the teachers and staff. What they received were statements like: "Boys will be boys." He became a loner and had no friends. He ended up truly hating school. He was labeled as weird or different. Yet, those who knew him best found him to be very sensitive and intelligent. On one Monday morning his mother found him dangling above his bunk bed, dead. When he took his own life, he took much of the families also. His mother said, "our hearts have been broken forever. Life really hurts now!" The family exclaimed they are sorry that the world has to be so cruel.

In this world of revenge and bitterness, Steve Seskin and Allen Shablin presented the pathetic poem, "Don't Laugh at me!"

"Don't laugh at me, don't call me names,
Don't take your pleasure from my pain,
I'm a little boy with glasses, the one they call geek.
A little girl who never smiles because I have braces on my teeth.
And I know how it feels to cry myself to sleep.
I'm that kid on every playground, who's always chosen last,
A single teenager mother, trying to overcome my past.
You don't have to be my friend
But is it too much to ask: Don't laugh at me
Don't call me names.
Don't get your pleasure from my pain.
Don't laugh at me; I'm fat, I'm thin, I'm short, I'm tall
I'm deaf, I'm blind, hey aren't we all!"

Many adults view taunting and teasing as a childhood rite of passage. Yet, there is clear evidence that shows such early isolation can follow children throughout their academic careers. All you need to do is think back. You will probably remember some of the cruelties emanating in your own childhood: "four-eyed Freddie," "stuttering Sally," and "metal-mouthed Melanie." Or maybe you were one of them—one of the kids always being hit by the dodge ball, one of the kids who just never quite fit in the group, or the one who usually wound up sitting next to the teacher at lunch to escape the severe taunting and tormenting from classmates. I can still remember the shame and humiliation my cousin felt when the kids in grade school routinely called her "football head." This happened when my aunt fixed her hair in a certain way—she fixed the crown and fastened in double ball, glass barrettes. I watched her melt into her desk and disappear.

I watched it happen with my own family. I'll never forget the day I was standing in the checkout line of Albertson's Foods with the youngest two of my three daughters. Before a holiday, the store was jammed with people doing last-minute shopping. A large-sized, middle-aged woman entered the store and my little Michele uttered, "That's a BIGGGG lady daddy!" Not only did the woman hear this very public appraisal of her obese appearance, so did everyone else within a few hundred feet. Adults standing in line near us began to giggle and guffaw and the lady briskly walked away, her face burning red with anger and total embarrassment. I stood there stunned, half wanting to run after her and apologize for my daughter's words. I also felt like giving the adults around me a piece of my mind about their rude and thoughtless reactions to my daughter's innocent, yet embarrassing, remark. But, I did neither.

After finally making my purchase and heading to the car, I did have a private chat with both of my daughters about not making loud comments about other people's appearances because it could be embarrassing for them. But I knew I needed to do more. Three questions came in my mind:

- What could I as a parent teach my daughters about tolerance and acceptance of differences and empathy for the feelings of others?
- What message did the behavior of those adults send my daughters about large people?
- What could those adults be teaching their own kids?

The fact of the matter is kids of all ages are attuned to picking up the differences of other people. It is perfectly normal. But, how kids respond to these differences is impacted largely by how adults react in their lives. If parents and teachers convey the notion that being overweight is bad or something to be ashamed of, kids not only internalize this message but also project it in their interaction with others.

My daughter's non-malicious comment is magnified three times over in classrooms, lunchrooms, playgrounds, or riding the bus to school every day. Perhaps, it is magnified ten times online. Large children are frequently singled out, ridiculed teased and bullied by their peers because of their size. Studies show that overweight children are even treated differently by teachers and other adults. We live in a society where television commercials, magazine covers, music videos and other teen outlets of popular culture flaunt and celebrate images of the wafer thin, supermodel or the muscle-bound hunk. Day in and day out, our kids are programmed to believe these models represent reality. As parents, we must work to help our kids create their own reality.

This type of verbal put-downs is apparent for all our children. A number of schools report kids hashing out their conflicts online. There is a form of verbal fighting. Sometimes it is ignited at school. One school found two girls following up their online fighting with physical fighting at school. In addition, others video taped the fight and posted it on YouTube for everyone to see. Several girls were suspended for a few days as a consequence.

No matter how open-minded or accepting we believe ourselves to be, and no mater how good a job we think we are doing when it comes to raising tolerant children, this fact remains that children will develop prejudice and biases. Yet, it is from the home most biases are learned. The personal biases we hold as adults significantly influence what we teach, and don't teach our children about valuing difference. Some of us may have internalized negative attitudes about our identity groups because of the discrimination that we experienced growing up. As such, we sometimes pass these negative attitudes along to our children, or we are reluctant to have open, honest dialogue about their discrimination because these conversations are too painful.

Others of us may have been raised in families where parents and other relatives dealt in discriminatory attitudes about other groups of people. Even if we do not openly accept their behavior, it may affect our beliefs about others on a subconscious level. Knowingly or unknowingly, we can pass along many of these unspoken beliefs in our children. Simply living in a society in which discrimination-at times, legal- has played such a major role affects us all on some level.

We know that biases are learned. We also know that we as parents impart many of the most important, lasting lessons in our children's lives. If we hope to pass on lessons that encourage acceptance and tolerance, we have to be willing to live those values ourselves. This calls on parents and teachers to institute the crucial work of reflecting upon and addressing our own personal biases. It is work that is essential, needed today, and work that must be ongoing.

The parents of Alex Schmid. a thirteen year old from Atlanta Georgia, were told by both educators and friends that Alex was in serious trouble. He had become a well-known victim at Kittredge, which is a magnet school for high achievers. Parents felt that bullying was merely a rite of passage and were too late to save their beloved child from bullycide.

A similar situation was seen with Travis Retherford an eleven year old from Kansas City, Missouri. On the Notre Dame playground he was virtually a victim of a bullying problem every day. It took all he could muster to share this with his parents. Despite being very intelligent, he had trouble focusing on routine school work. For the parents, they transferred Travis to another school in hopes of saving their son.

Special education students are a prime target for all types of bullies. Stephen Klunder, age ten, experienced ADHD. Coming to or from classes he was often teased by a growing group of misfits. He turned into a cornered animal. In Kindergarten he stabbed another with a pencil. This only led to increased peer pressure. He now became the bully. In 2nd grade he was pulled off another student after Stephen had stabbed him in arm. Little counseling was warranted according to the educators. His verdict was an exaggerated course in anger management.

Shelby Troiani. of Kansas City, Missouri was similarly bullied. She, too, retaliated by becoming a bully herself. She had no models at home for her to follow. Her mother was a certified drug addict. The courts gave Shelby to her grandparents for custody, but they had already raised children who were not role models. The situation went from bad to worse.

November 20, 2000 in Mission, British Columbia, fourteen year old Dawn Marie Wesley hanged herself with her dog's leash in her bedroom. She left a suicide note naming three girls at school who she said were "killing her" because of their bullying both at school and online. She said, "If I try to get help it will get worse. They are always looking for a new person to beat up and they are the toughest girls. If I ratted, they would get suspended and there would be no stopping them. I love you all so much." The girls named in the note were merely suspended from school.

He traded shots with four Red Lake police officers. Then he shot security guard Derrick Brun and then walked down the hallway shooting and went into a classroom where he shot a teacher, Neva Rogers, and more students before turning the gun on himself. Only ten minutes had elapsed. The security guard, a teacher, and 8 students were shot. 15 others were wounded. Police later said there were so many bullets found that they could not keep count. After the shooting, one girl echoed the sentiments of the majority," I don't want to go back to that school." Grief poured forth at tribal and religious ceremonies.

Within forty-eight hours after the shooting, students and teachers began receiving counseling. One girl echoed the sentiments of many students: "I don't want to go back to that school." Yet experts say that a return to school and routine is therapeutic for traumatized students. Another student said, "I don't even want to talk to counselors about going back there." Principal Chris Dunshee said he is concerned about some students saying they don't want to go back to the school. "For a lot of people and not just kids, the impact of this is so great and so powerful; there is naturally a lot of fear."

In Holyoke Colorado in January 2001, fourteen year old Miranda Whittaker killed herself with a gun in her family's home. Her parents filed a suit against local school officials for their failure to "deal seriously with the aftermath of the sexual assault" of their daughter. They accused the school district of "failing to provide their daughter with a safe and secure learning environment free of sexual harassment." In this case, a sixteen year old popular boy athlete raped her. He pleaded guilty to second degree sexual assault and was sentenced to four year's probation and a deferred judgment. After this the online and school bullying really began with students calling her a "slut" and a "whore." A couple of teachers joined in the verbal attack. They blamed and shamed her for being a rape victim of a star athlete.

"I'm tired of it and can't take it any more!" This was the final resolve of fifteen year old Brian Head in his high school economics class in March 1994. Taking a 9mm semiautomatic pistol to school in his book bag, he pulled it out in his classroom as students jumped under their desks. Yet, his message was one for his classmates to be reminded of for a lifetime. Instead of aiming the gun at them, he turned it on himself, killing him immediately.

His mother, whom he told every day how much he loved her, was shocked and devastated. Brian was a victim of major bullying at school for a number of years. He was overweight and wore thick glasses. Classmates saw him as an easy target. In the lunch room students threw apples at him and broke his glasses. Others slapped him on the back of his head and pushed him into the lockers. They liked watching him cry. Students said he seemed always mad while at school and had been bullied since the first grade by other unthinking students. Riding the bus, walking to or from school, were repeated horrendous experiences. He did not want to go to school at all. His friend said Brian asked for help many times from teachers, but it was seldom given. The same friend indicated he was reading the Bible when Brian uttered "what for? Everything goes wrong anyway." He was a good poet, yet one of his poems he entitled "shadows" spoke of his dreary existence which other students had put him into the shadows of life.

The day was typically boring in the small farming community of Cazenovia seventy miles northwest of Madison Wisconsin. The silence was disturbed when fifteen year old Eric Hainstock burst into Weston High School with a shotgun blazing, Principal John Klang was the target. Eric had been repeatedly bullied. Turning his rage inwardly, Eric was confronted by a custodian and teachers trying to stop the onslaught but he broke free and with a handgun shot the beloved principal three times. Two hours before the principal died of his wounds, the superintendent of schools choked up as he read a hastily prepared handwritten statement from teachers and staff describing the principal as a kind, compassionate and soft-spoken man. Authorities said fifteen year old Eric had complained about being bullied and teased by other students. A group kept calling him names and rubbing up against him. Others threw food at him and used terrible profanity against him. Eric said he tried repeatedly to get help from the principal and teachers, but none would help him. No one cared! On the previous day Eric tried to ward off his bullies, but the bullies' lies made the principal severely discipline and suspend Eric instead.

In the first month of 2008 came a major tragic story from Newport Beach. Two teenage girls were arrested for investigation of participating in the videotaped beating of a thirteen year old girl that was posted on the social networking Web site MySpace. They were taken into custody for investigation of battery and conspiracy to commit battery. Their names were not released because they are minors.

A teacher in Arizona was placed on administrative leave pending an investigation for doing a cheerleading routine. In Kent School District in Washington, Joyce Mong found herself the subject of a video entitled "Monzilla" which was shot by her students to make fun of her. Legal experts say school districts tend to ignore videos that are simply embarassing to a teacher, but do not when the taping is a threat to the school or the teacher or is disruptive to the learning process. A student who commits non-sexual assault or battery on a school employee is not subject to mandatory expulsion.

Yet, the number of teachers and staff who are threatened at school and online is continuing to grow. For instance in the legal case of Evans vs. Unified, the Court ruled that a teacher must always expect public dissemination of his classroom communication and activities. In another case, Roberts v. Houston, the Court found that video taping a teacher's classroom performance by a school did not violate the teacher's privacy rights.

In one case, a headshot of a teacher was pasted on to a naked body and posted online. The major attorney for National School Boards Association (NSBA) said, "If a kid has a photo and posts it on YouTube, modified or unmodified, it is hard for the school to show disruption because of it. That's First Amendment speech." All this with the understanding that such a photo could be devastating to someone's career. Even though this could be considered libelous and inaccurate, it can totally undermine the teacher's confidence to the point that they become ill. It is particularly hurtful for young, vulnerable teachers who are very unsure of themselves and just want to fit in.

It has gotten so bad in England that the teachers union has called for a ban on YouTube. While the website might be blocked from access on the school's network, teachers are obviously powerless to dictate what is viewed in the home. The Norwich England Evening News found several fake profiles of teachers in city schools on the Bebo social networking site, which is very popular with youngsters. This included teachers from the Hewet School and Sprowston High School. Here the student made derogatory comments about teachers' private lives, personal hygiene, teaching methods, size, ethnicity, sexual orientation and dress, using vile and abusive language. The sites encouraged others to post vicious and offensive abuse about the individuals.

Around the globe, questions are lingering over whether schools should have jurisdiction over what a student posts in the privacy of their own homes. At the North Eugene High School in 2006, several students posted racially charged photographs and statements about a black student at the school, including depictions of lynchings. The site was incendiary and disruptive to the learning environment though the postings were not made during school hours. Free speech advocates like the Oregon ACLU, though, are leery of expanding the boundaries of a proposed law, and school boards do not want to find themselves caught up in expensive legal disputes over speech issues, especially if that speech takes place off school property.

An eighteen year old high school student in Great Falls, Montana, was suspended for publishing a web site about "the hottest freshmen girls." A district court judge issued a temporary restraining order to stop the school from suspending the boy, and about fifty of his peers staged a peaceful sit-in in protest.

In 2001, a popular site, www.schoolrumors.com, had to be closed down for technical reasons after receiving 70,000 visits in just a few weeks. Visitors to this site could click on a particular high school and post their own insults of real students using a false name.

Ceclia met Andrew in a chat room. Andrew wrote: "bring a gun to school, ur on the front of every..I can't imagine going through life without killing a few people..If I don't like the way it look at me, u die..I choose who lives and who dies." (In reality, Cecilia reported her online conversation to her father, who contacted the police. The police found that Andrew had many weapons, including an AK-47. He is now in prison.)

Greg set up an anonymous IM account and sent a threatening message to his older sister suggesting that she would be killed the next day at school. (Greg's sister told her parents, her parents told the school, and the school went into "lockdown." Greg was identified easily and arrested for making a threat.

For teachers and children alike, the scars of being bullied last forever. Most cyberbullies easily escape punishment and repercussions because adults do not realize what is happening to the victim. Children who are bullied spend a lot of time thinking up ways to avoid the trauma and have little energy left for learning.

Many adults who were previously bullied kids often lament "I'll never forget the pain of high school (or middle school)." They became so very tired of being a loser. They are tired of being made fun of. A successful adult in today's technological world will find it difficult to call his public school teachers by name. They will find it difficult to even name their friends in school. But, they can remember by name, by day and month and year, those individuals who bullied them.

The National Association of School Psychologists belabors the point that many of our heroes of today were bullied in their school years. Victims suffer lifelong problems. They still complain about their scars. Phil Collins, Harrison Ford, Mel Gibson, Tom Cruise, Michelle Pfeiffer, Frank Bruno were but a few. Erika Harold, Miss America of 2003, was the victim of pervasive and severe racial and sexual bullying. She said," teachers and school officials were cognizant of the harassment and took no steps to intervene." Bill Gates was bullied but today he utters "do not pick on the nerds. You'll probably end up working for one." Former National Teacher of the Year, Guy Doud, and motivational speaker Frank Peretti still visualize and can name their tormentors to this day. Everything we say and do has the potential to shape another's dreams.

One of these present-day heroes was a repeated victim of bullying. Recently he gave a speech. His name is Frank Peretti. He wrote a book about "*Wounded Spirits.*" Speaking of the pain he went through as a youngster he acknowledged the fact that many other kids are experiencing this type of victimization today. Frank loved monsters growing up. Frankenstein, Dracula, The Thing, the Creature from the Black Lagoon. Like King Kong who became a circus freak, he felt the same way in school. He idolized "the Hulk" who had the advantage of turning green and breaking things when others bothered him. These monsters had the power. Other typical monsters have come a long way since then.

When Peretti was born, the doctor was absent. Another amateur helped with the delivery. It caused him serious physical harm. It created a tumor on his neck which, in turn, spread to his tongue. The tongue became a huge growth that hung from his mouth. It was big, black and scaly making it very difficult to talk.

Living at home he knew his family loved him! But then he had to go to school. Everyone makes you go to school. For many victims like Frank, it is a helpless trap. At school and online the kids were quick to remind him of his tongue. Despite numerous surgeries he dealt with it until graduating from junior high school. Speech therapy was vital and he improved, but the damage was already done. He was small because of his medicines. He became introverted for fear of what the bullies said to him. They trapped him and robbed him of his dignity. Bullies constantly kicked and stabbed him. Frank offered it was like when cutting your finger. It hurts for a short while and then it will heal. But when he was hurt inside, it created within him a broken spirit. His soul was deeply wounded.

How can teachers or parents put a bandage on a child's wounded spirit? Injury to his body will heal, but a wounded spirit can stay wounded for years. There were the little pricks and barbs and stabs and he couldn't do anything about it. The bullies gave him a name, not his own, which labeled him as stupid. Being smaller and weaker, they would spit on him, stomp on his ankles from behind, spill his food on him. Physical education was a nightmare. Every student has to take physical education. Here he was slower and weaker. He could not throw a football or catch a ball. Worse, he had to take a shower in front of his assailants, naked. Naturally, they pointed out all his physical imperfections.

Frank hurt every day. Others would inappropriately try to put bandages on the hurt. They would tell him to "just ignore them." There was no choice. In his culture if he told on them he would be labeled as a "wimp, a snitch". His parents were also authority figures, just like the teachers. Peretti was forty-eight years old and still remembered the names and faces of the jocks today. He is a grown, very successful man, yet he still feels the wounds.

He thought about leaving suicide notes. Like many other victims of bullying, he admitted to having a fantasy world in which he would blow away all the jocks. He demonstrated that hate can grow out of open wounds. He attested that his thoughts became an act and could have brought forth death very easily. He understands how it can, and has, led to school shootings.

Television's Dr. Phil Show emphasized bullying. One young man named Mark shared that he was kicked, shoved and spit on every day at school. A girl named Tess shared that a group of girls who she thought were her friends started making her life a living hell. The mother of a girl named Rochelle shared that her daughter committed suicide due to bullying at school. Dr. Phil ended the show by exclaiming that if we do not help the persons who are being bullied, then we are validating the actions of the bully.

The experience of coping with the anguished families of young suicide victims who took antidepressants has had a lasting effect on mental health professionals, researchers and federal regulators. One of the first drugs that will require testing for psychiatric side effects before it can be approved in the United States is rampant, an anti-obesity drug used in about 20 countries. The FDA has asked rimonabant's maker, the French pharmaceutical firm Sanofi-Aventis, to use a new yardstick to detect and measure suicidal side effects.

Scientists long have known that many drugs used to treat symptoms below the neck enter the brain also and that the receptors and chemicals on which they work in organs such as the heart, blood vessels or liver are present in the brain as well, although they may have different functions there. That these drugs might have an incidental effect on mood, then should not be terribly surprising. Other drugs in Japan, Tamiflu and Relenza, have been widely used to shorten the duration and ease the symptoms of influenza, raised serious alarms. Taking one of these drugs, two children- a boy and a girl- fell to their death from high rise apartment buildings in suspected suicides and two 12 year olds were injured from falling from buildings. Delirium, hallucinations and psychotic behavior caused one child taking the drug to bolt into traffic to his death.

In all, an FDA advisory panel was told there have been twenty-five deaths and three hundred sixty-five cases of abnormal behavior in people younger than twenty-one who have taken Tamiflu since it was approved in 1999. Under scrutiny is the use of Singulair, a pill used to treat asthma and allergies. Also being carefully reviewed is Chantix, an anti-smoking drug. (Melissa Healy. Los Angeles Times. April 27, 2008).

REACTION TWO: *Explosion.* Victims will go home and bring a weapon back to school causing major loss of life. Victims utilize deadly violence in their misguided and painful efforts to even the score. Even though crime rates are down, the lowest they have been in thirty years, homicide by firearms is up. So why are more and more kids carrying guns and knives illegally? To protect themselves, to engage in gangs, and to gain respect. twenty-five percent of all adults and forty percent of American households own at least one firearm. There are about twenty-two million children in the United States living in homes where there are firearms. More than five hundred thoursand guns are stolen every year from legal owners.

The U.S. Secret Service reported between 1992 and 2002, one hundred sixteen people were killed in ninety-three incidents by students in U.S. schools. The Chicago Sun-Times reported that in the thirty-seven highest profile school shootings and violent eruptions in this country, two thirds of the aggressors cited persecution and bullying as the direct cause. Past fistfights have become gun fights.

SUGGESTIONS FOR GUN OWNERS:
- *Store guns unloaded and locked up*
- *Store ammunition separately*
- *Hide any keys in places where children will not think to look.*
- *Use trigger locks to keep it from firing*
- *Use cable locks that prevents ammunition from being loaded*
- *Use gun safes and keep them locked*

1.
AWARENESS
Child feels he is going nowhere
No opportunities

4.
ANGER
Feeling like a victim
Not caring what happens

5.
VIOLENCE
Anger is building. Phys./emotional danger

2.
FRUSTRATION
Feeling
Powerless to change his situation

3.
FEAR
Reality of being in danger.
Things will never change

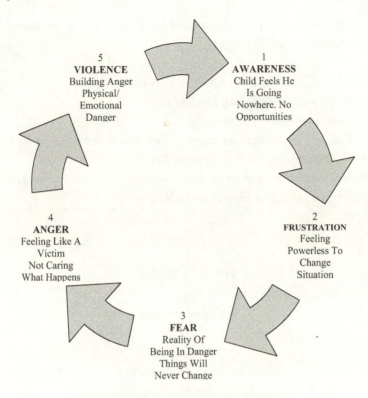

THE CYCLE OF VIOLENCE

Most bullying fires are fueled by fear, anger and frustration. It rages openly, smolders, and burns a path of devastation. I became a school administrator at Lindhurst High. This was one of the first schools in the United States where a child's bullying vengeance took the lives of others. Unhappy with the treatment he received and constant bullying he received from other students, Eric Houston became a ticking time bomb. He came back to the school as Juniors and Seniors were talking excitedly about the upcoming prom. He blamed the bleakness of his life on the students who taunted him and teachers who didn't really care.

Houston entered "C" building with a twelve-gauge shotgun and sawed off .22 rifle. Donning a camouflage hunting vest, he shot Robert Brens, a popular history instructor, who had flunked him in Civics. He then shot Judy Davis a current student of the teacher. Later in the hallway he shot Jason White in the chest as the boy was trying valiantly to stop him. He continued his rampage shooting anything he could think of as a target. At one point Eric pointed his shotgun at a female student, but before he could pull the trigger, Beamon Hill pushed her aside and took the blast to the side of his head. Students huddled on the floor of the commons room and hid in bathrooms and elevators. He took eighty-four students hostage for eight hours before giving up to authorities. In his murderous wake were three students and one teacher killed and ten others wounded. Wayne Bogus was one of the severely injured students and could never walk again. About 10:30 p.m. he walked out and surrendered to police. Eric has been on death row since he was convicted in 1993. In the years that followed the rampage, Houston's trial, the civil lawsuits and a bizarre series of bomb threats plagued the school, driving down morale. An award winning band dwindled in membership. No seniors were interested in going on the senior trip. A traditional championship football team was totally weakened and the school was ripe as gangs spilled onto the campus.

The school and the small town talk in terms of the journey, but there is not a blueprint where they are supposed to be even today. The people in this community will never forget. There is still a survivor's guilt readily seen. Teachers who were there at the time constantly relive it. Certain mundane events trigger the memories. Just passing a church where one attended a memorial service will bring on anguish of a high level. Weather, similar to that terrible day, can trigger bad memories for some.

(Plaque dedicated to teacher and 3
students killed at Lindhurst High School)

Bullies tend to be impulsive and unsuccessful in school. Studies have also shown that young bullies tend to remain bullies in adult life, without the proper early intervention. Adolescent bullies tend to become adult bullies who have children who are bullies.

*1985: a fourteen year old junior high school student in Kansas killed the principal and wounded three others. He identified as his motive the fact that he was bullied and beaten by other students for years.

•1988: A sixteen year old in Virginia took a pistol and firebombs to school in retribution for being called racist names. One teacher was wounded and one was killed.

•1993. Lindhurst High. Eric Huston. Killed teacher Robert Brens. four killed.and ten injured.

•1995: A sixteen year old from South Carolina, who indicated that he was bullied, wounded a teacher, killed another, and then killed himself.

•1996: A fourteen year old in Washington killed a peer who had teased him, another student and a teacher.

•1997: A sixteen year old in Alaska killed his principal, another student and wounded two more students. He had repeatedly reported to school staff that he needed help to stop the bullying.

•1997: A sixteen year old in Mississippi with a long history of family disruption and instability, killed his mother and two classmates and wounded seven other students. He remembered being bullied all the way back to the third grade.

•1999. Columbine. Eric Harris and Dylan Klebold.held a massacre in Colorado. fifteen dead. thirty injured.

•2001. Santee, California. Charles Williams killed two classmates and wounded thirteen others.

•2002. Halifax, Nova Scotia. A popular student Emmet Fralick killed himself.

•2002: Twelve students and one teacher were killed. Twenty-three were wounded and the two gunmen committed suicide. Cited specifically by parents in testimony investigation of the massacre was their belief that school administrators had failed to respond to the intimidation, assaults, bullying and taunts by student athletes toward a specific group of students.

•2003: A plot in New Jersey was foiled. Someone other than the intended targets are often injured or killed. The innocent victims get in their way. It is blind rage.

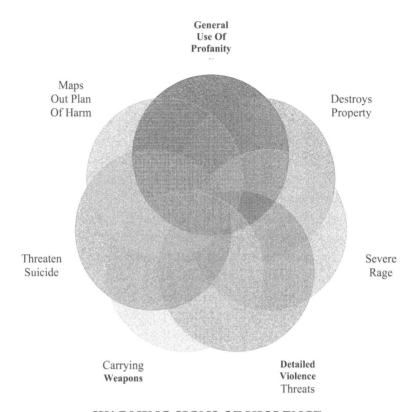

General
Use Of
Profanity

Maps
Out Plan
Of Harm

Destroys
Property

Threaten
Suicide

Severe
Rage

Carrying
Weapons

**Detailed
Violence**
Threats

WARNING SIGNS OF VIOLENCE

Student violence is escalating. People like Cho-Seung Hui, Ed Allaway, Charles Whitman, Sara Weeden, Wendy Percastigai Mejia names permeate our nation's airwaves and Internet. Today's parents and school leaders worry about terrorism and gun violence. Victims are more likely to carry weapons to school for self-defense. We live in a world of a new normal. Past fistfights have become gunfights. Now schools emphasize color-coded terror alerts as part of the fabric of life. School lockdowns have become as familiar as fire and earthquake drills.

The most notorious act of revenge came at Columbine High School. April 20, 1999 Eric Harris and Dylan Kleboll were considered outsiders at their

Littleton Colorado high school. Students reported that these two boys had been bullied and cyberbullied for years. Students, especially "jocks", continuously made fun of them. On this day horrendous killings would take place. At lunch, some students poured ketchup over them. They were called "faggots." This all happened while teachers watched. It became the catalyst. They had been called names for years. Other disrespectful things were continuously done to them. The two boys folded into a group of their own called the "Trench Coat Mafia." Slowly, but surely, their rage began to surface. They posted angry messages on the Internet and had brushes with the law. On this fateful day, students were happy and carefree rehearsing for the school play and thinking about graduation. The two arrived at school carrying two duffel bags filled with propane bombs. They tried to detonate these in the cafeteria, a location they had come to despise, but a loose connection prevented their detonation. They then pulled two sawed off shotguns, a HiPoint 9mm carbine, an illegal TEC DC9 semiautomatic and a plethora of homemade bombs and made their way to the outside staircase. At the top of the staircase, Eric began the massacre by killing Rachel Scott and injuring Richard Castaldo.

Popular students were targeted, especially the jocks who had relentlessly harassed them. Firing was at random. Students cried for help in heaps of blood. They fired at the principal shattering a plate glass window behind him. The principal said to himself, "Oh my God! I'm going to die! What is it going to feel like to have bullets pierce my body?"

The killers caused over $1 million in damages. Fifteen lost their lives and twenty-three were seriously injured. In a suicide note left by Eric, it was apparent that he and Dylan felt bullied and alienated, and in their minds it was "payback time." The memories shattered the lives of students and teachers. Today, Columbine still struggles to put the attack in the past. Even the years after the massacre, the reassuring routines of the present and the horrific memories of the past are inextricably entwined. Cited specifically by parents in testimony investigation of the massacre was their belief that school administration had failed to respond to the intimidation, assaults, bullying and taunts by student athletes toward specific groups of students. The killings were brutal, but so was the intense bullying the killers had undergone. For a year following the massacre, the tragedy was replayed by the entire national newscast, Internet, and some daily papers. There was a sixty percent rollover of the faculty. It takes a long time to heal. It is worse for the teachers who remain. Even today, many have not faced their grief yet.

Recently Darell Scott, the father of Rachel Scott, a victim of the Columbine High School shootings was invited to address the House Judiciary Committee's subcommittee. What he said to our national leaders during this special session of Congress was painfully truthful. They were not prepared for what he was to say, nor was it received well. His courageous words are powerful, penetrating and deeply personal.

The following is a portion of the transcript:

"Since the dawn of creation there has been both good and evil in the hearts of men and women. We all contain the seeds of kindness or the seeds of violence. The death of my wonderful daughter, Rachel Joy Scott, and the deaths of that heroic teacher, and the other eleven children who died must not be in vain. Their blood cries out for answers.

The first recorded act of violence was when Cain slew his brother Abel out in the field. The villain was not the club he used. Neither was it the NCA, the National Club Association. The true killer was Cain, and the reason for the murder could only be found in Cain's heart. In the days that followed the Columbine tragedy, I was amazed at how quickly fingers began to be pointed at groups such as the NRA. I am not a hunter. I do not even own a gun. I am not here to represent or defend the NRA-because I don't believe they are responsible for my daughter's death. Therefore, I do not believe that they need to be defended. If I believed they had anything to do with Rachel's murder I would be their strongest opponent. I am here today to declare that Columbine was not just a tragedy-it was a spiritual event that should be forcing us to look at where the real blame lies! Much of the blame lies here in this room. Much of the blame lies behind the pointing fingers of the accusers themselves. I wrote a poem just four nights ago that expresses my feelings best.

Your laws ignore our deepest needs,
Your words are empty air.
You've stripped away our heritage,

You've outlawed simple prayer.
Now gunshots fill our classrooms,
And precious children die.
You seek for answers everywhere,
And ask the question "Why?"
You regulate restrictive laws,
Through legislative creed.
And yet you fail to understand,
That God is what we need!"

Men and women are three-part beings. We all consist of body, mind and spirit. When we refuse to acknowledge a third part of our make-up, we create a void that allows evil, prejudice and hatred to rush in and wreak havoc. Spiritual presences were present within our educational systems for most of our nation's history. Many of our major colleges began as theological seminaries. This is a historical fact. What has happened to us as a nation? We have refused to honor God, and in so doing, we open the doors to hatred and violence. And when something as terrible as Columbine's tragedy occurs- politicians immediately look for a scapegoat such as the NRA. They immediately seek to pass more restrictive laws that contribute to erode away our personal and private liberties. We do not need more restrictive laws. Eric and Dylan would not have been stopped by metal detectors. No amount of gun laws can stop someone who spends months planning this type of massacre. The real villain lies within our own hearts.

As my son Craig lay under that table in the school library and saw his two friends murdered before his very eyes, he did not hesitate to pray in school. I defy any law or politician to deny him that right! I challenge every young person in America, and around the world, to realize that on April 20, 1999, at Columbine High School prayer was brought back to our schools. Do not let the many prayers offered by those students be in vain. Dare to move into the new millennium with a sacred disregard for legislation that violates your God-given right to communicate with Him. To those of you who would point your finger at the NRA- I give to you a sincere challenge. Dare to examine your own heart before casting the first stone! My daughter's death will not be in vain! The young people of this country will not allow that to happen!" (Scott,. 2008).

Scott's message vibrates throughout America as bloodshed surfaces. Eight days after Columbine, a copycat shooting took place at a high school in rural Alberta. This demonstrated that this is clearly not a "big-city" problem or an "American" problem; it was everyone's problem. It became apparent soon afterwards that the young people who committed these heinous acts were relentlessly bullied and teased throughout their young lives.

In Sacramento County (May 22, 2006) more than thirty young people have been killed. They are the victims of youth-on-youth violence. In 2000, twenty young people ranging in ages from fourteen to twenty-four were gunned down in Sacramento County, most in gang-related altercations. In 2005, the number jumped to forty-six. Between 1997 and 2005 the collective toll was two hundred sixty teenagers and young adults. Finally, Area Congregations Together (ACT) have launched a campaign called "Stand Together" to focus on early intervention. (Sacyouth.com). In Sacramento County California, last year twenty-seven people who were twenty-one or younger were shot to death. Of thirteen homicides, twelve were shot to death. It has become a nightmare for patrol officers. It is more difficult to stop a fifteen to sixteen year old more so than a hardened criminal because this child often just reacts to the situation. Sacramento City police took away eight hundred ninety-nine guns last year. The Sacramento County Sheriff took one thousand two hundred ninety-eight guns last year.

Weapons have gradually seeped down from the high schools to the middle schools and even the elementary schools. As an assistant principal in a low income area at Martin Luther King Middle School in Sacramento, I personally took away three handguns and seventeen major switch blades from kids in a mere two years time. Children are changing. Their standards and morals are left in the shadows. Many do not offer any feelings for their classmates.

The terror of weapons on any campus is a daily worry for administrators, teachers, and parents alike. The news media seems filled with various incidents of violence. Recently in Knoxville, Tennessee a high school student fatally shot a fifteen year old classmate as other teenager classmates watched in horror as the victim clutched his chest and fell to the floor. Ryan McDonald, a sophomore who lived with his grandmother was the shooter. Tracing the problem, police found that Ryan had alopecia, a condition that left him bald since he was three. As such he was the automatic target of endless teasing and bullying. Ryan had the dubious distinction of being charged with first degree murder yet was held in the juvenile detention facility.

For teenagers living in a shelter for abused and neglected children, school can provide a daily dose of normalcy, a place to fit in, a chance to be just another kid. It didn't turn out that way for fifteen year old Lawrence King. In Oxnard, California, 60 miles northwest of Los Angeles, Brandon McInterney, a 16 year old at E. O. Green Junior High shot King in the head. For the area itself, there were seven shootings in one week's time. King was openly gay and found no refuge from his tormentors. Not in the classroom, the quad, the cafeteria. Not from the day he enrolled at school in Oxnard. The anti-gay taunts and slurs that King endured from his male peers were constant. The stinging words were isolating. The name-calling had begun long before he told his small circle of confidants that he was gay, before problems at home made him a ward of the court, and before he summoned the courage to further assert his sexual orientation by wearing makeup and girl's boots with his school uniform. To make maters worse, he flirted with some of his mockers. One of them was McInerney, who seethed over it. McInerney was tall and strong for his age. He excelled in athletics and academics. He was one of the "cool" kids and could be unfriendly. If you weren't part of his privileged group, it was like you didn't exist. Many called him a real jerk. He was one of the school's most notable bullies. The shooter had personal bullying issues and was in foster care for neglected children. McInterney had his own troubled home life when he was younger. His parents accused each other of drug addiction. There were many physical assaults in the home according to court records. The year before McInterney was born, his father allegedly shot the boy's mother in the arm, shattering her elbow.

McInerney has been charged as an adult with premeditated murder and a hate crime. The cold blooded nature of the killing: two shots to the head in an attack carried out at 8:30 a.m. in a roomful of twenty youngsters unpacking their books. King was brain dead. Earlier in the year, King began hitting on McInerney remarking for all to hear that he thought McInerney was "cute." Other boys then ribbed McInerney by saying he must be gay. Brandon had told a close girl friend that he was going to kill Larry. She, however, did not tell any school official. Everyone thought it was a joke. King was shot the next day.

The family has established a Web site in King's memory, with a photo gallery that shows King throughout his childhood: on his first plane ride, getting a haircut, dressed as the Great Pumpkin for Halloween. On the site, hundreds of sympathetic comments have been posted.

In Los Angeles (May 15, 2006) two Quartz Hill teenagers (ages seventeen and fifteen) meticulously planned a Columbine-style attack on their old high school. They stockpiled ammunition and bomb-making materials then practiced detonating improvised explosives in the Antelope Valley desert in anticipation of an attack. Luckily a sixteen year old girl told authorities. The bullies said they were planning on cutting off her arms and legs during the attack. A judge has ruled that the older boy, Johnny Casas, is unfit for rehabilitation in a juvenile setting and should be tried as an adult. The boys confessed to deputies that they were going to make the attack because of their peers school and online ridicule and bullying of their Goth attire and life-style. The student they chose to victimize was in special education and was really a gentle soul.

In Santee California, Charles Andrew Williams, a freshman, brought a gun to school. He shot and killed two schoolmates and wounded another 13. Friends said he was picked on constantly. He was very skinny and some called him "Anorexic Andy." Peers felt he was dumb, skinny and a faggot. He had many items stolen, more recently two skateboards. One classmate said we abused him pretty much all the time.

One young man from Mississippi, sixteen year old Luke Woodum had suffered repeated bullying. He began to hate his condition more every day.

Returning to the school's cafeteria, he opened fire and assortment of those who were harassing him. When a heroic assistant principal sacrificed his life and tackled him down. There were two killed and seven wounded. Lying amongst the dead was Luke's ex-girl friend who had recently joined the chorus of hecklers. The home life was not much better because prior to the slaughter at the school, he was upset because he received no help at home. He took a butcher knife to his mom while she lay sleeping in bed. When questioned, he said, "she never loved me!"

Bullying usually takes place out of sight of adults. Most victims are reluctant to report the bullying for fear of embarrassment or retaliation. Most bullies deny or justify their behavior. Victims often suffer lifelong problems with low self-esteem. They are prone to depression, suicide, retaliation by shootings and other mental health problems. Youth less than twenty-one years old constitutes less than a third of the nation's population, but they commit half of the known bias crimes. Boys who were identified as bullies later on have one criminal conviction by the age of twenty-four while forty percent of those identified had three or more arrests by the age of thirty.

Jeff Wiese, age fifteen, had been harassed and teased for a number of years. He became a loner and began to wear a black trench coat all the time. On top of this his father committed suicide four years earlier and his mother lives in a nursing home after suffering brain injuries from a car accident. In trying to prevent the repeated bullying at school, he began to spark fear among some of his fellow students. He began to paint his face. Teachers found him in art classes drawing pictures of skeletons, skulls and playing sorrowful tunes on his guitar. One drawing was a sketch of a guitar-strumming skeleton with a caption that read, "March to the death song till your boots fill with blood."

A few students continued to bully him. He responded physically and was suspended from school. Jeff drove his grandfather's squad car to the front door of the school. Armed with a twelve-gauge shotgun and a .40 caliber handgun and .twenty-tow- caliber handgun, he walked into the Red Lake High School on the Indian Reservation wearing his grandfather's bulletproof vest and opened fire. Students scrambled under desks. One girl pleaded, "No Jeff, quit, quit. Leave me alone. What are you doing?" Jeff wrote in his blog: "I'm a retarded (expletive) for ever believing that things would change. I'm starting to regret sticking around. It takes courage to turn the gun on yourself, takes courage to face death."

Rumors about school problems can quickly be circulated through student text messages and on MySpace and Facebook. Recently, about four hundred parents picked their children up from Galt High School (California) before the school day because of rumors of an impending gang fight. The rumors stemmed from a fight on campus earlier in the week. Retaliation circulated quickly through Facebook, MySpace and student text messages. Kids became in a panic and began calling parents saying guns were on campus. The Superintendent said that if there had been a problem the district would have let parents know. After all, they have an autodialer system which can call every parent's phone number and leave messages in both Spanish and English within twelve minutes.

Kids can devalue their victims by using the Internet. Kids profile could get online. Parents are warned that data are scooped up from many sources. Jane Yang, a thirty year old marketing coordinator was curious the other day to see what would turn up if she searched for herself on Reunion.com, a Los Angeles-based social networking site. Sure enough, there was her name. Under her "friends and family" was listed her husband's name. It also listed the town they were from. But then it startled Yang to see the name of her four year old son. It made her really, really angry and really worried. She was scared knowing that there are predators out there.

The incident serves as a cautionary tale for anyone who thinks kids' personal information is excluded from the data smorgasbord that is the Internet. There is no telling what can turn up as vast databases of sensitive information are bought and sold by private companies. This company recently purchased records on millions of people from a data broker. A supervisor told Yang that her son's name probably came from state vaccination records or from the Centers for Disease Control and Prevention. Reunion.com is no stranger to privacy issues. They send emails to all their contacts saying that so and so was searching for them, even when no such search was performed. The practice helps privately held Reunion.com register 1.3 million new members each month, an important statistic to advertisers and affiliates. The site now boasts about forty million registered members. The Better Business Bureau gives Reunion.com its lowest grade of "F", mostly due to its emailing of people in members' address books. The site now has decided to build its own database by acquiring files for as many as two hundred sixty million people from a private data broker.

The most reasonable assumption is that if one minor slipped through, then others might also have gotten in. It is up to teachers and parents to monitor online directories such as Reunion.com and make sure their names aren't present. Parents might also want to think twice about using their kids' names for children's magazine subscriptions or online gift registries. Once a name is in a corporate database, it can be bought and sold.

Chapter 4:
Your Child May Be a Bully

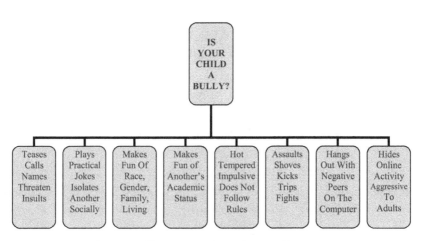

Your Child May Be a Bully

Former President George Bush wrote: *"I have learned that our children are a mirror, an honest reflection of their parents and their world. Sometimes the reflection is flattering and at other times, we simply do not like what we see; but we must never turn away."*

Dr. Bill Meyer interviewed a former bully in the Sullivan Correctional Facility in New York. It was the convicted serial killer, David Berkowitz, the media's "Son of Sam". Berkowitz acknowledged much pain due to bullying as a child in his home. It led to a level of intense anger. Later it resulted in people being killed in cold blood. He admitted to being a bully from an early age. He was eight years old when he remembered really getting involved in bullying. From time to time there were certain guys he would pick on, just because he was mean. He said, "they never did anything to me. Over the years I have never been able to forget them nor their faces. I, too, was tormented because even I have a conscience. I am so sorry. I had no right to be cruel to these guys!"

Beckowitz was an admitted **physical bully**. Bullies can be physical. This type is action oriented. It is linked more to boys than girls. It involves hitting, kicking, damaging property. It is easy to identify. The entire neighborhood and school are aware. The older they get, the more aggressive they become.

Another type is the **verbal bully**. When a bully taunts her target, there is no playfulness in the attack. Verbal bullying can be name-calling, taunting, belittling, cruel criticism, personal defamation, racist slurs and sexually suggestive abusive remarks. Lying and false witness is vicious. This type is easier to inflict on other children and can occur in the least amount of time. It leaves no visible scars but can be even more damaging.

The third type is the **relational bully**. In the teenager's world where peer acceptance is prime, this type of excluding or rejecting certain students from a circle of friends can be devastating. It is linked to verbal bullying and is more common among girls. The bully princess is alive and well. She will use techniques like ignoring, isolating, excluding or shunning. Also included will be aggressive stares, rolling of the eyes, sighs, frowns, sneers, snickers and hostile body language.

One of the hardest parts of being a parent is when someone may tell you your child is a bully or cyberbully. Parents are told that their own offspring is creating chaos, panic, and pandemonium. No parent wants to hear that his child might be a bully. Too many parents want an eye-for-an-eye.

The bully is someone's child also. Remember that failure is an event-not a person. Both children in this situation might need help. If you are the one which feels a need to contact a parent about his child being a bully, handle it very carefully. Emphasize that you are trying to teach your child both at home and at school to help develop a positive environment where every child is valued, accepted, safe and free to learn. Explain that you have been exploring the increases in bullying in your area. Tell them that some behaviors you have noticed about their child might be worthy of watching. Then give them examples of why you think so.

Educators and parents should be aware that evil can come in the form of secret student conspiracies or an ambush of weaker students. Bullies want to catch targets unprepared. Bullies tend to have a defiant swagger that simply screws up lives. Bullying is a conscious, willful and deliberate hostile activity intended to harm, induce fear through the threat of further aggression and create terror. The bully makes and breaks the rules. Bullying is simply arrogance in action. Bullies are mean. Bullies are scary. Bullies are a pain in the brain and every child needs to know what to do when confronted by one. Every teacher and parent needs to know how to help children in dealing with bullies and cyberbullies.

Just about any child may be transformed into becoming a bully or a cyberbully. They are an inflammatory bunch. They want to annihilate everything in their path. Cyberbullying may also indicate a tendency toward more serious adrenaline-pumping behavior. They light up the blogosphere in varying degrees of nastiness. Unlike regular bullying, online bullying can occur any time of the day or night. Anyone can blog. While bullying has always been an unfortunate reality, most bullies grow out of it. Cyberbullying has not existed long enough to have solid research, but there is evidence that it may be an early warning for more violent behavior.

Research has found that identified bullies in their early teens have one criminal conviction by the age of twenty-four. Forty percent had three or more arrests by the age of thirty. Children who bully others tend to have difficulties with other relationships, such as those with friends, parents, and teachers.

A study by scientists at York University and Queens University, looked at eight hundred seventy-one students for seven years from ages ten to eighteen. Each year they asked the children questions about their involvement in bullying or victimizing behavior, their relationships and other positive and negative behaviors. The research found that most children engage in at some point bullying during their school years. Almost a tenth (nine point nine percent) said they did so. The study found that children who bullied tended to be aggressive. They lacked a moral compass. They experienced a lot of conflict in their relationships with their parents and other adults. Their relationships with friends also were marked by a lot of conflict and they tended to associate with others who bullied. They said," by providing intensive and ongoing support starting in the elementary school years to this small group of youth who persistently bully, it may be possible to promote healthy relationships and prevent their career path of bullying that leads to numerous social emotional and relationship problems in adolescence and adulthood. (Pepler, 2008).

Cyberbullying is well known by many professional organizations. The National Education Association indicates that every two seconds a student is physically attacked in school and that a typical child has a twenty five percent chance of being involved with bullying on campus. Even though most bullying occurs at school, bullying is a broader social problem that often happens outside of the schools, on the street, at shopping centers, the local pool, summer camp, and online. At any given time, about twenty-five percent of American students are victims and twenty percent are engaged.

No teacher or parent wants his/her child to be identified as a bully or a cyberbully. How can you, as a caring adult discover these tendencies? The child may be a bully if he/she:

- Values aggression. Assaults other children with shoving, kicking, tripping or fighting.
- Tends to have average or above average self-esteem. Likes to be in charge.
- Tends to be impulsive, hot-headed personalities who lack empathy, have difficulty conforming to the rules and have

positive attitudes toward violence.

- Shows no empathy for others. Are even aggressive toward adults. Are tough or shows no sympathy for other children who are being bullied.
- Teases, name calls, threatens or insults other children
- Plays practical jokes or isolates another child socially
- Makes fun of another child's race, gender, living conditions or family's financial situation. Is impulsive.
- Makes fun of another child's academic status.
- Arrogant and boastful winners and poor losers in competitive games
- Fights often with siblings. They are given opportunity in your home to dominate siblings through verbal, physical, social or sexual abuse. They will try to wield these controls outside of the home as well.
- Have been involved in other anti-social behavior, such as vandalism and theft.
- Consistently uses profanity and nasty comments. In a study at the London School of Economics, nasty comments were reported online by one third of British children ages nine to nineteen years old. Only seven percent of parents were aware that their child had received sexual comments and only four percent that their child had been bullied.

By using things like the new line of camera phones, the cyberbully can perpetrate their victim with even nastier stuff. Any youngster can now sneak into a bathroom or locker room, snap a few photos and upload those photos directly from her phone to a Web site that caters to multi-media messages. There, anyone in the world with a computer and an Internet connection can view download, and archive the images. All this mischief can be accomplished in seconds.

When both parents work outside the home, it is an open invitation for the child to begin cyberbullying or bullying. Yet, bullies may also come from a privileged family where parents are overly permissive. Bullies bully because they can and because they can get away with it.

The relative anonymity of the Internet is appealing for bullies because it enhances the intimidation and makes tracing the activity more difficult. They have no fear of detection. Some bullies also find it easier to be more vicious because there is no personal contact. They do not see the other child's reactions before they realize the situation has gone too far. Unfortunately, the Internet and email can also increase the visibility of the activity. Information or pictures posted online or forwarded in mass emails can reach a larger audience faster than more traditional methods, causing more damage to the victim. Because of the amount of personal information available online, bullies may be able to arbitrarily choose their victims. (US-CERT, 2008). For this reason, most cyberbullies easily escape punishment and repercussions because parents and other adults do not realize what is happening to a victim.

Cyberbullies use email, instant messages (IM's), cell phones, text messages, photos, videos and social networking sites to humiliate and threaten others. Most cyberbullies have Internet access from home. Boys more commonly cyberbully by sending messages of a sexual nature or by threatening to fight or hurt someone. Girls more often bully by spreading rumors, sending messages that make fun of someone or exclude them. They also tend to tell the secrets of others to harm them.

Cyberbullies feel great if they can put other people down. It makes them feel powerful. Since most have a low self esteem themselves, why not attack someone else who they feel is lower than them? They prefer to publicly harm and humiliate their victims in cyberspace rather than resolve their issues through communication because of the fear of peer confrontation. Oftentimes, these misguided youth are generally too frightened to face the other person.

Cyberbullies may disclose victims' personal data (e.g., real name or workplace/schools) at websites or forums, or may attempt to assume the identity of a victim for the purpose of publishing material in their name that defames or ridicules them. Some cyberbullies may also send threatening emails and instant messages to the victims. The content in these messages are often so strong that a victim may commit suicide.

Repentance for an act of cyberbullying should be in the sorrow for the deed, not for getting caught. Once you think child might be a bully, what can teachers and parents do?

* Take it seriously. It is important for children to know parents take harassment seriously.
* Set good examples. Be aware of your own behavior, as it sets the standard for your children. Do not call the person who cuts you off in traffic an ugly name or yell taunts or names at opposing teams during sporting events.
* Know your child. Do not treat bullying as a passing phase. Another child is being hurt. What pushes your child's buttons or makes him/her most likely to respond aggressively? Role play with your child and suggest ways he/she can interface assertively and without resorting to bullying and name calling.
* Examine your discipline tactics. Never discipline your child out of anger or use punitive discipline when your child misbehaves or makes mistakes. Children who use verbal harassment and bullying require discipline that is non-violent, consistent and logically given.
* Help build empathy for others and talk to your child about how it feels to be bullied. Use the famous adage: "If you can't say something nice, don't day anything at all." Foster empathy. Encourage your child to help others who need it. Provide opportunities for your child to be of service to other groups by volunteering at a shelter, making cards for sick children, cleaning up a neighbor's yard. Encourage your child to always think about how it might feel to stand in another's shoes.
* Ask yourself if someone at home is bullying your child. Do not bully your children nor bully others in front of them.
* Teach kids to solve problems without using violence and praise them when they do.
* Show disapproval. Let your child know taunting and name calling are unacceptable with you. Express disappointment or concern if you know your child has taunted someone and make them apologize to the person he/she taunted.
* Give children positive feedback when they behave well.

   *   Support bully-prevention programs at your school. Encourage
         frankness.

Finally, remember that bullying and cyberbullying are learned behaviors.
As such, they can be changed. Experts say that between the ages of two
and five, children become cognizant of differences in other children's gender, race, ethnicity and disabilities. They also become aware of and even
pick up considerable negative biases, which not only impacts how they
view others, but how they view themselves. Make certain the impetus of
your child's bullying is not due to problems involved in the home.

Bullies often come from families where parents choose more physical
forms of discipline. They are coupled with parents who are rejecting
and hostile or overly permissive. N. M. Floyd found that many bullies
at school are, in fact, victims in their own homes. It may not be a happy
home. These homes report three times more family problems than their
nonbullying peers. Violence in the home may be a frequent occurrence.
Their parents often do not keep up with their whereabouts. Family in-
teractions are often disengaged. Positive role models are scarce. No one
apparently has shown them how to get along with others.

In a bully's home discipline is generally inconsistent and arbitrary. Punishment
is often harsh and meted out according to parental mood. Little empathy is
present as the children are bombarded with negativisms. The transmission
of aggression through the child is often intergenerational. There is harsh and
capricious punishment. There are frequent blow-ups after minor infractions.
The home has violent and emotional outbursts by adults. The home tends to
ignore the child for long stretches of time and has a definite disinterest in the
child's welfare. There is no praise, no encouragement, no humor. The home
resonates with put-downs, sarcasm and criticism which makes certain that the
child feels insecure and rejected. Aggression in this home is viewed as good
because parents want them to take care of themselves without bothering the
parents. The entire family enjoys watching violent and aggressive movies.

Barbara Coloroso in her work *"The Bully, The Bullied and the Bystander"*
encountered three kinds of families;

➤ **Brick Wall Families.** In this family, learning takes place in an atmosphere of fear. In order to get affection and approval, children are expected to do as told. In this family children are controlled, manipulated and made to mind. Their feelings are often ignored, ridiculed or negated. The parent always wins. There is rigid enforcement of rules. Brute force is often used. There seems to be an attempt to break the child's will and spirit with fear and punishment. Parents use humiliation. They often threat and bribe their children to guarantee observance of rules. In this family, there is a heavy reliance on competition. Children are taught what to think, not how to think. These parents often make disparaging comments about people in their community or school. Thus, they teach their children intolerance, bigotry, and hatred. A bully is born!

➤ **Jelly Fish Families.** A jellyfish parent tends to become enmeshed in their children's lives. They are always there to smooth out problems and rescue them from any responsibility. This family basically lacks a firm structure. Children become obnoxious and spoiled and or scared and vindictive. The parent doesn't know how to create a healthy structure with consistency and safe boundaries for their children. There is no structure at the critical points of family's day-to-day life: mealtime, bedtime, chores, and recreation. The parent has personal problems that keep them centered almost totally on themselves. Punishments and rewards are arbitrary and inconsistent. Second changes are arbitrarily given. Threats and bribes are commonplace. Emotions rule the behavior of parents and children. Love is highly conditional. A victim is born!

➤ **Backbone Families.** Rules are simple and clearly stated. Consequences for irresponsible behavior are either natural or reasonable. This type of family allows teachers at school to receive total assistance. Here parents do not demand respect- they demonstrate and teach it. Children learn to love themselves and have empathy for others. Their slogan is most often: "I believe in you. I trust you. I know you can handle life's situations. You are listened to and you are cared for. You are very important to me!" Democracy is learned through experience. Discipline is handled with authority that gives life to children's learning. Children get second opportunities. Children are motivated to be all they can be. Children receive lots of smiles, hugs and humor. Children learn to accept their own feelings and to act responsibly on those feelings through a strong sense of self-awareness. Competency and cooperation are modeled and encouraged. Love is unconditional. Children who feel loved, wanted and respected are more willing to celebrate differences and welcome others into their circle of caring. Children are taught how to think. They are spoken with, not to. They are listened to, not ignored. Children are buffered from the possible impact of a bully or from the need to be a bully by the daily reinforcement of the message: "I like myself; I can think for myself; there is no problem so great it can't be solved." Being a backbone parent is not easy. There are no quick fixes, no sure answers, just lots of opportunities to grow.

In families parents must become the sentries to help their children gain knowledge, skills and values to make safe and responsible choices in online activity. Smart parents know what to say as well as what not to say to their children. Disastrous bad remarks towards your child can create havoc. Three bad remarks towards your child may include:
- A self-righteous "Didn't I tell you" statement
- A negative label and a blank condemnation of his future
- A parent's own anger and frustration, demeaning and alienating your child makes a bad situation worse

A persistent pattern of such remarks may do lifelong damage. Children learn most of their communication skills in the home. Cleveland State University's Michael Beatty explained that "Kids who are chronic targets of insults and criticism grow into adults who tend to resort to the same negative language."

Teasing that comes from adults is the most painful says Dr. Carole Lieberman, psychiatrist in Beverly Hills. "Children look to their parents as a mirror to tell them who they are in this world." Teasing creates uncertainty because a child never knows how serious the teacher or parent is.

Teasing and belittling creates an epidemic of inferiority besetting our children. It hurts deeply and permanently. Parents and teachers do not need to add to the demise of the child. They need to learn how to express anger without being hurtful. Criticize the child's behavior instead of the child. Avoid gender labels such as calling a boy a "sissy" or "crybaby." Children respond best to acts and words that they perceive as encouraging, and worst to punishment and degrading comments which inflict discouragement. Adults who cannot control their temper are teaching children that it is okay to yell, scream, and use physical violence to get their way. It is hard, but the adult needs to allow children to express feelings about you. Let him respectfully blow off steam, argue, and state opinions that are different from your own. Then reconstruct what needs to happen in your own home.

Fran Litman, director of the Center for Parenting Studies at Wheelock College in Boston says parents may say "if you don't put away those toys right now, I'm going to whack you!" Yet the parent probably would never do it. False threats undermine a parent's credibility. Try replacing a threat with a promise. The idea is to build motivation and encourage the desired behavior. Emphasizing the positive by giving the child a logical reason for doing something works with children of nearly every age.

CHAPTER 5:
OUR CHILD MAY BE A VICTIM

Most On-Site
Are Boys
Girls Most
Cyberbullies

Carry
Weapons For
Protection.
Talks Of
Suicide

Most Victims
Are Younger
Than The
Bullies

Sad, Anxious
Depressed,
Moody. Low
Self-Esteem

Victims Tend
To Have Few
Friends

**Bullying/
Cyber-
bullying
Victims**

Don't Want
To Go To
School.
Declining
Grades.

Do Not Stand
Up To Bullies
Or Fight Back
Physically
Weaker

Become
Quiet,
Sensitive,
Exhibit Fear
Or Anxiety

Lack Social
Support From
Peers, Adults.
And Parents

Sometimes
Academically
Different.
Smarter Or
Not As Smart

BULLYING CYBER-BULLYING VICTIMS

For some children, having friends and positive support can help make them more resilient to the slings and arrows from bullies. But other children take the words and abuse more to heart and begin to believe what's being said about them. Those types of negative thoughts are actually believed to be at the core of things like depression and anxiety.

A child's friendships are very serious at any age, but especially during junior high and senior high school years. They need friendship. Your child needs to build friendships. They need healthy relationships. They need to know that other children are going through the same thing that they are. They need to learn from the wisdom of others. Sometimes teachers and parents forget this. Without this, children are at risk.

Acknowledging that there is a possible unprecedented battle for their child's survival, an educator or parent might ask, "Is my child at risk?" The answer is simply "maybe!" Since victims tend to have "roller coaster" emotions, there are a few things a parent or teacher can check. For instance, has their behavior changed recently. If you suspect your child is being teased or bullied, look for the signs. Keep an eye out of reluctance to go to school, silence on what is happening at school, frequently losing objects or possessions and a frequent "everything on me" attitude, or low self-esteem. They have been made to feel dumb or stupid and it affects their ability to perform. Among the most-often expressed emotions are panic, anxiety, denial, ambivalence, irritability and anger, frustration, fatigue, hopelessness and helplessness and guilt.

Roller coaster emotions are often normal. How an adult deals with them helps to decrease stress. This is what counts. Parents and teachers must take charge by showing interest by asking questions less likely to be answered with a brief yes or no. Don't ask," How was your day?" Try asking, "What important things did you do at recess today?" or "What happened at lunchtime today?" Talk to your child about your own childhood experiences about being teased or bullied. Talk about how it made you feel and how you handled it. To help a child, parents and teachers can make lists and check items off as each one is accomplished. A person cannot keep everything in your head because you will undoubtedly forget something important.

Children between the ages of nine and eleven were asked why other children are bullied or cyberbullied? Basically their comments fall under four general headings.

<u>Physical Attributes</u>:

She is very skinny.

He smells a bit and is dirty.

He is fat.

She comes from a different country.

He is poor and he has eczema.

She is very tiny.

<u>Learning Problems</u>:

She cannot read well.

He is not very good at things.

Some kids cannot do things as well as others.

They are sometimes rubbish in work habits.

<u>Emotional Disposition or Reaction</u>:

She gets moody easily.

He is sensitive and does not stick up for himself.

She appears considerably stressed out.

He gets picked on because he is new to the school.

<u>Retaliation</u>:

She is so bossy- she makes horrible remarks and is just a pain.

He thinks he is better than people.

She shows off and lies and about people.

He picks on you first.

She keeps telling off people for being stupid and showing off.

The educator or parent can look for warning signs that the child may be a victim or that they are misusing the computer:

> Your child may be spending long hours online, especially at night.
> You, or your child, begin to receive phone calls from people you do not know. Devices can be purchased that show telephone numbers that have been dialed from your home phone. The last number dialed from your home phone can be retrieved provided that your phone is equipped with a redial feature.

> ➤ Your child is receiving unsolicited gifts in the mail.
> ➤ Your child suddenly turns off the computer, or changes screens, when the parent walks into the room. When this happens, parents should ask "why?" Regardless of the response, start monitoring computer time more closely.
> ➤ Your child appears to be withdrawing from family life.
> ➤ There is reluctance by your child to discuss his/her online activities.
> ➤ The parent finds pornography on the child's computer.
> ➤ The parent discovers that your child is using an online account belonging to someone else.

Once discovered, realize that your child generally will refuse to report victimization. Children do not report cyberbullying to adults for a variety of reasons. Among them are fear of retaliation, feelings of shame for not being able to stand up for themselves, fear that they would not be believed, not wanting to worry their parents, not having confidence that the situation would change for reporting it, thinking their parents' or teachers' advice would make it worse, fear that the adult would tell the bully who reported the incidents, and thinking they would be considered a "snitch."

Children are at the highest risk of being the victim of a violent crime in the four hours following the end of the school day. Many bullies seem to have brazen disregard of the presence of an adult-any adult. Oftentimes, the adult does not understand the world of the child, particularly the teenager. The inability of adults to understand their children is a large part of what teenage rebellion is all about.

Dogged by a ruthless enemy, victims of bullying and cyberbullying are often fearful of telling others about being bullied because they fear that the bullying may actually become worse if they tell. Children know that if the bully is merely suspended for the day, they may come back and "kick my butt!" Victims are often also afraid to report to adults about being cyberbullied, as they also fear that adults will over-react and take away their mobile phone, computer and Internet access. This is something that is increasingly unthinkable for the "Always On" generation as not being online means not being able to socialize or communicate with their peers and this fear of exclusion is paramount in the lives of most adolescents and teens. They are caught in a deadly cross fire.

Respect where the child is. Parents often want to act immediately by calling the teacher or a school administrator. This can sometimes make the situation more difficult for your child if he/she is being bullied. If your child asks you not to do anything about the incident, respect this wish and work instead on making him/her feel empowered enough to attack the situation on their own.

One good way is to try role-playing. Reenact the bullying and help your child practice aggressive ways to handle it. Brainstorm about witty or humorous comebacks, utilize preventative tactics such as reporting aggressive, abusive behavior and seek friends or adult supervisors.

As these forms of social Internet communication increase in popularity, it is likely that cyberbullying will spread even more to our defenseless children. Victims are often perplexed as to how to respond. In most cases, cyberbullies know their victims, but their victims may not know their cyberbullies. With the advent of mobile, wireless Internet access, communications have become more ubiquitous. As a result, cyberbullying can happen any time and any place. For many children, neither the home nor the school is a refuge from negative peer pressure such as schoolyard bullying. Children need to turn to adults for help. Teachers and parents are urged to maintain their sense of humor. And most importantly, trust their gut feelings as to what should be done. Do not use someone else's values.

Educators and parents need to help children believe in themselves. If they do, other children will notice. If they are confronted by either a bully or a cyberbully, they need to tell them that your child does not like what they are doing. It may be hard to believe, but some kids might not know that they are considered a bully. Help your child develop the ability to speak firmly so they will not be afraid. Explain they should not get mad. If they do so, the bully wins. Instead of getting mad, your child may get funny. Humor is one way to stop bullies. It will also show the bully that your child is confident. Therefore, they can practice comeback lines. Keep them short and do not say anything mean. Definitely, do not fight back. It will only make matters worse.

Bullies try to upset kids. Stay calm and try to calm the bully. Help your child to check out the way they look. Slouching, looking to the ground or their feet, fidgeting shows they are not confident. Instead, hold your head up, stand up straight, and look people in the eye. Look assertive and the bully will be less likely to pick on them.

Parents and teachers can help the child who is a potential victim by help-ing them understand some common truths:
- I do not have to put up with bullying.
- It is okay to tell on bullies.
- It is okay not to bully.
- Bullying hurts my body and my feelings.
- I am an individual.
- I respect people's possessions.
- We are all different, yet share a great deal.
- I have rights and with them come responsibilities.
- There are people I can ask for help.
- There are things I can do to stop bullying.
- I can play safely without hurting others.
- You have to be a friend to have a friend.
- I am responsible for my own actions.
- I can help make my class and school a bully-free zone.

Cyberbullying is very capable of creating deep, emotional wounds from which many cannot recover, ever! It hurts feelings and destroys self-es-teem. Each educator or parent must get involved. You have a genuine responsibility to view the child's actions online. They may become profiles into your child's soul. It leads victims to not want to come to school or face their peers. It often causes stomachaches, headaches, depression, which, most assuredly, impacts the child's school attendance and school academic performance.

These wounds can create many different health problems. An important study by Dr. Louise Arsenault of King's College, London, identified one thousand one hundred sixteen sets of twins between 1994 and 1995. The importance was that this study targeted the kids who are more likely to develop depression. The research offers strong evidence that children can develop depression and anxiety. Among identical twin pairs in which one experienced bullying between the ages of seven and nine and the other did not, the bullied twin was significantly more likely to have symptoms of internalizing problems at age ten. Internalizing problems are psychological problems in which negativity is directed inward toward the self, such as depression, worrying, being withdrawn and feeling overly guilty as opposed to outwardly, such as conduct disorder. The study proves beyond a shadow of doubt that bullying is bad for a child's health. The fact that children were having these symptoms which include frequent crying, fear of being alone, and stomach aches- at such a young age-strongly suggests that they need help.

When dealing with emotional health problems sit down and truly communicate with your child. Dr. Sarah Shea, Director of the Child Development Clinic suggests that teachers and parents "ask your child indirectly how he or she spends lunch hour; or what it is like walking to school, walking home or taking the school bus. Ask what they are doing online and who causes them the most problems? Without personalizing it, ask if there are any other children online at school who are bullies?"

When dealing with cyberbullying, some teachers and parents express their biggest concern. Basically, it can be labeled "the 4P's": privacy, predators, pornography and pop-ups. Adults must take the time to really listen to the complaints and actions of each child. If they are being bullied online or at school, it can become tragic for your child and yourself.

Generally a victim is different from other kids. Size, race, sexuality or different interests than other kids appear to be some of the reasons. Victims seem to be weaker, either physically or emotionally. A child who is in special education classes is an obvious target. Victims tend to be insecure at home and at school, desperately want approval, and generally will not reveal to adults that they are being bullied. Parents and educators need to be observant of their children's behavior, appearance, and mood both for the signs of being bullied or engaging in bullying behavior.

So what does the teacher or parent look for? Kids speak in a number of basic ways: with the body, face, eyes, tone of voice and words. You should look for:

- Withdrawal and depression. Children who cause trouble at home or at school may actually be depressed but not know it. Because the youngster may not always seem sad, adults may not realize that troublesome behavior is a sign of depression.
    - Difficulty with Relationships. The ultimate insult among children is to be rejected by one's peers. Rejection by peers is a kiss of death in Kid World. A child who used to play often with friends may now spend most of the time alone and without interests. There is social isolation and poor peer communication. No matter how cutting an adult's comment might be, the same words yielded by a peer cut deeper and heal slower. Peer rejection in the form of verbal taunts and ridicule is the equivalent of a public stoning.
    - Trouble with School Grades. There is poor classroom performance and a significant drop in grades and refusal to do homework. They are reluctant to go to school and there are frequent absences. The child loses interest in school and talks negatively about school experiences. The child has poor concentration and a feeling of hopelessness.
    - A Battered Look. The child experiences torn clothing, ripped book bags, personal papers written on. The child may suffer bruises on parts of his/her body.
    - Loss of appetite. A major change in eating and/or sleeping patterns is the norm.
    - Physical Illness. There are frequent complaints about physical illnesses such as headaches and stomach aches. The child has mood changes, persistent boredom, and low energy.
    - Sadness & Crying. Frequent sadness, tearfulness, crying. Tears appear as the silent language of a child's grief.
    - Indifference to Activities. A loss of interest in activities he/she

previously enjoyed. Things that were once fun now bring little joy to the depressed child.

- <u>Need for Additional Money</u>. A required need for extra money above and beyond previous expenditures.
- <u>Unexpected Violence</u>. Child turn to violent behavior as a protection
- <u>Negative Talk</u>. Child talks to siblings or friends about efforts to run away from home.
- <u>Alcohol and Drugs</u>. They may find a way to abuse alcohol or other drugs as a way to feel better.
- <u>Bullycide.</u> Child expresses thoughts or expressions of suicide or self-destructive behavior. They may say they want to be dead.

If your child is overly stressed and feels depressed or has personal problems, make certain they know they can get help at: Lifeline on 131114, Sane on 1800 18 7263, Kids Helpline 1-800-551-800 or Mensline Australia on 1300 789 978 or log on to www.beyondblue.org.au or phone 1300 224 636. There is also a free suicide prevention hotline: 800-273-TALK (8255). This group will provide immediate assistance to individuals in emotional distress or suicidal crisis. It is ready twenty-four hours a day, seven days a week. www.suicidepreventionlifeline.org.

Children with special needs often display a number of the signs listed above. Students with special learning needs fall into the category of being higher-risk targets as they may exhibit many of the characteristics of which predators are likely to notice. They are different. They stand out by virtue of behavioral, vocal, or physical challenges. They may have social skills deficits that are readily noticeable. They may react or overreact to the smallest of taunts or intimidations. If one is struggling with an impediment they are ripe for becoming a victim.

One young lady struggled with a speech impediment that kept her from properly forming the words that she is trying to say. Other kids would ask her derisively, "What language do you speak?" No amount of speech therapy or special education induction can match the power of meeting other children who intrinsically understand and accept them. A peer support group means your child can be among children who understand hurtful comments all too well. Its peer acceptance and patience that kids need.

Unfortunately, children with special needs are an automatic target for bullies early in their life into adulthood. For instance, on a recent drive home from a party parents asked their five year old daughter who she had played with. With tears in her eyes, their little girl responded that "no one had played with her because they don't understand me." Their daughter has a speech disability that impairs her pronunciations. She understands everything she hears, and she always has the appropriate response. Her words, though, are often a challenge to understand. Parents have tried to come to her aid but the therapist now wants to triple the number of sessions, which triples their expenses to nearly $1,000 a month. The insurance provider will not pay. Most parent's resources are limited despite how much they desire to help. Parents and teachers watch as the parents' daughter grows increasingly introverted at school. Bullying is destroying their daughter.

She is being effectively ostracized. Actually ostracism is used by lions, wolves, primates, and bees where the intended target generally dies. Homo sapiens continue to use it in our modern world. The government can call it banishment; tribes call it social death; churches call it excommunication; the military calls it silencing; education calls it time out; and prisons call it solitary confinement. In the workplace it can be called sidelining, shelving or closeting where the individual is given minimum responsibilities but kept on the payroll.

To be ostracized as a child, they suddenly become like a container without any contents. It becomes like a social death or social annihilation imposed because of a lack of activity. There is the trauma of meaninglessness by being powerless and non-productive. It is the beginning of psychological breakdown and leads to disorientation and mental breakdown. The individual's self esteem is affected. They become ashamed of themselves and oftentimes go into complete silence.

To emphasize this point, the research done by Kipling Williams suggests that even in our loving families, seventy percent of our loved ones use ostracism at one time or another. In looking at this subject, Williams' research selected three individuals in a game he called "ball tossing." The three would sit around in a circle and toss the ball to each other. All were involved. Then, at a cue, two of the individuals refused to toss the ball to the third child. The results was alarmingly similar to what happens when a child is ostracized at school or in their student group. They begin to lose self-esteem. They get angry. They have been left out and they do not like it. This same procedure was transformed to another venue called "cyberball." Here the one individual was again receiving the cyberball on his computer from two others. Suddenly, everything changed and he was not receiving the ball again. His negative reactions solidified the researchers' assumption that a child's self esteem is greatly damaged.

Another researcher discovered similar results when he used an elevator for his review. Picked people were placed in the elevator. The door was then opened for the unsuspecting person entering the elevator. In the first sequence the presenter merely made eye contact and nodded to the person coming into the elevator. Next, the person stared straight ahead and made no eye contact at all nor any visual sign that he even saw the incoming individual. The results were that everyone has a need to be noticed. The current mood and self esteem of the person entering the elevator is greatly affected for the remainder of the day. It was discovered that it does not take much to affect a person.

William James concluded that ostracism for any child might be even worse than physical bullying. You can take your bruises to the police, but you cannot take silence. It signals to the recipient a reflexibility that is detected as pain. It will thwart belonging, self esteem, control, and a meaningful existence.

One legal case recently brought a new degree of concern for ostracism. Let us call this case that of Lori and Tammy. They worked in a government agency. Lori was walking down the filing cabinet aisle. Tammy quickly opened one of the filing drawers into Lori's stomach driving Lori into the wall. Lori filed for workplace harassment. Yet, in the court the lawyer was able to prove that Lori had been using ostracism for one full year previously against Tammy. It was driving Tammy crazy. Lori's friends had been solicited to join in. The legal questions of serious proportions became "Who is the target?" and "Who is the source?" The court found in favor of Tammy.

Kids are reluctant to share experiences of ostracism with adults. Further, kids are reluctant to share their private life online with parents or teachers. Why tell an adult when they have the whole world to listen to them? According to one telephone survey of preteens and teens (Fight Crime: Invest in Kids, 2006), fifty-one percent of preteens but only thirty-five percent of teens who had been cyberbullied had told parents about their experience. Twenty-seven percent of preteens and nine percent of teens told a teacher. Forty-four percent of preteens and seventy-two percent of teens told a friend. Thirty one percent of preteens and thirty-five percent of teens told a brother or sister. Sixteen percent of preteens and teens actually told no one.

Even by following the suggestions of this book, educators and parents may find they can come into the room, even the kitchen, and the child's computer screen will suddenly go black. Schools and the home may use filtering software, but kids are very sharp. When the adult comes online to check where the child is located, he will simply go to the Website "Britannica" and the investigator will think the child is doing research for school.

Adults are encouraged to not let children try to win the battle by themselves. Things like staying home just isn't worth it. Just watching television or being on the computer all night are not good solutions. Every child needs other children. They are not the Lone Ranger-although even he had Tonto. Every child needs the proverbial "hug." Often they feel because they have been hurt and broken, they are not of much use. But there is always someone who is walking where they have already walked. Your child needs you to remind her there is hope.

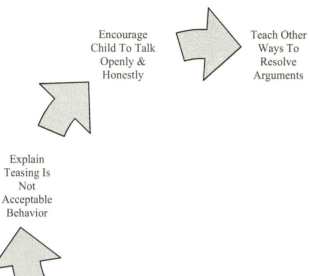

Encourage
Child To Talk
Openly &
Honestly

Teach Other
Ways To
Resolve
Arguments

Teach How
To Negotiate
In Assertive,
Nonaggressive
Ways

Explain
Teasing Is
Not
Acceptable
Behavior

Demonstrate
Self-
Protection
Skills

Talk Openly
About
Bullying &
Cyber-
bullying

Encourage
The
Buddy
System

HELPING YOUR CHILD COPE

PART III
What Can Parents Do?

Chapter 6:
Bully Proofing Your Child

It is recommended that every teacher and parent devise a personal "top ten" list for their classroom or family. These are top ten ways an adult can instruct children in handling the cruelest bullies. For instance, a suggested list might contain the following:

1. **Stay cool and calm.** He who angers you, controls you.
2. **Tell an adult.** Outer agitation reveals inner instability.
3. **Stand up for yourself.** Do not run
4. **Hang with your friends.** Keep part of that group
5. **Be clever** ("Don't I know you from my science class?")
6. **Just walk away**
7. **Don't keep it a secret**
8. **Don't be a bystander**
9. **Don't respond with violence**
10. **Act confident**

Item number four bears further inspection. Everyone needs friends. Friends are like pockets. Everyone needs them. Good friends are like stars. You don't always see them, but you always know they are there. Some people come into our lives and quickly go. Some people become friends and stay a while, leaving behind beautiful footprints on our hearts. And we are never the same, because we have made a good friend. Everyone hears what a child says. Friends listen to what they say. Best friends listen to what they don't say and respond anyway. And as Ralph Waldo Emerson said," the only way to have a friend is to be one."

WHAT CAN TEACHERS AND PARENTS (THE ANTI-BULLY) DO?

Children who experience chronic bullying pain need parents and teachers to remind them that they love and value them. A caring adult can effectively share a child's burden and strengthen the parent-teacher-child bond in the process.

- **Online habits**. Protect your children by teaching them good online habits. Reduce their risk of becoming cyberbullies by setting guidelines for and monitoring their use of the Internet and other electronic media like cell phones and PDAs.
- **Self Esteem**. Help build their self-esteem by providing positive feedback. No one can make them feel inferior without their consent. Victims must be able to draw upon a reservoir of hope, faith, and self-confidence stored up inside them through the love and encouragement of friends and families. They must become a friend to themself. Know they are a good person. As Eleanor Roosevelt once said, "friendship with oneself is all-important, because without it one cannot be friends with anyone else."
- **Communication**. The ability to listen is an underrated yet crucial part of helping your child. Keep lines of communication open with your children so that they feel comfortable telling you if they are being victimized online. Children sharing about their pain need the adults to listen respectfully, without judgment. Be open. Accept what they say, realizing that strong emotions often accompany this bully pain. Listen to your children. Ask about their day. Listen to them talking about their day, social events, classmates, and any problems they are having. Stay calm and give your child plenty

of time to tell you how he or she feels. Make it clear it is not your child's fault. Hear what they say. Be quick to hear, slow to react, and slow to give your personal opinions.

- **Speak With Compassion.** Bullying pain can bring a wrenching sense of loss followed by the same emotions experienced when a loved one dies. Your child may be in a cycle of denial, anger, depression and guilt. Acceptance comes last. Avoid saying things like "Cheer up, it'll get better," or "I know how you feel." Such phrases minimize your child's experience. Instead say, "I'm sorry it is so difficult" or "It must be rough." Affirming that the bullying pain is real comforts the suffering child.

- **Do Not Tell.** Never tell your child who is being bullied to "just ignore it." Yet, seek to ascertain if your child just might be doing something that encourages bullies to pick on him.

- **Concerns Are Serious.** Take their concerns seriously. Many children are embarrassed when they are being bullied. Acts of violence are never justifiable. Many times if kids are not taken seriously the first time they ask for help, they do not ask again.

- **Stop Bullying.** If you see any bullying, stop it immediately. A caring adult will take the blinders off, think the unthinkable, and see what is happening in the painful downside of a generation that is losing its way.

- **Support School.** Support your school's bully prevention programs. If your school does not have one, consider starting one up with other parents.

- **Impressionable Moments.** Capture impressionable moments of accomplishment. Self-confidence is affirmed through thought, feeling, action and imagery. When your child accomplishes something, help them hold that image of accomplishment by recounting the experience to you.

- **Display Memorabilia.** Having pictures or memorabilia of accomplishments are material for boosting confidence. Take many pictures and videos. Leave positive notes everywhere..

- **Praise.** Celebrate your complete child and all his and her admirable qualities. Praise your child's ideas. Discuss local events and get your child's perspectives and solutions. Show

your child that you are confident in them. As they prove
their worth, give them greater privileges to demonstrate your
ongoing confidence in them.

- **Laughter.** Playing, living, laughing and doing things together
  with family and friends makes every step of the journey
  easier. Research shows that bullying pain is a sensation and an
  emotion. Find things to laugh about. Share humorous stories.
  Watch a funny video or go to an entertaining play. Laugh
  with them when they are in the "funk" state. Some may be
  laughing on the outside but are dying on the inside. Laughter
  helps boost serotonin levels which act as a natural pain reliever.
  Learn a new hobby together for a refreshing change of pace.

- **Stop Rudeness.** Make sure your children do not respond to
  rude and harassing emails, messages, and postings. Keep a
  record of them in case you need proof.

- **Avoid Escalation.** If your child is a victim, explain that
  they should avoid escalating the situation. Responding with
  hostility is likely and could escalate the situation. Depending
  on the circumstances, consider ignoring the issue. Often
  bullies thrive on the reaction of their victims. Other options
  include subtle actions, like changing their email address.

- **Diagnosis/Medical Alert.** Early diagnosis and medical
  treatment is essential for depressed children. This is a real
  illness that requires professional help. Comprehensive
  treatment often includes both individual and family therapy. It
  may also include the use of antidepressant medication. If this
  is the case, parents should ask their physician to refer them to
  a child and adolescent psychiatrist who can diagnose and treat
  depression. Each state has an organization to assist parents.
  For instance, in California, it is:

Educational Partnerships Office
California Department of Education
721 Capitol Mall
Sacramento, California 95814
916-657-5342
Http://www.cde.ca.gov/cyfsbranch/lsp/fphome.htm

* **The Bully's Parents.** Consider contacting the cyberbully's parents. These parents may be very concerned to learn that their child has been cyberbullying others, and they may effectively put a stop to the bullying. On the other hand, these parents may react very badly to your contacting them. So proceed cautiously. If you decide to contact a cyberbully's parents, communicate with them in writing- not face to face. Present proof of the cyber bullying (e.g., copies of an email message) and ask them to make sure the cyberbullying stops. Consider contacting an attorney in cases of serious cyberbullying. In some circumstances, civil law permits victims to sue a bully or his or her parents in order to recover damages.

* **ISP & Police.** Call law enforcement and inform your Internet Service Provider (ISP) if necessary. Report these if there has been threats of violence, extortion, obscene or harassing phone calls or text messages, harassments, stalking or hate crimes or child pornography. If your child is being harassed or threatened, report the activity to the local authorities. Law enforcement agencies have different policies, but your local police department or FBI branch are good starting points. Unfortunately, there is a distinction between free speech and punishable offenses, but the legal implications should be decided by the law enforcement officials and the prosecutors. Depending on the activity, it may also be appropriate to report it to school officials who may have separate policies for dealing with activity that involves students.

A wonderful program to help parents and teachers work with children who are being bullied is called "Be Cool." In this approach, it is reported that victims generally react to bullying in one of three ways: be cold, be hot, or be cool. This is an excellent way in teaching children how to deal with bullies in a nonviolent way. It will help your bullied child act with self confidence. Under the guidelines of this program, you are encouraged to:
* Don't encourage your child to fight. This could lead him/her getting hurt, in trouble at school, and beginning more serious problems with the bully.

* Help your child learn to walk upright, look peers in the eye, and speaking clearly.
* Adults are solicited to involve children in activities outside of school. This way they can make friends in a different social circle.
* Help them learn to not act in haste. Count to one hundred. Try to avoid anger-there is enough aggression already.
* Encourage your child to approach a teacher with whom they feel comfortable.
* Encourage activities that help the child to forget the bullying. Try to build their self-confidence. Teach your child self-respect. Tell him to carry himself confidently. Instruct him to walk with his shoulders back, his head held high. The weaker they feel about themselves, the more vulnerable they are going to be to bullies.
* A teacher or parent should never try to minimize a child's disappointment and thus suggest their feelings do not count. For instance, the day that your daughter does not make the cheerleading squad or your son does not make the basketball team, saying, "well it could have been worse. The other child needed it more than you." When your child expresses acute disappointment or a negative emotion, don't contradict it. Merely acknowledge his or her feelings with respect. Once the feelings have been acknowledge, he or she can begin to deal with them. In fact, they may even be able to find their own solution.
* Help your child avoid the situations that expose him to bullying. Help them find a safe route to and from school. Point out places the child may go for help. Make sure your child knows that his safety is always more important than possession.
* Educators and parents are encouraged to not "blow smoke" in constant praise of children. It may lead to a huge letdown later. Children who receive a constant stream of adult compliments are likely to experience a big letdown in the cyberspace world. Oftentimes, they will learn to expect a lot of praise and really begin to worry when they do not get it. Youngsters need

positive feedback when they do well, but parents and teachers need to temper praise with honesty. When a girl is told constantly she is the most beautiful little princess in the world, but the boys in school constantly make fun of her, she will pick up on the inconsistency. She may even conclude that her parents and teachers do not expect much of her.

* Help your child grow a funny bone. Develop a safe, no confrontational method to disarm the bully. Help your child to not take themselves so seriously. Help him to think up one-liners to use when he is being teased. It can be something as simple as, "Thanks for sharing," and merely walking away.

Controlling a child's temper is essential. Adults may develop another "ten list" for helping children control their tempers. Examples might be:

1. Recognize your anger signs
2. Turn anger into positive energy
3. Count to ten and cool off
4. Talk about it, do not act it out
5. Breathe deeply and relax
6. Share your feelings with a friend
7. Punch a pillow, not a person
8. Recognize your anger can hurt others
9. Don't let it build
10. Pretend the world is watching

Adhering to these lists, children will try to live up to their teachers' and parents' expectations of them. Janet Christie, social worker from Boca Raton, Florida talked about a parent calling her young son a "real animal." At school and later on the Internet, he tried to live up to his mother's expectations and built upon his previous behavior. Most children believe what their parents and teachers tell them. When a parent tells their son he is a loser, he sees himself as a loser. Then when the bullying and cyberbullying emerges, and bad things happen to him, he tells himself he deserves them because he is a loser. On the other hand, when positive things happen, it is just because he got lucky.

L. Wayne Reid, Ph.D.

PATHWAY OF PAIN

As I watch you each day in the hallways,
I can see into your soul.
Behind the boastful laughter, there is fear of exposure-
That someone will discover your weakness.

You seek to cover your secret flaws at the expense of
Those you taunt
Unaware that each cruel act
Lays bare your own shabby character.

Now you can push a button and roam the corridors of cyberspace,
Seeking more victims to devour,
Unseen, unknown, unobserved in your
Role of destroyer, purveyor of lies, seedy merchant of menace.

The attacker always wounds himself, and
Inevitably, you will someday see your reflection in a glass,
A despicable, empty shell with missing pieces,
Lost on the pathway of pain you dispensed.

Carole Karber Reid

CHAPTER 7:
THE MOVE FROM THE
CLASSROOM TO ONLINE

High tech, split second technology has caught most adults off guard in relation to their children. Many youngsters in elementary grades are badgering their parents to convince them they need to have a cell phone. "You'll be able to call me anytime you want when I'm outside or riding my bike." "You can even call my phone to tell me to come and bring the television remote, instead of yelling from another room." And the favorite line is: "All my friends have one!" This really isn't an exaggeration. I have seen 9 and 10 year old friends toting cell phones with hip ring tones and flashy face plates. Still, I am convinced this is a very ominous threat. I am not convinced third-graders have a real need for personal communication devices.

The same goes for the Internet; such as, MySpace, YouTube, Facebook, Friendster. Nearly every teen in America is on the Internet every day, socializing with friends and strangers alike, trying on identities, and building a virtual profile of themselves-one that many kids insist is a more honest depiction of who they really are than the person they portray at home or in school.

Hundreds of millions of people communicate through email with family, friends, and colleagues around the world. The majority of people in developed nations go online to exchange electronic mail and instant messages. Others use chat areas to make new friends who share common interests. They post and read messages in social networking sites and blogs, "surf" the world-wide web.

As an educational and entertainment tool, users can learn about virtually any topic, visit a museum, take a college course, or play an endless number of computer games. Creating content of all shapes and sizes is getting easier and easier. High bandwidth Internet access and expanded computer memory and storage continue to grow. Children can now be collaborators in the creation of large storehouses of information. Already, most parents are bracing themselves for their child's next likely request—a computer in their bedroom.

Our children live in a world identified by the Internet as the "Always On Generation." Today, the Internet isn't simply a convenient way to research or have fun after school; it is a major part of the child's life. Our generation of school-age children cannot remember life without the Internet. As such our kids know they are more savvy than their parents and teachers and tend to exploit this power. The National Center for Education Statistics reported that ninety-nine percent of all American public schools have computers connected to the Internet. Technology doubles every six months. Educators and parents have come to realize that children are in a new world of interaction and need to be prepared for even more technological advancements.

Personal computers are no longer the only method for accessing the Internet. Kids can go online from almost anywhere. They surf the Internet and send messages from a home computer or one at a friend's home, library, or school. Kids connect at coffee shops and other "hotspots" using laptops and wireless connections. Internet-enabled, video-game systems allow them to compete against and chat with players around the world. Cell phones enable kids to surf the web and exchange messages, photos, and short videos from just about anywhere. Instant messaging (IM) is facilitated through programs such as ICQ, AOL, MSN, or Yahoo.

As a child's interest in cyberspace grows, a parent and teacher rightly must be worried about how the latest technical gadgets and advancements will affect their child's safety. And statistics tell every parent and teacher, they have a right to be worried. A 2005 study revealed about eighteen percent of students in sixth through eighth grades reported being cyberbullied at least once in the past two months. They are being wounded from afar. A *Netday* survey of March 2005 discovered that eighty-one percent of students in grades seven through twelve have email accounts, seventy-five percent have at least one Instant Messenger (IM) screen name, and ninety-seven percent believe strongly that technology use is important in education.

The Internet is no longer the safe environment it once was. It's hostile territory now. The increasing trend of cyberbullying has transcended the playground. Like the technological wizards, adults need to also utilize cunning and expertise to escape the clutches of cyberbullies. And the sooner we equip our kids with the terms and tools they need to navigate safely, the better. (Vuko, 2004). Unfortunately, the same advances in computer and telecommunication technology that allow our children to reach out to new sources of knowledge and cultural experiences are also leaving them vulnerable to exploitation and harm by merciless terrorist cyberbullies and computer sex offenders. (Louis J. Freech, FBI)

Misuse of technology has caught parents and teachers off guard. Like any endeavor- attending school, cooking, riding a bicycle or traveling- there are some risks and annoyances. The online world, like the rest of society, is made up of a wide array of people. Most are decent and respectful, but some may be rude, obnoxious, insolent, or even mean and exploitative. Over a quarter of teachers and principals are the subject of mocking blog posts or doctored images. Children are no exception. In fact, they are more likely to be online than adults. Children get a lot of benefit from being online, but they are also targets of crime, exploitation and harassment.

Children come across sites containing adult images or demeaning, racist, sexist, violent or false information. There have been some highly publicized cases of exploitation involving the Internet and cyberspace. A major problem is that children most often feel it is safe. It is hard for children to distinguish reliable sources of information from less reliable ones. Some believe because information is posted online it must be true.

In this age of information, knowledge is plentiful but wisdom is often scarce. The technology that has so dramatically changed the world outside our schools is now changing the learning and teaching environment within them. Every day young persons manipulate their world by pointing and clicking their way to experiences and knowledge. This is your child's digital world.

What makes cyberbullying so easy-and tempting- is the mask of anonymity the Web provides, along with a potentially huge audience. There is a lack of social norms when children use technology to communicate. Cyberbullying can be a complicated issue, especially for adults who are not as familiar with using the Internet, instant messenger, or chat rooms as their children. Lacking familiarity with popular teen Web sites, many adults are unable to monitor their children's online activities and thus find it impossible to intervene in cyberbullying. Their child, the victim, often has received many offensive messages or images before becoming desperate enough to complain to adults. And the cyberbully often has more than one victim and will continue their offensive behavior until they are caught.

The Internet is like a bathroom wall. Secrets and privacy do not exist online. Kids want their privacy, but worried parents and teachers want to keep track. There are no censors on the Internet. Anyone in the world can publish material on the Internet. A service provider will link you to these sites, but it cannot control what is on them. It is up to individuals to make sure that they behave in a way that is safe and appropriate.

An interesting turn of events has found parents and teachers turning themselves more to the Internet's MySpace and Facebook. One young lady was shocked when her mom sent her a "friend" request on Facebook. She didn't believe her mother had enough computer experience to take her past emailing her family and friends. The girl felt Facebook was her world and would never be compromised by adults.

Not anymore, many concerned parents and teachers are flocking to social networking sites. At Facebook, which was originally created for college students, the number of users ages thirty-five to fifty-four more than tripled in the last twelve months. A number use it to monitor their children. Many parents feel they need to monitor their children online. A few demand being included as a friend when their child signs up for MySpace and Facebook. They want to make certain the child is not posting anything inappropriate or revealing too much personal information. Others are using it as a communication tool much like their children use. The key is to make certain there is open communication online and off about the actions between children, parents, and teachers. A large number of children today actually like hanging out with their parents to being holed up in their room. This development can easily extend to social networking sites

Experts warn parents and teachers that if they "friend" a child without being invited, it can send teenagers the message that adults do not trust them. Some experts feel that these sites are like a new mall, a place where teenagers can hang out without authority figures. Michael Solomon at St. Joseph's University in Philadelphia says teens who post suggestive photos or inappropriate messages will block their parents anyway from accessing the information. He feels that being a friend can backfire at times. It can embarrass the kids and their friends and create resentment for both parents and teachers. Author Anastasia Goodstein believes parents and teachers should keep a discreet distance on social networking sites. Where it gets tricky is what's happening on social networking sites is really conversations between teens and their friends. The adult is not just listening in on their own child. Suddenly, the parent is hearing what all their friends are doing as well. Adults should remember that their teenagers are watching them back.

However, as children grow and enter college, using this network system is an easy way to interact with the child and to keep up on the child's life when they are away from home. Actually, it is a lot easier than making a phone call.

Photo Gallery

Portion of Lithuania's elementary principals. A three week workshop in preventing bullying for secondary and elementary principals was directed by the author.

As administrator at Martin Luther King Junior High in Sacramento, California, the idea of peer development to help curb bullying was born.

Typical screen PowerPoint presentation utilized in national and international conferences where Dr. Reid was the presenter.

Picture of a Latino family. It is vital that parents know the dangers of the Internet so that they are the major protectors of their children.

Small boy. Boys are much more inclined than girls to bully their targets physically, especially weaker or defenseless individuals.

Girl. Girls are much more inclined to create rumors, cast insinuations about others on the Internet, and to ostracize other girls which can lead to victim suicide.

Lindhurst High School's nationally recognized "Ambassadors" began with only 20 students but grew to over 160. Their goal was to stop bullying and to improvement the environment and reputation of their school. The advisor was Dr. Reid.

Lindhurst High School in Oliverhurst California was the first school where a major school shooting in the United States occurred. Because of a student being bullied he retaliated! This is the monument dedicated to the three students and one teacher who were murdered. Ten others were seriously wounded.

Students from one of a number of elementary school presentations who assisted Dr. David Karell and Dr. Reid in their anti-bullying program.

Dr. Reid and Dr. Karell have appeared on several instrumental live and Internet programs sponsored by Sacramento's Channel 10 ABC on the topic of bullying and cyberbullying.

CHAPTER 8:
DEFINITION OF TERMS:
UNDERSTANDING THE INTERNET

Teachers and parents alike need to understand the terms used by children when using the Internet.

*<u>Web Site</u>. This is a site (location) on the World Wide Web. Each Web site contains a home page, which is the first document users see when they enter the site. The site might also contain additional documents and files. Each site is owned and managed by an individual, company or organization. Cyberbullies can create Web sites that mock, torment and harass others. If these are published on a local regional Internet Service Provider, you should copy and print out these Web sites and then contact the ISP. Webcam sessions and photos can be easily captured, and users can continue to circulate those images when online. In some cases people believe they are interacting with trusted friends, but later found their images were distributed to others or posted on web sites. Kids may come across offensive or inappropriate images and videos while surfing the web. Users may not know what they have downloaded until it is on their computers. By sharing files kids can unknowingly end up downloading and distributing harmful viruses and even illegal material such as pornography.

*Internet Service Provider (ISPs). You can go online by signing up with an Internet Service Provider which will provide you with access to the web sites and other areas of the Internet. Many Internet service providers offer filters to prevent children from accessing inappropriate sites. Parents are encouraged to talk immediately to your ISP about what safe-search options they offer. As a customer, you have a right to choose an ISP with the services meeting your family's needs. If you have a problem with cyberbullying, give your ISP a chance to respond. Unfortunately, some ISPs are not as responsible and you may have great difficulty in not only finding their AUP or abuse reporting options, but even in getting them to acknowledge your concerns, let alone have the defamatory Web site taken down. Equally unfortunate, some ISPs may not respond or take action unless you tell them that you are contacting the police, the media or a lawyer. Many ISPs offer filters to prevent kids from accessing inappropriate sites. Talk to your ISP about what safe-search options they offer. Before you sign up with an ISP, research the effectiveness of its spam filters. You may also purchase spam-filter software separately. Once you are connected to the Internet, you are able to exchange information with people who use other providers unless you are using a service that offers restricted access such as blocking mail from outside the service or from people who aren't preapproved by a child's parent. Many sites use "cookies" that track specific information about the user, such as name, email address, and shopping preferences. Cookies can be disabled but you need to ask your Internet Service Provider for more information.

*Internet Relay Chat (IRC). These networks enable computer-to-computer access. Tim Berners-Lee had a grand vision for the Internet when he began development of the World Wide Web. Writing to the Web required knowledge of the HTML code that make Web pages work and of the protocols to get those pages up and running on the Internet.

*Microsoft. This is an American multinational computer technology corporation. It develops, manufactures, licenses and supports a wide range of software products for computer devices. Their best product is Microsoft Windows. One of Bill Gates key visions is to get a workstation running their software onto every desk and eventually into every house. It launched their online service, MSN (Microsoft Network) as a direct competitor to AOL. Microsoft's "content advisor" prevents kids from viewing inappropriate content and lets parents set up an approved group of Web addresses. Thee is a "restricted zone" of forbidden sites. "Client filtering" prevents kids from playing specific Internet games and restricts Web surfing time.

*<u>AOL</u> Formerly America Online it is an American global Internet service and media company operated by Time Warner. It is perhaps best known for its online software suite which allows the user to enter the worldwide Internet. AOL has developed AOL Guardian which reports who their kids exchange messages with and what Web sites they visit, monitor chat rooms for kids 13 and under and an IM safe list restricting people with whom a child can talk.

*<u>Yahoo.</u> This site attracts more than 110 million visitors a month. Users typically stay on the site for more than three hours to search for real estate, check email or shop. Yahoo's "parental controls" package allows parents to set different limits for each child using the Internet. There are four levels available: one for kids 12 and under, one for teens 13-15, etc. Yahoo offers a weekly "report card" of the child's online activities during the prior week.

*<u>Google</u>. The search engine tends to be the home page of choice. It draws in more than 124 million users every month for as long as an hour and a half. Users can search for maps, check their e-mail or chat. Choose search engines carefully. Some are specifically designed for children, and others offer kid-safe options.

To search the Web, the kid can try services from Google, Yahoo and 4INOFRO. Google can be reached by sending a text message to 466453. For Yahoo text 92466. For 4INFO text 44636. Each service has unique features. For instance in finding local businesses, Yahoo includes cross streets. 4INFRO lets you set up customize alerts to your cellphone.

Google sends you driving directions if you text this: "directions from (address or city) to (address or city)."

There are also additional search engines an individual can utilize. One of the most recent is called "Cuill," pronounced "cool." Cuill's search index spans 120 billion Web pages. This is approximately three times the size of Google's index although Google maintains its' site is the largest index. A search index's scope is important because information, pictures and content cannot be found unless they are stored in a database. Cuill has a different method for identifying and displaying pertinent results. Rather than trying to mimic Google's method of ranking the quantity and quality of links to Web sites, Cuill's technology drills into the actual content of a page. Thus their results will be presented in a more magazine-like format instead of just a vertical stack of Web links. Cuill's results are displayed with more photos spread horizontally across the page and include sidebars that can be clicked on to learn more about topics related to the original search request. Cuill is just the latest in a long line of Google challengers. The list includes swaggering startups like Teoma (whose technology became the backbone of Ask.com), Vivisimo, Snap, Mahalo, and Powerset (which has been acquired by Microsoft Corporation.)

__Instant Messaging (IM)__ allows instantaneous communication between a number of parties simultaneously, by transmitting information quickly and efficiently, featuring immediate receipt of acknowledgment or reply. It enables the user to create a private chat room with another individual. Typically, the instant messaging system alerts you whenever somebody on your private list is online. You can then initiate a chat session with that particular individual. There are several competing instant messaging systems such as ICQ, AOL, Messenger, MSN Messenger, Yahoo! Messenger, etc. Unfortunately there is no standard, so anyone you want to send instant messages to must use the same site. Cyberbullies can and do use IM to send harassing and threatening messages to the targets of their hatred and loathing.

IM has become a very large part of the social lives of our young people. The relationships they form with others in school and in other facets of their lives are extended and maintained through IM-ing. The conversations and conflicts that arise online often give rise to behaviors that are acted out in person during school or at the local shopping mall. Users of IM should create a buddy list of only people you know and trust well.

*YouTube. It is a personal journal site. It is a free video sharing site where users can upload and view video clips. Fifty seven million users view videos approximately two hundred fifty million times a month. They spend about ten minutes per visit watching video clips. YouTube.com alone consumes as much bandwidth (high speed Internet) as the entire Internet consumed in 2000. Users upload sixty-five thousand new videos every day. Using this device, students can elaborately edit videos shot over several days to make fun of students or teachers. Another similar site is called "Xanga."

*MySpace It is a dating site, blog, and forum site all merged into one site. This is the world's largest online social network with two hundred million users worldwide. It is a hugely popular online hangout for kids. Up to one hundred sixty thousand new members join the site every day. It is the third most viewed Web site, generating more hits than Google, eBay, AOL, and Hotmail. The king of social networking has visitors looking at friends' personal pages and updating profiles. Users spend about half an hour every month looking at pages. (Kurtz, Rod, Inc.com). This website has a data base that members can look through in order to find other people who live in the same city or state. Children can find out if someone has worked or gone to school at the same places you have. They can find other kids who like the same music, movies or books that they enjoy. The site offers blogs so a child can make entries about their everyday life which can be read by others. Many students get on MySpace looking for relationships. MySpace has taken a number of different online concepts and compressed them into a single whole.

Entering MySpace, the child will begin to add "friends" to their site. When friends sign up, the owner is automatically connected to their friends. When you are on MySpace, you can contact your friends and meet people who have interests or views which are much like your own. The site offers blogs so that you can make entries about your everyday life. Your child cannot send messages, post comments, post bulletins or add friends until they verify their email.

Kids love showing off their "MySpace" profiles to their friends- friends of friends are welcome too. Our youth spend anywhere from fifteen minutes to five hours daily on "MySpace." Kids have the incredible misperception that it is only their friends who are going to stumble across their pages. Teens sometimes forget that their profile is public. When they post a picture they may get people IM-ing them with rather inappropriate come-ons.

In checking with a young ladies' MySpace account, Gabriella has a sexually suggestive photo of herself. Her name is Gabriella. Her profile says she is twenty-six years old from Hampton, Virginia. She adds that she "needs a big fine country boy." Tom became one of her immediate friends. Another was Lacie who says "hey fellas! My name is Lacie. Im twenty and am very grounded woman with my head on straight. I love to snuggle, camping, fishing, swimming and all kinda stuff but hey if you are lookin for a real woman to talk to." She was sharing herself with the world.

Hemanshu Nigam, security officer at MySpace, feels cursing and profanity is all but mandatory. Vindictive children can easily spread gossip and rumors. Parents of one teenager looked into her "MySpace" pages. They felt cursing was all but mandatory, a king of generic password into the teenagers vernacular. Sheer volume and repetition has made even the most profuse profanity muted and stale. The sliding scale of profanity, with words that were forbidden only a few years ago are now accepted in even polite technological circles. It has left most expletives with little weight.

Many young people are literally stunned when they discover what other people are saying about them. The victim is deeply hurt. Most can never imagine that such a dastardly thing could possibly happen to them. Still, our children generally do not want their parents looking into what they are posting.

Safety for young users of MySpace has always been a concern for parents and safety experts, but the issue was thrust even further into the limelight when the mother of an Austin, Texas teenager, who claims she was raped by a man she met through the site, filed a thirty million dollar lawsuit against MySpace. The mother claims that the social networking giant was short in protecting its teenager users even though there were warnings of possible dangers. The girl bumped up her age. He allegedly posed as a high school senior. Pete Solis was a nineteen year old guy. She was a fourteen year old girl.

*****Facebook**, launched by Mark Zuckerberg in 2004, is the world's second largest social networking Web site. At number five on the Alexa list of most popular Web sites in the United States, it is closing in quickly on its rival MySpace. The network has grown quickly from 2004 when it started at Harvard and a few other schools as an online version of a college yearbook. In early 2006, high school students signed on and then so did employees with many companies. By the end of the year, people were sharing photos and videos, posting updates about their personal lives and creating causes and groups across the social networking platform. It has more than eighty million active users worldwide. It will connect the user to the people around them. Here children can upload photos, publish notes, get the latest news from their friends, post videos on their profile, tag their friends, use privacy setting to control who sees their information or join a network. This social site becomes addictive to users. More than thirty million visitors a month spend as long as twenty minutes per visit taking quizzes, poking friends, checking out profiles and updating their pages. It is a site originally designed for college students to connect with each other. People who were friends were able to keep tabs on people in their network, send messages and even connect with friends of friends.

It has grown exponentially in recent years. Teenagers make up a large part of their membership. This has created a new potential venue for sexual predators who lie about their age to lure young victims and for cyberbullies who send daggers to their victims.

Today, the fastest-growing segment of Facebook's estimated eighty million users are people ages twenty-five and older. (Aratani, 2008). Montana Miller, an assistant professor of popular culture at Bowling Green State University in Ohio is an expert on Facebook. She points out that policies are still developing, and legal issues surrounding social-networking sites have not been settled. There is very little precedence to go on. Kids sometimes compete to see who has the greatest number of contacts and will add new members to their lists even if they don't know them in person. Children are more willing to say things on Facebook than they ever would to a person's face. If two kids are name-calling, their friends are on Facebook too, watching it- then they try to incite the situation.

Facebook allows the child to post unlimited photos on their page and see other friends' photos. Everything the child publishes on Facebook gets shared with others. This includes developers of "widgets" and other applications that their friends download onto their Facebook pages. These widgets, which are free to download, are goofy, but hard to resist. To date, twenty-four thousand applications have been built by four hundred thousand developers. About ninety-five percent of Facebook users have installed at least one.

Like most other computer companies and programs, Facebook changes at least every six months. The popular online social hangout is setting up a new system that will allow its users to take their personal profiles with them as they surf other Web sites. Users will be able to automatically copy pictures, personal information and other customized applications established on Facebook to other Web sites without extra effort once the changes take place.

Facebook is more about entertainment than work. They are watching soap operas of people they sort of know. One young lady explained that "It sucks you in!" The public conversations are really digital eavesdropping.

Fortunately for parents and children alike, Facebook is adding more than forty new safeguards to protect young users from sexual predators and cyberbullies under an agreement with officials nationwide. The measures include banning convicted sex offenders from the site, limiting older users' ability to contact subscribers under eighteen, and participating in a task force set up to find ways to verify users' ages and identities. Officials from Washington D.C. and forty-nine states have singed on. Facebook now lets users block online bullies. They can also conceal their "online now" status and use privacy controls to limit who can view their images.

There are real privacy issues. Facebook comes with various privacy settings that allow users to limit what information is available to the outside world. Even so, novices often have trouble with these settings or make whopping errors in judgment. Today, Facebook is both very useful and a genuine privacy threat. In Facebook you can visit a friend's page and check their interests and their friends. It is like a constantly changing yearbook page, mostly written for friends but with the understanding that others could see what was posted.

Of course parents grow concerned that their kids were revealing too much personal information. Schools, too, sanctioned students for posting unflattering comments about teachers. Others warned that potential employers might be turned off by photos of beer-soaked T-shirts. The big privacy issues with Facebook is always in the defaults. When Facebook creates a new service or changes a privacy setting from pot-in to opt-out, it has an enormous impact on millions of Internet "accept" button on several friend requests.

State attorneys general investigated cyberstalking. They urged Facebook to crack down on predators. As Chris Songhoian, a cyber-security researcher told the Washington Post," You want to be social with your friends, but now you're giving twenty guys you've never met vast amounts of information."

Facebook has potential booby traps. One British young man had an up-and-coming professional soccer career. Ashley-Paul Robinson told his one hundred ninety-four Facebook friends that he was trying out for a rival team. The only problem: The message went out to 2.7 million members of the London network, getting him in trouble with fans and bosses.

Another girl has a lot of friends. Facebook will allow you as many as five thousand "friends." Enduring realities impose far more significant limits. A whole lot- one thousand two hundred ninety-five to her latest Facebook count. Yet, if she ran into some of her "friends" on the street, she might not remember their names. Taking individuals off their accounts is not easy. It is called "defriending". The biggest value-added for Facebook friends is that it helps maintain relationships-somewhat superficial but not worth getting rid of. Some are selective in acceptance of friends. These have on the average one hundred thirty-one on Facebook. But if she had a relationship blow up, on the shoulders of how many could she cry? Probably, like twenty. Real world friendship just sort of drift apart, but not on Facebook. Here decisive action has to be taken. Defriending cements that a friendship is over. Massive emailing and tongue wagging ensue. It is futile to try to erase latent traces of Friends Next. The digital trails of an online friendship-true or not-really do last forever. Its evidence is stored on servers indefinitely, beyond the control of the persons involved.

Other social networking Web sites like Facebook include MySpace, Flickr, Twitter, Bebo. Never before has it been so easy to keep up with so many people with whom you otherwise would have lost contact. This is the world of participatory surveillance. Real online friends watch over each other-mutually, voluntarily and enthusiastically. One friends' theme to others was: "I'll be there for you, when the rain starts to pour. I'll be there for you because you are there for me too."

*<u>**Profile.**</u> This is the page where children list their personal statistics. The profile page is very important. It is here that the child describes himself and posts friends. They accumulate friends. With this posting, many try to see who can collect the most friends and turn it into a competition. A few go as high as two thousand friends on their site; however, they really know only about two hundred friends and are best friends with only about fifty. Children update their profiles on YouTube quite often. There is a Web site called "Club Penguin" which seven year olds can access about how to socialize online.

*<u>**Amazon.com**</u>. One of the first major companies to sell goods by the Internet. Workers enjoy online shopping while at work- fifty-one million users a month. Users shopped for about twenty-five minutes per visit last month, which is considered the off season. It began as an on-line bookstore, but soon diversified to product lines of VHS, DVD, music CDs, MP3 format, computer software, video games, electronics, etc.

*<u>**Chat rooms**</u> are virtual online rooms where a chat session takes place.

They are set up according to interest or subject such as skiing or a favorite TV show. Because children can communicate to each other alone or in a group, chat rooms are among the most popular destination on the Web for kids. Once a chat has been initiated, either user can enter text by typing on the keyboard and the entered text will appear on the other user's monitor. Most networks and online services offer a chat feature. Young kids should not be in chat room unless a trusted and responsible parent is sitting with them at the computer. Older kids should be only in moderated chat rooms and even moderated chat rooms can lead to compromising, embarrassing and harassing situations. Kids should not exchange email with someone from a chat room or arrange to meet someone from a chat room without a parent or guardian present. Users may pose as someone else-a different person or person of a different age-without others knowing. Such users have taken advantage of this and social-networking profiles to entice or sexually exploit kids.

Kids cannot "take back" the online text and images they have entered. Once online, chat as well as other web postings become public information. Many web sites are "cached" by search engines, and photos and text can be retrieved long after the site has been deleted. Kids do not need to enter a chat room to "chat" via the Internet. They also communicate with others on gaming sites, on IM sites, and via Internet Relay Chat (IRC) networks, which enables computer-to-computer access.

Any cyberbully generally finds another child who is vulnerable. They are very skilled in what they do in manipulating children. They know their likes and dislikes and know which buttons to push. And they are patient for even months. The cyberbully will invite the child into a private area of the chat room to get better acquainted. His first tactic is to create a comfort level, typically posing as a young person about the age of the intended victim. He may even send a doctored photo of himself. Next comes private chat via an instant message service followed by email, phone conversations and finally face-to-face meeting. Children who are relatively quiet in online chats are especially targeted. The perpetrator will sometimes say my father will pick you up so the victim feels safe getting into the adult's car. A child needs to know when they enter a chat room, others will know they are there and can even email them once you have started chatting. ChildNet operates an excellent Web site that provides parents with advice on chat rooms. www.chatdanger.com.

*Bash Board. This is the nickname for an online bulletin board, or virtual chat room, where teenagers can go to anonymously and write anything they want, true or false, creating or adding mean-spirited postings for the world to see. People are not always who they appear to be or who they say they are in chat rooms. Senders sometimes disguise themselves, pretending to be someone else- a friend or acquaintance, a well-known bank, a government agency-for illicit purposes. This is known as "phishing." By using the site- www.schoolrumors.com- children can click on a particular school and post their own insults of real students by even using a false name.

*Voting/Polling Booths. Some Web sites such as www.freevote.com, offer users the opportunity to create online polling/voting booths. Cyberbullies can use these Web sites to create Web pages that allow others to vote online for "The Ugliest, Fattest, Dumbest Boy or Girl at any school." While such Web sites may state that they do not condone the use of their Web sites for such purposes. We commend them for having clear abuse policies and a clear abuse reporting system, the reality is that most of these pages are not regulated by the Web site creators. They are supposed to be overseen by the volunteer "maintainers" who are supposed to be the quality-control gatekeepers, but most of these positions are listed as "abandoned." A user can set up a poll on whatever topic he chooses including the biggest nerd in the school band and send results to the whole school via listserv.

* Email. Email is relatively private-but not completely. Children and adults alike use email to communicate rapidly and cost effectively with people all over the world. Email transmits messages, documents, and photos to others in a mater of seconds or minutes. The messages can be notes entered from the keyboard or electronic files stored on disk. Cyberbullies can and do use email to send harassing and threatening messages to the targets of their hatred and loathing. It is often possible to trace which email account the message was sent from, however, it is almost impossible to prove who actually used this email account to send the offending messages. Messages sent from accounts with local/regional Internet Service Providers can be more easily traced and acted upon than messages sent from large Web-based email accounts such as Hotmail, Yahoo, Mail, etc. Most email programs allow you to use email filters that will block or automatically delete messages from undesirable senders. It is almost impossible to stop unwanted email messages such as advertisements, SPAM, etc. Kids can set up private accounts through free web-based, email services without asking permission from parents. Anyone using email is vulnerable to receiving "spam," messages from people or companies encouraging recipients to buy something, do something or visit a particular web site. Spam can be sexually suggestive or offensive in other ways. Children should not put anything into an electronic message that they wouldn't want to see posted on a neighborhood bulletin board. Children are encouraged to learn to recognize junk email and delete it. Don't even read it first. Never download an email attachment from an unknown source. Opening a file could expose your system to a virus.

Email still has many advantages over other modes of communication. Email is easy to ignore. You can deal with email at your leisure. It doesn't have the same and insistence that other platforms, such as instant messaging, do. With instant messaging there is the expectation that you will always be there and you will answer right away. That can get pretty exhausting. Email is an office mainstay. It is easily saved, stored, and searched and it provides a record of our conversations in ways that some other mediums can't. It is considered as good as paper in a business sense.

***Blog**. A blog, short for Weblogs, is a personal diary, a daily pulpit, a collaborative space, a political soapbox, a breaking-news outlet, a collection of links. It can be your own private thoughts- memos to the world. A child's blog is whatever they want it to be. It can be easily created and is easily updateable. There are an estimated 25 million of them, in all shapes and sizes, and there are no real rules. Blogs can become a hotbed of cyberbullying and cruelties. With blogs you can make entries about your everyday life which can be read by others. Blogs are very popular web diaries kept by children and teens. Statements to the recipient include such things as: "I hate you"; "Wish you were dead!"; "You are so ugly and so obese."; "I'm going to get you on the way home tomorrow."; "I have pictures of you that I'm going to post online."

TWITTER.COM. This microblogging site lets you keep up and communicate with friends via one hundred forty character posts that are logged via your computer or cell phone. You can follow friend updates. It is great for checking the status of what they are doing. You can also use it to ask a bunch of people a question at once- it is like a quick instant message service.

SKYPE.COM. This VolP (Voice over Internet Protocol) lets users bypass land lines and mobile phones to make telephone calls via the Internet. Other features include instant messaging and video conferencing.

BEENUP2.COM. Users of this El Dorado Hills-based company's application-think of it as the love child of Twitter and Flickr-communicate via cell phone photos. The idea is simple: Users upload cell phone photos to keep up with friends on the microblogging site.

LIVEJOURNAL.COM/BLOGGER.COM. These popular Web log sites let you post thoughts on any and every topic imaginable-and the "comments" function lets readers holler right back atcha.

FACEBOOK.COM/MYSPACE.COM. Seems like everyone and their grandmother's using one of these two social networking sites-both of which allow intra-site messaging, chat, comments and mobile phone options. E-mail? Sorry but that's just sooo twentieth century uncool.

***P2P**. This is called a peer to peer system. It makes it possible for your child to exchange files without having to go through a web site or other centralized system. P2P systems allow kids to exchange music, videos, movies, photographs, documents and software.

***Texting** is similar to IM but whereas IM is more closely associated with computers and related Bluetooth applications, texting is associated with cell phones and applies to short messages of one hundred sixty characters sent to another cell phone subscriber. Some common phrases used are brb (be right back), gtg (got to go), and ttyl (talk to you later).

In Japan, five of the top ten best selling novels of 2007 were originally written as cellphone novels. Writers create such works by typing out snippets of their stories on their cellphones in text messages and sending them to a Web site, where readers can follow and react to the works in progress. Text messaging requires the writer to limit each sent message to about 160 characters. Students believe the idea that novels have to come in books and that people have to read a large amount at once, is an old-fashioned concept. There is actually an art to creating a message for a cell screen.

*__Webcam.__ Webcams, microphones, and digital cameras allow kids to post videos, photos, and audio files online and engage in video conversations. Kids often use this equipment to see each other as they IM and chat. Webcams are often used by extended families to help kids stay in touch with distant relatives, traveling parents, and other family members and friends.

*__Podcasts__, unlike traditional broadcasts, it allows the user to download a program from the Internet when convenient and listen to it on their iPod whenever and wherever your child chooses.

*__iPhone, BlackBerry, Treo__. Termed "smart phones," iPhone is a technological product from Apple Inc. The Blackberry (current Curve model) was developed by Research in Motion Ltd. They have a new high end model called the Bold (or 9000). Treo smart phones are produced by Palm Inc. Each has more internal memory and adds corporate strength Wi-Fi capabilities to third generation cellular and Bluetooth technology. They have a horizontal screen above a trackball and a keyboard with one letter per key. Most cellular telephones sold today come with a web browser, email, and some form of instant or "short" messaging system (SMS).

The burning question today is: are you an iPhone or are you a BlackBery? There was a time when only Bay Street regulars, Parliament Hill staffers and technology company executives carried around cellphones capable of sending emails and surfing the Internet from the palm of their hand. But all that has changed. Today, the smart phone is the fastest growing segment of the cellphone business and as consumers trade in their aging mobile phones. Many are opting for those of the Internet-enabled "smart" variety as replacements. The two most visible leaders in this new marketplace are Research in Motion Ltd.'s family of built-for-typing BlackBery devices with their QWERTY keypads, and Apple Inc.'s media-friendly iPhones with their colorful touch-sensitive screens. Next-generation advances are forthcoming. RIM announced its Bold device, while a redesigned 3G iPhone is next. BlackBery is working on a touch screen known as the Thunder.

*Wikis are websites that can be written upon and edited by multiple users at once. They are collaborative websites where anyone can add content and anyone can edit. They allow the creation of simple web pages that groups, friends, and families can edit together.

*Wikipedia (www.wikipedia.org) is a multilingual, web-based, free content collaborative encyclopedia project built on a wiki (a type of collaborative website) that anyone with an Internet connection can use to publish to and edit. It is considered the quick fact site which shows up when people search for information on Google. 55 million visitors a month check this page for an average of 18 minutes per user. Wikipedia can be referred to as a black hole because people continue looking for more facts. Wikipedia's articles provide links to guide the user to related pages with additional information. Volunteers from around the world write it collaboratively. Wikipedia's articles provide links to guide the user to related pages with additional information.

Unfortunately, such companies as Microsoft, Yahoo, AOL and Google presently allow people to use some of their powerful communication tools without requiring any verifiable information about the user. Representatives from these companies, claiming privacy issues, will not give parents or school authorities information about user accounts and IP addresses.

Even though companies that provide Internet access strive to provide their subscribers with an enjoyable, safe and rewarding online experience, it is not possible for these companies to monitor everyone who uses their service anymore than a local government can control the behavior of the people within its' borders.

New Technology

This is especially true when one considers the myriad of technological wizards graduating from our universities today. A case in point is the Massachusetts Institute of Technology (MIT) students who designed an application of Google's new *Android* system that lets users automatically adjust settings according to locale. Due to their brainstorms, phones will soon challenge the Internet as a source of innovation. The class is a glimpse of the future and the not-so-distant future. Other student projects include *Re:Public*, a social networking program that helps people make new friends in their area. *Loco* offers a way to find events around town and invite other people, *Snap* guides users to interesting places in their vicinity. *KAEAI* has software that enables a cell phone to unlock your car.

Internationally, a new digital divide is developing. The lack of high speed Internet access in some areas of the United States has been hotly debated, even as that digital divide has narrowed. But a new, wider gap is being created by technology that will make today's broadband feel as slow as a dial-up connection. The next generation of Internet connections will allow for vivid, lifelike video conferencing and new kinds of interactive games. The most promising route to super fast home broadband is to extend the fiber-optic lines that already form the Internet's backbone all the way to homes. Existing fiber-to-the-home (FTTH) connections are already ten times faster than vanilla broadband provided over phone or cable lines.

Other new tricks are appearing today on your child's cell phone. Parents just get caught up with innovation and it whirls away again at monumental speeds. One thirteen year old child in the Ft. Worth area dashed into her father asking him to watch what she could do. The radio was playing "Jordin Sparks, 'No Air'". She showed her father her screen which had the words to the song. "Pretty cool," she said. She then dialed 866-411-7664 as the father put on a CD of songs. One was Alain Souchon,"Les Regrets." Words came again. The technology used by 411-SONG is licensed from a British company called Shazam. The inventor has launched a signal-boosting business called repeaterstore.com. The song recognition works by recognizing a "musical fingerprint" from the music being sent, and matching it to a database of more than two and a half million songs. The service uses patented technology from Shazam that can recognize songs even when cell phone audio quality is very low.

Parents certainly never realized their child's cell phones could recognize songs. But there are other things the cell phone can do. 1)Your cell phone can cut short a meeting or a date or other unpleasant activity. When you register with www.popularitydialer.com, you can program it to call your cell phone at a specific time, or times. Your phone rings, you answer it, and then you go through a pre-recorded, entirely fake conversation with prompts. You get 5 calls free. 2) You can send reminders to yourself to take your medicine, or buy bread, or anything. Jot.com is a dictation and transcription service that lets you call in messages to yourself. After you have dictated a 30 second message, it turns it into an email or text message to your chosen end destination. So when you dictate "Pick up the kids from preschool" into your phone while you are driving, it winds up as an email on your office computer. 3) You can update your blog from your cell phone. Once you set up an account at www.blogger.com, you can post updates and photos via your cell phone by sending missives to go@blogger.com. From there you get additional routing directions. You can also create a new blog via cell as well. The service is free. 4) You can settle a wager or dispute with your cell phone. All you have to do to get the answer to anything, at any time, from any place, is to register with www.mosio.com. 0000000Members of the Mosio "Qniverse" (question universe) are standing by to look up your answer. You can ask about locations, recommendations, trivia, etc. Pretty cool and it's free.

Today's modern technology doubles every eighteen months. The cost is cut in half every six months. (Moore's Law). Our children are faced with keeping pace each and every day. For instance, the first IBM three sixty mainframe computer was launched in 1964. Now, the iPod sells for four hundred dollars and has four gigabytes (two hundred ninety-nine dollars for two gigabytes). It fits into the palm of your hand and is five hundred twelve times more powerful than the IBM 360 mainframe.

SPOT Technology reported in 2004 that Bill Gates personal watch now costs $400 and has 512 megabytes capacity. He can project an image on the wall which includes a keyboard. It is wireless and has a global positioning system.

Now the Web's social network sites are contemplating mingling their tribes. Online social networking today is more about hanging out with friends behind gated communities than exploring the World Wide Web. Visit another site and you will have to rebuild your profile from scratch. This is like having to get a new driver's license for every state you drive through. Although the walls that keep users from taking their data wherever they go are starting to erode, recently announced programs aim to help users move among networks. The two leading online hangouts, News Corp's MySpace and Facebook, have promised to release tools in the coming weeks for Web sites to incorporate profile data, friend's lists and other social functions. Google followed with its own program for bridging various networks. MySpace users, for instance, can soon have their biographical information appear on eBay Inc. profiles. A social network focused on skiing will be able to incorporate Facebook photos and friend lists rather than build its own. It is all done through software hooks that let eBay and others grab profile data from MySpace and Facebook. The new programs come as users increasingly complain about having to retype basic profile information over and over. It also allows social circles to travel from site to site, much as friends going bar hopping together do not have to start conversations afresh at each pub. Google's new Friend Connect comes close to merging those lives. Some startups like Minggl and Zude promise to help user's aggregate data. Users still must agree before a third party site can access their data. Email addresses and other non-profile data are off limits under the programs.

MySpace and Facebook are adding a bunch of splashy user features to do a one-ups-manship over the other competitors. A significant investment from Microsoft Corporation gave Facebook an eye-popping fifteen billion dollars valuation. MySpace, which attracted one in four Americans, no longer seemed the jewel. Facebook developers were dreaming up all kinds of features, ranging from the practical, such as buying music or scouting vacation spots, to the quirky, such as biting your friends to turn them into zombies. The features spread quickly because users could alert their friends when they added them. Facebook awoke the sleeping giant. So MySpace went to Silicon Valley to get its mojo back. Before Facebook allowed users to throw food at each other (called FoodFight) or join social or political causes (called Causes). In a two month period, MySpace had about one thousand new applications from more than ten thousand developers. Earlier some major Internet players-Yahoo Inc., eBay Inc., and hot startup Twitter- backed a MySpace initiative that lets users bring their profiles and network of friends to these sites. MySpace and Google Inc. announced *OpenSocial*, which established a common set of standards for developers to write programs for social networks. One offshoot, RockYou, wrote a Web application that could turn anyone's photos into a slide show.

Investigators said they found eighty-eight news groups devoted to child pornography in an investigation over six to eight months. More than eleven thousand images were collected using software that identifies child pornography by tracking patterns in the pixels of the images. People are very creative and there is a market for this filth.

Internet providers Verizon, Sprint and Time Warner Cable have agreed to block access to child pornography and eliminate the material from their servers, New York's attorney general said. The companies also will pay $1.1 million to help fund efforts to remove the online child porn created and disseminated by users through their services. The changes will affect customers nationwide.

Experts say there are now more than three billion cellphones in use around the world, meaning nearly half the planet owns a mobile device. Companies now need to persuade customers to upgrade their devices. Analysts say there are more than one hundred fifty million smart phones already in the hands of users with the number expected to grow to more than one billion by 2010.

Recent technological advancements across Asia have made touch screens easier and less expensive to manufacture. South Korea based LG already has its touch screen Vu and Shine models available in Canada. The company added the LG Secret to its roster of iPhone killers. Taiwanese manufacturer HTC is also earning an international reputation for its devices which include the HTC Touch and Touch Dual that resemble BlackBery devices with touch screens instead of keypads. Nokia-which commands about forty-three percent of the global smart phone market despite holding less than two percent of the U.S. market-has the touch screen N95 and smart phones like the E71.

New devices include push email (a process that wirelessly connects a smart phone to a server that can automatically update email inboxes). Sony Ericsson Mobile Communications AB's XPERIA Xi has a new flip and sliding design.

A number of companies have developed hybrids known as Mobile Internet Devices (MIDs) which aim to replicate the laptop experience as closely as possible while making them a lot smaller. The Nokia N810 is slightly smaller than a paperback novel and features a 4.13 inch touch sensitive screen and a sliding QWERTY keyboard. It can connect to the Internet through both Wi-Fi and WiMax networks and includes a USB 2.0 port, Webcam and 2GB internal memory.

The Samsung Q1 is one of many ultra mobile PCs on the market and includes a tablet interface, forty GB hard drive as well as a seven inch touch screen display. It is billed as a mobile storage device and media player but also features Wi-Fi capabilities.

The Apple's high end iPod Touch is available in eight, sixteen, and thirty-two GB models. The touch screen device is equipped with Apple's Safari browser and connects to the Internet over Wi-Fi networks.

The latest version of Sony's mylo (which stands for My Life Online) mobile Internet device is similar to the IPod Touch, but it includes a sliding QWERTY keyboard in addition to a touch sensitive screen. The mylo also supports Skype for VoLP calling (voice over Internet protocol) and features a 1 GB hard drive for storing movies and music.

Kids are encouraged to tap into their cellphone's smart potential. Yes, even their boring old cellphones. For email, there is a free service (TeleFlip) that lets them send and receive email via text messaging. It works with any email account that doesn't require a secure connection to the Web. It includes Yahoo Mail, Hotmail, and Gmail. They sign up at www.teleflip.com/ which takes less than five minutes. All they need to enter is their email address and password, their cell phone number and a confirmation number that TeleFlip sends to their cellphone (via text message of course.)

The new iPhones initially to be introduced in twenty-two countries are designed to work over so-called 3G, or third generation, wireless networks and have global-positioning technology built in. They will also support Microsoft Corp.'s Exchange software. These new iPhones download data twice as fast as the older ones. New applications range from video games that use the iPhone's motion-sensing technology to guide characters to study tools for medical students and a program that lets users find nearby cell-phone-carrying friends on a map. One program brings real-time video highlights and game stats from MLB.com; another creates an Associate Press news feed based on the user's location and lets users submit news tips to the wire service.

Apple also announced a new Web-based service called "MobileMe," which the company describes as "Exchange-for the rest of us," a consumer-friendly way for people to link their iPhones to their home and work computers so updates entered into one device automatically appear in the others.

Scientists unveiled the world's fastest supercomputer, a one hundred million dollar machine that for the first time has performed 1,000 trillion calculations per second. The breakthrough was accomplished by engineers from the Los Alamos National Laboratory and IBM Corporation on a computer to be used primarily on nuclear weapons work, including simulating nuclear explosions. The computer, named Roadrunner, is twice as fast as IBM's Blue Gene system at Lawrence Livermore National Laboratory. Blue Gene is three times faster than any of the world's other supercomputers. Roadrunner could have a wide range of other applications in civilian engineering, medicine and science, from developing biofuels and designing more fuel-efficient cars, to finding drug therapies and providing services to the financial industry. To put the computer's speed in perspective, it has roughly the computing power of one hundred thousand of today's most powerful laptops stacked one and a half miles high. Or, if each of the world's six billion people worked on hand-held computers for twenty-four hours a day, it would take them forty-six years to do what the Roadrunner computer can do in a day.

CHAPTER 9:
THE DANGERS OF THE
INTERNET REVEALED

Adolescents love new technologies while adults, who foot the bills, often remain oblivious to the dangers for misuse. With the advance of modern communication technicalities, such as email, instant messaging, Internet chat rooms and electronic gadgets like camera cell phones, cyberbullies can meticulously direct and spread hurtful images and or messages at warp speed.

Innovation and modernization are fostering hatred and harassment in cyberbullies rather than promoting intellectual growth and knowledge. In the world of cyberspace, students believe there are not laws. Masterminds behind these cyberspace terrorist plots can open your home and your school to computer bullying.

Recently in a billion dollar court clash between new and old media giants, the Judge ordered YouTube to give Viacom the log-on names and Internet addresses of all viewers.

A federal judge told YouTube to hand over the log-on names and Internet addresses of every person who has ever viewed material on the Web's top video site. With such cases, privacy fears are substantiated.

Judge Louis Stanton of U.S. District Court in New York, ordered Google, which owns YouTube, to turn over to Viacom its records of which users watched which videos. The order raised concerns about YouTube users and privacy advocates that the video viewing habits of tens of millions of people could be exposed. Viacom also said that the information would be safeguarded by a protective order restricting access to the data to outside lawyers, who will use it solely to press Viacom's copyright lawsuit against Google. The move raised concerns among privacy advocates that Internet companies like Google are collecting unprecedented amounts of private information that could be misused or fall unexpectedly into the hands of third parties. It reminds folks that companies like Google are sitting on top of a lot of personal information that they can't always control.

For every video on YouTube, the judge required Google to turn over to Viacom the log-in name of every user who watched it, and the address of their computer, known as the IP or Internet to protocol address. In many cases, technology experts and others have been able to link IP addresses to individuals using other records of their online activities. The amount of data covered by the order is staggering. In April alone, eighty-two million people in the United States watched four point one billion clips there, according to comScore, a market research firm which tracks Internet use. Lawyers for Mountain View-based Google estimated the information would total twelve terabytes of data-equivalent to the text of roughly twelve million books.

Users should have the right to challenge and contest the production of this deeply private information. That right is protected by the federal Video Privacy Protection Act. Congress passed this law in 1988 to protect video rental records, after a newspaper disclosed the rental habits of Robert Bork, then a Supreme Court nominee.

In another case, after AOL released for research purposes the search records of thousands of anonymous users, reporters from New York

Times were able to track down one person by analyzing her search queries. Anonymous viewing habits may similarly yield clues about the identity of viewers.

One of the most difficult roads to navigate in the world of the Internet is how to balance the safety of the child with the benefits that come with students taking ownership of the work they learn and publish online. Today's homes and schools are faced with a difficult dilemma that pits a student body that has grown up immersed in technology against parents and a teaching faculty that is less facile with the tools of the trade.

For instance, an eight year old may log on to a search engine and type in the word "Lego." But with just one missed keystroke, he/she might enter the word "Legs" instead and be directed to thousands of websites with a focus on legs-some of which may contain pornographic materials. These elusive terrorist cyberbullies are aware of this. Most adults know that there are chat areas, newsgroups and web sites that have material that is hateful, violent or contains other types of material that parents and teachers might consider inappropriate. Falling to the diabolical plans of pornographers, it is possible for children to stumble across this type of material when doing a search using one of the web sites that is specifically designed to help people find information on the Internet. Most of these sites are called "search engines." They do not, by default, filter out material that might be inappropriate. Also the Internet contains newsgroups, web sites, etc. for adults who wish to post, read, or view sexual explicit material including pictures, stories, and videos. Many make no effort to control access. .

In Placer County California, Sheriff Ken White discovered that a fourteen year old girl was staying home from her school at Loomis' Del Oro High. She was busy however. First she submitted five threats to her school via the Internet. Later, she created a special MySpace account complete with pictures of herself and submitted it to online. One hundred fifty "friends" appeared on her website, including thirty-five adult males. Like many parents, her parents were oblivious to their child's Internet activity. Most adults who attend Sheriff White's presentations are shocked to find that so many of their children have created MySpace accounts. It creates children who think differently from their parents and teachers. Unlike their children, who seem able to tune into many different media at once, the Digital Immigrants (adults) don't multitask well. All of this paints a picture of a home environment and an educational system which is out of touch with the way its children learn. The gap is widening.

Instead of an incident being seen or heard by a few surrounding students, embarrassing moments can be caught on video or camera from a cell phone and broadcast to the entire school, community and across the nation. At Lindhurst High School several years ago, a girl's soccer match had just concluded. Girls were disrobed and showering when another, so-called friend, came with her cell phone which also doubled as a camera. The bully carefully shot uncompromising nude pictures of one of the girls, took it home, posted it on the Internet, called a couple of friends to see it, and before school opened the next morning at least fifty percent of the student body had already seen the material. This fine young lady simply could never return to our school. Even the slightest perceived misstep can be humiliating for an adolescent struggling with developing self-esteem. But with the widespread use of technology, those missteps can be broadcast to the world. It was devastating.

On another occasion at Martin Luther King Junior High an awkward seventh grader was walking down the hall when suddenly one of the bullies tripped him. It could have been considered an accident, but it wasn't! One of the eighth graders quickly took a picture of the young man sprawled on the floor with his belongings thrown to the wind. Now with this type of camera phone, this very moment can show up on YouTube for the entire world to see. This victim now can become humiliated over and over again every time another peer sees the incident.

At another middle school in Pennsylvania, some boys created an animation on a Web site where they virtually "beat up" one of their classmates on a regular basis and invited others to join them in the beatings. Yet, another incident saw some of the middle school girls pictured on a "Hot or Not" list that were emailed to other classmates to be voted on

A documented cyberbullying instant message follows:

Divagirl:"Hey, loser, watch your back"
Surferchick:"What r u talking about?"
Divagirl:"Why don't you kill yourself while u r ahead?"
Surferchick:"Why can't you just leave me alone?"
Divagirl:"Ugly girls like you need to be put in their place."

Through the ubiquity of Facebook and YouTube a call from a student became a rallying cry for students' First Amendment rights. It also showed the generation gap has become quite large in this technological chasm. There was a three inch snowfall at Lake Braddock Secondary School in Burke,Virginia. On his lunch break, senior Devraj Kori, seventeen, an intelligent three point nine seventy-seven grade point average student, used a listed phone number to call Dean Tistadt, chief operating officer for the Fairfax County system to ask why he had not closed the schools. He left his name and phone number and got a message later in the day from Candy, Tistadt's wife.

"How dare you call us at home? If you have a problem with going to school, you do not call somebody's house and complain about it. Snotty-nosed little brats and get over it kid and go to school!" Not long ago that would have been the end of it, but the frenetic pace of students online networking, it gets harder for adults to have the last word. Kori took the message left on his cell phone and posted an audio link on a Facebook page he had created after he got home from school called "Let them know what you think about schools not being cancelled." The Web page listed Dean Tistadts work and home numbers. The Tistadts received dozens more calls that day and night. Most were hang-ups. At one point they were coming every five minutes. At the same time, his wife's response was spreading through cyberspace. Within a day, hundreds of people had listened to her message which was also posted on YouTube. A friend of Kori's sent it to a local television news station and it was aired on the nightly news. As of Tuesday, more than nine thousand people had clicked on the YouTube link. Hundreds of comments had been posted on Facebook. Claiming he was exercising freedom of speech, Kori was called into the principal's office but not punished. (Chandler, 2008).

In another case a school district in Missouri is being sued by parents of Brandon Myers, a twelve year old boy, who killed himself. They claim that he committed suicide as a result of the constant harassment he endured while at school and they are suing the district for failing to stop the "incessant bullying." It was ascertained that Brandon was teased in class on the day he died for acting depressed. The boy was screaming for help. The Blue Springs School District has had an anti-bullying policy since April 2004 (expanded in 2006). When angry parents confronted the school board in the weeks after Brandon's death, officials explained they adhered to the policy.

"Principals should be a powerful role model for bullied students and take action," said Bill Bond, National Association of Secondary School Principals' (NASSP) specialist for school safety. "Allow a bullied student to see that you care about him/her and give them the hope that the situation will improve." (NASSP, 2008).

In April 2008, in Fresno California's Hoover High School a student rally was cancelled because of an anonymous text message that threatened a campus shooting. It affected students across town at Sunnyside High and Ayer Elementary schools went into a thirty minutes lockdown for the same reason. Someone had threatened students via anonymous text messages. The threats were the latest in a string during the week that caused concern in Valley schools highlighting what officials say is a growing problem- a high tech version of pulling the fire alarm. It appears to be a new fad. In fact it appears this new fad of text messaging becomes the youthful generation's version of the phone bomb scare. (Sac. Bee, 2008).

The most recent bullying case to hit headlines in April 2008 is characterized by senseless violence and questionable Internet safety. The incident left six Lakeland, Florida girls and two boys in jail and another, sixteen year old Victoria Lindsay, in the hospital recovering from a concussion, as well as partial hearing and vision loss They were charged for allegedly beating another teen in an "animalistic attack" so they could make a videotape to post on the Internet through YouTube and MySpace.

At a supposed friend's home, Victoria, the cheerleader, was struck on the head several times and then slammed her head into a wall, knocking her unconscious. She was defenseless against the attackers' multiple blows. The clip of the video saw the teens blocking a door and hitting Lindsay. After the attack, three of the teens forced the victim into a vehicle and drove her to another location, where she was told she would be given a worse beating if she contacted the police. Lindsay was treated for a concussion, damage to her left eye and left ear, and numerous bruises. The reason these girls ganged up on the victim? They were allegedly seeking revenge for slurs the teen had posted about them on MySpace. In return, the teens had planned to post a video of the beating on the social networking site before it was recovered by police.

The disturbing facts of this case have left millions of parents confused and concerned. Could this happen to my child? The sad twist is that this is the same online social networking activity in which many children participate. Psychologists and other child development experts are urging parents and teachers to take this opportunity to talk with their teens about bullying. Internet safety can become the potential link between the teachers and students and parents and their children. (Sorentino, 2008).

At Waycross Georgia a group of third graders plotted to attack their teacher, bringing a broken steak knife, handcuffs, duct tape and other items for the job and assigning children tasks including covering the windows and cleaning up afterward. The plot involved as many as nine boys and girls at Center Elementary School. Police said it was a serious threat. School officials alerted police after a pupil tipped off a teacher that a girl had brought a weapon to school. Students apparently planned to knock the teacher unconscious with a crystal paperweight, bind her with handcuffs and tape and then stab her with the knife. They told police they did not intend to kill her, but police said they could have accidentally killed her. The children were apparently mad at the teacher because she had scolded one of them for standing on a chair. The children are too young to be charged as adults and probably too young to be sentenced to a youth detention center. They were given discipline; up to and including long-term suspension.

March 15th, 2008 found three middle school students in Deland Florida charged with plotting to kill their classmates and themselves. Two boys and a girl, all 13, were taken into custody shortly after the plan was discovered. Their mental health was evaluated before they were transferred to a juvenile detention center. The ring leader claimed he was being teased, bullied and picked on by other students. He threatened to lock the cafeteria doors during lunch and shoot everyone in sight. The ringleader's MySpace page also expressed admiration for the teenagers responsible for the Columbine High School killing spree.

Many youth are extremely intellectual and technologically gifted. They are capable of causing serious havoc. In 2000, a juvenile cybercriminal "cOmrade" a sixteen year old in Miami Florida hacked into the military computers at DOD for three months. He intercepted names, addresses and three thousand three hundred email messages network used by the Defense Threat Reduction Agency (DTRA). He also hacked into thirteen computers at NASA's Marshall Space Flight Center. Here he downloaded the Space Station's proprietary software for controlling temperature and environment. It forced NASA computers to shut down for twenty-one days. It comprised the software valued at one point seven million dollars. Another forty-one thousand dollars came as a result of computer shutdown. He was given six months in a detention facility. It was the first time a juvenile hacker served detention.

In 2003, a nineteen year old sophomore at the University of Chicago, Illinois was charged under the 1996 Economic Espionage Act, of stealing trade secrets from DirecTV and spreading them on the Internet. Secrets included technical specifications and architecture of satellite smart-cards. As a result DirecTV is spending twenty five million dolalrs on R&D to combat piracy. The student faces possible ten year prison sentence and two hundred fifty thousand dollars fine. (Vuko, 2004).

In referencing the Florida case above, a student at UC Davis, Michelle Satterlee, reported that she had been recently victimized by someone who used her own MySpace page against her. She reported that her freshman year of college was a typical roller coaster of mixed emotions, confusion and self-discovery. She had graduated from the protected world of St. Francis High

School, an all-girls high school in Sacramento. Her parents had warned her of the dangers of MySpace and the nightly news proved their concerns. Yet less than a month after leaving home, she found herself mesmerized by the attractive profile of a "new friend request" from someone named "Jason". He was nineteen and said all the right things. It appeared as if he knew her. Accepting his request would allow him to chat with Michelle on her MySpace page. Jason told her he was a friend of an acquaintance and found Michelle on one of her MySpace friends list. She felt an instant attraction to him, even with her parents warnings still ringing in her ears. She messaged her friend that Jason said he got her name from. She assured her that Jason was a great guy. Conversations began and they seemed fun, flirty, interesting and thrilling. Jason never ceased to impress her. Though he offered few details about his job, school and family, she overlooked such secrecy and accepted his ambiguity. She trusted him because she wanted to believe what he was telling her. Jason told her she was beautiful, intelligent, confident and strong. He began mailing handwritten letters, postcards while on vacation, pictures and he text-messaged her cell phone often.

Though Michelle knew her relationship with Jason was in no way legitimate, she felt a strong devotion to him. She turned down dates, cutting off potential real relationships for the glimmer of hope he held just out of reach. She began to seclude herself from her family and friends because talking to Jason became more important than her most cherished relationships. She admitted that somewhere in the back of her mind she knew she was being foolish, but she tricked herself into believing that if she gave up everything she loved, Jason would understand how much she cared for him and would visit her. They planned to meet a dozen or more times. Every time she was stood up. As the months dragged on, their relationship began to eat at her self-esteem. She convinced herself that she wasn't pretty at all or nice enough to be with someone so wonderful and handsome as Jason. She never felt so lonesome.

Her parents began to notice her sullen moods and wondered fitfully if they were connected to the hefty phone bills that came each month. Their suspicions led them to investigate Michelle's changed behavior and they found that the phone number she had sent thousands of text messages to came from a high school girl three years younger than Michelle. As details unfolded, Michelle learned she had spent a year of her life talking to someone who didn't exist. Jason was a fictional character created by her childhood friend with whom she had verified his acquaintance.

Looking back, Michelle says she is disgusted with herself and embarrassed. Yet, she appears confused as to why anyone, especially a teenage girl, would do something so malicious and deceitful. Jason had deceived a half-dozen other girls around the country, and in an effort to make me jealous, told me the name of one of his ex-girlfriends. Michelle emailed and called her. She learned that the girl had been given a story line similar to what Michelle had heard and to this girl; Michelle was the evil ex-girlfriend. She even flew across the country to meet him, only to be stood up at the airport.

What goes through a person's mind to make them manipulate others with their imaginary world to the extent even close friends do to them and other girls. If not for her parents' watchful eyes, other parents and educators might ask how far things might have gone. MySpace and Facebook have created an addicting virtual reality that lures people into an anonymous world, separating its users from the authentic world. One danger which Michelle and her parents and teachers now realize is that networking sites embolden users to act out of character, going so far in some cases as to create false identities and false lives for themselves. And for some users, that's just too much power.

MySpace, Facebook and other online networks have created a way for sexual predators to lie about their age and lure young victims like Michelle to chat, share images and sometimes meet in person. They have also empowered cyberbullies, who send threatening and anonymous messages. Online bullying gained national attention after recent high profile cases.

One of the worst cases of cyberbullying occurred in October 2006, thirteen year old Megan Meier of O'Fallon Missouri was found hanging in her bedroom of her home as a result of being cyberbullied. (Bullycide) Megan had depression and attention deficit disorder. What makes this case so preposterous was the fact that the tormentor was a forty-nine year old mother, Lori Drew. Drew created a MySpace account under the name "Josh Evans" in 2006. He was supposed to be a sixteen year old boy. Prosecutors said she used the social networking account to contact a young girl named in the indictment as M.T.M. with sexually charged messages from "Josh." Megan was a former friend of Drew's daughter. After weeks of chatting, "Josh" began to send Megan nasty messages, via the MySpace accounting, ending with one that suggested "the world would be a better place" without her. The boy suddenly ganged up on her online with her friends. Megan crumbled, reminding teachers and other adults how vulnerable teenagers are to social pressure and how the agony of being singled out escalates with the wider forum provided by technology. Megan, believing she had been rejected by "Josh" committed suicide.

Drew has been charged by a federal grand jury in California after prosecutors in St. Louis felt there was not enough evidence. Drew was charged with one count of conspiracy and three counts of accessing a computer without authorization and via interstate commerce to obtain information to inflict emotional distress. Each of the four counts carries a maximum penalty of five year in prison. Megan's mother believes media reports and public outrage helped move the case forward for prosecution. The case made worldwide headlines and prompted calls for social networking sites to crack down on cyberbullying. The case was brought to California because MySpace is a unit of Fox Interactive Media which is based in Beverly Hills and its' server is there.

Federal prosecutors decided to wield a federal statute that is generally used to prosecute fraud that occurs across state lines. It is an extremely aggressive indictment because cyber crimes are a relatively new area. The statute applied in this case because by violating the user agreement of MySpace, which prohibits phony accounts, Drew was seeking information "to further a tortuous act, namely, intentional infliction of emotional distress." U.S. attorney for the Central District of California, Thomas O'Brien said that this was the first case of its kind in the nation. Another sad point is that Tina Meier, mother of Megan, acknowledged Megan was too young to have a MySpace account under the Web site's guidelines. Even though Megan also sent mean messages to others before her death, Tina felt she had been able to closely monitor the account. (Steinhauer, 2008).

After the incident became widely known, the Drew family were shunned by members of the community, targeted for abuse on the Internet and had their small advertising business vandalized. As a result of this tragedy Missouri legislators approved a law banning cyberbullying. Other children have been the subjects of harassment campaigns, including whole sites set up to deride them. The bill updates state laws against harassment to keep pace with technology by removing the requirement that the communication be written or over the telephone. Supporters say the bill will now cover harassment from computers, text messages, and other electronic devices. It was approved one hundred six to twenty-three votes in the House and thirty-four to zero votes in the senate. Governor Matt Blunt urged lawmakers to pass the bill. Repeat offenders and someone who is at least twenty-one years old could be charged with a felony and face as many as four years in prison if they harass a minor. Other instances of harassment would remain a Class A misdemeanor, which carries penalties of as long as a year in jail and fines as much as one thousand dollars. (Columbia Tribune 2008) As a result of the Meier case, many schools have been compelled to develop cyberbullying policies. Even so, some school officials still do not understand the impact such harassment can have on the lives of the children and the families they live with.

During the hearing, Tina Meier said she told senators "laws being in place are not going to save a child's life, but certainly no family should ever have to go through sitting here on a daily basis and knowing that these people are still next door and knowing what they've done." (Steinhauer, 2008).

In Northern California's Sylvan Middle School, a thirteen year old was booked into juvenile hall after she posted threats against another student on MySpace.com. Earlier the girl had threatened the other student with a piece of glass she picked up in the schoolyard. But it was the taking of the dispute into cyberspace which really got her in trouble. The girl was charged with a felony count of making terrorist threats. An arrest summary indicated a misdemeanor charge of brandishing a weapon.

In the area the Citrus Heights Police Department maintains that cyberbullying, stalking and other problems related to the Internet are increasing. Stalkers are becoming adept at surfing the Net- on the prowl for potential victims. Teenagers are posting revealing photos and far too much information about themselves on sites like MySpace. The police commander pleads with teachers and parents to learn how to check the MySpace pages maintained by their children and by friends of children. (Richie, 2008).

On February 27, 2008 a young sixteen year old girl from Wheatland with a diminished mental capacity was taken from her home and became the object of a major search created when the Internet was misused. Thirty-eight year old David Faboo met her on the Internet and communicated with her on more than one Web site, including the chat room of the popular online website. He thought the girl was a grown woman because she represented herself that way. She told him that she was coming out of an abusive relationship. She arranged to meet him. About ninety minutes after going missing, the girl sent a text message to a friend indicating she had gotten into the wrong car with the wrong guy. Fortunately, officers found her in a white truck going into Oregon near Grants Pass. Using the girl's cell phone provider, police tracked her location five hours after she was taken. Police chief Dan Boon said "we were very, very lucky." He emphasized the fact that parents and teachers need to be really aware where the child is spending time on the Internet.

Late last spring, fourteen year old Sara VanEssendelft of Mastic, New York experienced bullying worthy of a teen movie. She said," there was a group of five girls and they decided they didn't want me sitting at their lunch table anymore." One knew of her serious allergy to peanuts. To get Sara to leave, they all brought in peanut butter and jelly sandwiches and pushed them at her. For VanEssendelft it might as well have been arsenic. She had been isolated by these bullies but also suffered serious allergies which kept her away from school for weeks. Two weeks later a boy in the back of her class opened up a peanut butter cup. The smell was enough to trigger her peanut allergy and send her to the emergency room with breathing problems. Severe bullying and food allergies have emerged as troublesome issues for educators in recent year. When bullies target food allergies, kids face a serious problem. (Cox, 2008).

Like many other large cities around the nation, Sacramento California has discovered a most disturbing development in law enforcement. Underage prostitutes are now being marketed on the Internet. A fourteen year old girl named Jasmine could have sex with nine men a day. She would start posting ads online at two or three p.m., in time to set up appointments with early commuters. She would finish by 5:30 a.m., exhausted and disgusted. The money-about one hundred dollars per trick-went to whichever pimp was profiting from her lost innocence. Officers found Jasmine the same way so many men had: on craigslist. Well-known as a free online community bulletin board, craigslist has gained the dubious distinction of being a popular site for pimps to market young girls to customers, or "johns." The young prostitutes often are disguised behind photos advertising older women. It is difficult to estimate just how many children are being pimped out, either locally or nationally.

In 2003, the FBI reported about one thousand four hundred juveniles were arrested nationally for prostitution. Most law officials believe the number is much larger. What police departments around the country know is that the trade in sex with underage girls is thriving mostly due to the Internet. As prostitution increasingly moves to the Web, the girls are just getting harder for police to find. Frequently, the detectives say, pimps pass girls along a multicity circuit: their ads go up in Oakland one week, then Sacramento, then Reno. The unit has recovered girls shipped to Sacramento from Minnesota, Texas, Wisconsin and Montana. Some Web sites, such as myredbook. com, specifically showcase "adult content and sexually explicit material." By contrast, prostitution postings on craigslist are buried in one corner of the site, past the section for furniture and collectibles. Clicking on the "erotic services" link brings up a disclaimer releasing craigslist from any liability. Another click leads to a list of posts featuring scantily clad young women promising pleasure in exchange for "donations" or "roses." Craigslist bears no legal responsibility for the exploitation of minors. Since 1996, federal law has protected Web sites from such liability. Legal experts say sites such as craigslist-which has about 30 million free postings each month- cannot be expected to monitor such a large volume of content. (Wiener, 2008).

One officer opened up a browser window. Click. Click. "Sassy & Classy w4m-18" read one ad. "Come have some fun with Monica tonight-18", suggested another. "Just turned eighteen and ready for fun" posted another.

CHAPTER 10:
THE SERIOUS CONSEQUENCES
OF CYBERBULLYING

The same things that happen on the playground or in the commons, in the restrooms, coming to or from school blaze amidst a brutal conflict online. But it happens 24/7 for the victims. No place can they find rest from the onslaught. Young people often use the Internet to bother their victims in dark, mind-shattering conspiracies. Cyberbullying simply means being cruel to other kids online. This includes:

- The child may encounter messages via chat, email, on their social networking site or their cellular telephones that are belligerent, demeaning, or harassing.
- The child may be exposed to inappropriate material that is sexual, hateful, or violent in nature, or encourages activities that are dangerous or illegal.
- The child might provide information or arrange an encounter that could risk their safety or the safety of other family members. In some cases child molesters have used chat rooms, email and instant messages to gain a child's

confidence and then arrange a face-to-face meeting.

- The child may send someone mean or threatening emails, instant messages, text messages. Hate crimes based on race, religion, appearance and sexual orientation can occur.
- The child may exclude someone from a buddy list or blocking their email for no reason.
- The child may trick someone into revealing personal or embarrassing information and sending it to others.
- The child may break into someone's email or instant message account to send cruel or untrue messages while posing as that person.
- The child can create a website to make fun of a classmate, teacher, or another person. They can use one to rate peers as prettiest, ugliest, etc.
- The child may select teachers, and even parents to appear on their YouTube or MySpace account. They may doctor up photographs and place them online.
- The child may tell someone's secrets or spread rumors about them.
- The child could download a file containing a virus that can damage the computer or increase the risk of a "hacker" gaining remote access to the computer. This can jeopardize family privacy and perhaps jeopardize the family's safety.
- The child could do something that has a negative legal or financial consequence such as giving out a parent's credit card number or doing something that could get them in trouble with the law or school officials.
- The child may use Internet-enabled, video-game systems that allow them to compete against and chat with players around the world.
- Cell phones enable the child to surf the web and exchange messages, photos, and short videos from just about anywhere.
- Children can set up private accounts through free web-based, email services without asking permission of parents.
- Anyone using email is vulnerable to receiving "spam," messages from people or companies encouraging recipients to buy something, do something, or visit a particular web site.

Spam may be sexually suggestive or offensive in other ways. Senders sometimes disguise themselves, pretending to be someone else- a friend or acquaintance, a well-known bank, a government agency- for illicit purposes. This is known as phishing.

- Children should never give out their real names. A survey of ten to seventeen year olds revealed thirty-four percent had posted their real names, telephone numbers, home addresses, or the names of their schools online where anyone could see them. Forty-five percent had posted their dates of birth or ages, and eighteen percent had posted pictures of themselves. (Wolak, 2006).

- Webcam sessions and photos can be easily captured, and users can continue to circulate those images online. In some cases children believed they were interacting with trusted friends, but later found their images were distributed to others or posted on web sites.

Internet sites were not created so that adults could reach out to children. They were created for children to reach out to each other. Some children say and do terrible things to each other online because they do not see the direct effects of their actions. Children may tell you, "everyone does it!" Kids operate on the premise that "you can't see me, I can't see you". I Safe America conducted a recent survey about web safety. The survey included fifteen hundred fourth and eighth grade students. The survey discovered that forty-two percent have been bullied online. Fifty-three percent admitted saying mean or hurtful things to someone online. Seventeen percent were victimized by someone lying about them on-line. Ten percent were victimized because someone posted unflattering pictures of them online. (I Safe America,)

Like traditional bullying, cyberbullying can cause victims to have low self-esteem, skip school, have depression, and lean toward suicide. The methods used by kids to harass in cyberspace are limited only by their limitless imaginations, bandwidth, and technical skills. Online bullying can be more harmful than face-to-face bullying because there is no escape. It can happen 24/7.

In East Cleveland (Feb. 8, 2008) a twelve year old boy could not escape either. He battled cerebral palsy and seizures his entire life. He couldn't fight back when three students attacked him after a tutoring lesson. The sixth grader felt pain in his groin and had to have a testicle removed the next day. The three sixth graders-two boys and one girl- kicked him in the back and smacked him in the head after school safety people had left the building. The boy had often been targeted by other bullies because of his medical condition, a neurological disorder that impairs a child's ability to control their movement and posture. Earlier after another attack on him, the school had implemented a "no bullying policy". His mother exclaimed, "I'm praying that kids stop bothering him."

Another school from New York had a special trip planned for children to attend events at Madison Square Garden. Students belittled themselves by drinking, making sexual overtones, threatening others, and fighting. One mother was emailed a copy after someone had put these things online. Being a parent leader at the school, she immediately mailed them off to all other parents hoping to get a consensus of parental support in stopping this type of behavior. What she received went off the charts. About fifty percent of the respondents said a grateful "thank you." But the other half basically said "who the hell do you think you are?" What is worse, the kids were furious and went into orbit taking it out on her son. Now her son was mad at her and literally cut himself off from the family. This troubled youth maintained that his mother had ruined his entire high school experience.

Teachers and parents must act based on the facts of the situation. Sometimes adults are told they have a lifetime contract with Facebook. Not so fast. Some users have discovered that it is nearly impossible to remove themselves entirely from Facebook. Naturally, this causes a fresh round of concern over the popular social network's use of personal data. While the web site offers users the option to deactivate their accounts, Facebook servers keep copies of the information in those accounts indefinitely. They save your information without telling you in a really clear way. It means that users cannot disappear from the site without leaving footprints. Facebook web site does not inform users that they must delete information from their account in order to close if fully. Only people who contact Facebook's customer service department are informed that they must delete, line by line, all of the profile information, messages and group memberships.

No Wonder Stopping
Cyberbullying Is Difficult:

- It is cowardly. It becomes difficult, hurtful, time-consuming. It does not provide any tangible feedback. These bullies do not own their own actions. They appear anonymous. Children will say online what they will not normally say to others in regular life.
- It travels with remarkable speed. Increasingly, many are using high speed broadband connections such as Direct Subscriber Line (DSL) or cable modems.
- Law enforcement is unprepared.
- Free speech advocates like ACLU hold Internet use up as protected by the First Amendment
- Microsoft, Yahoo, AOL, Google, etc. require no verifiable user information.
- It has a very wide audience. Most go online anywhere, anytime.
- Most cellular phones sold today come with a web browser, email, and some form of instant or "short" messaging system (SMS).
- To a child, it may be nail-biting excitement. It can happen in any school, in any home.
- Search engines do not, by default, filter out material that might be inappropriate.

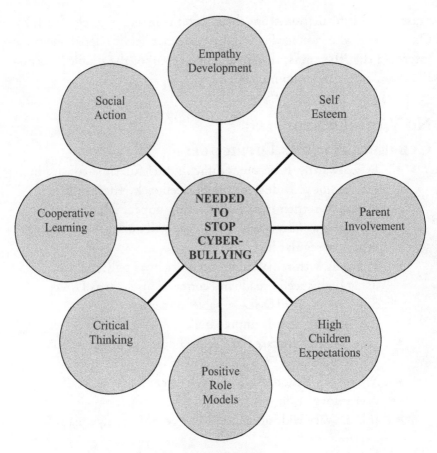

ESSENTIALS FOR COMBATTING CYBERBULLYING

Experts in the field agree that combating cyberbullying requires attacking both individual and systemic origins. The strategies that have demonstrated greatest effectiveness in changing children's attitudes and actions against victims are the following:

- **Empathy Development.** All children learn best when they are engaged. Children need opportunities to develop empathy by identifying and appreciating other children who are ostensibly different from themselves.
- **Self Esteem.** Probably the most effective approach parents and teachers can take to combat cyberbullying is to improve students' self concept. Children who feel good about

themselves do not need to denigrate others.

- **Teachers Need Parent Involvement.** Parents must take the early lead and continue to be involved in their children's online activities. Children benefit from positive, consistent role models, especially their parents and teachers.
- **High Expectations.** Educators and parents can help replace the images that society perpetuates of the low social potential of children. Set high expectations and then help them achieve it.
- **Critical Thinking.** Since faulty thinking and overgeneralizations characterize bullying, children who develop critical thinking skills are also the least likely to demonstrate prejudicial attitudes and behaviors.
- **Cooperative Learning.** Children, teachers, and parents need to work together on a common goal as a means of overcoming bullying. This will enhance children's attitudes toward each other and promote academic and social success.
- **Social Action.** Courage must overcome the prejudice of youth. The most effective way to combat cyberbullying is to eliminate discrimination. Bullying groups often do not change their negative stereotypes about their victims that they see as subordinate until the parents and adults of the subordinate groups social and economic status improves.

The wonder of the Internet has been tarnished by hundreds of Web sites that spew hate. Using the Net, hate mongers can reach into the room of any child who has a home computer. Their sites are often deceptive. Many attempt to disguise their message under a veneer of respectability. They use manipulation and lies to make their ideas sound almost reasonable.

There are chat areas, newsgroups and web sites that have material that is hateful, violent or contains other types of material that adults might consider inappropriate.

One parent-child-teacher activity has been developed by the Southern Poverty Law Center's Intelligence Project "Hate on the Internet." This project helps parents and teachers talk specifically to their child. They recommend the following:

- Prepare your children. "Daughter, I know that you go online a lot. We have talked about the 'bad stuff' that's on the Internet. I want you to be prepared, however, in case you ever come across this filth."
- Review some of the items you find offensive on the Internet. Help your children understand which items you have the most disgust for.
- Ask your children: "What symbols or terminology did you see that might serve as problems in the future? What might you look for to avoid these kinds of sites in the future?"
- If your children see information on the hate sites included in the discussion that disparages their own family or friends, remember to reassure your children: "Your father and I are not error proof either. And neither are you. We are a good family, and we are good citizens."
- Now bookmark equity and diversity websites on your home computer. Encourage children to be careful with search engines for any online research.

Another problem is verified by the investigation of web sites by the Federal Trade Commission. It revealed that only fourteen percent of the sample (six hundred seventy-four) reflecting United States commercial web sites provide any notice of their information collection practices. Only two percent provide a comprehensive privacy policy. Another survey found that eighty-nine percent of the two hundred twelve children's sites surveyed collect personally identifiable information directly from children. Only fifty four percent of the children's site discloses their information collection practices. FTC found that fewer than ten percent of the sites directed to children provide some form of adult control over the collection of information from their kids. The good news is that many of the major players in the technology industry do have privacy policies and do not provide any personally identifiable information until you read it. Parents and teachers are encouraged to check with the service provider to see if they offer age-appropriate parental controls. If not, consider using a software program that blocks chat areas, newsgroups and web sites. You can find a directory of the filtering programs at: Kids.getnetwise.org/tool/ Also the latest versions of both Microsoft Windows (Vista) and Apple's OSX have adult control tools that can limit what your child can do online.

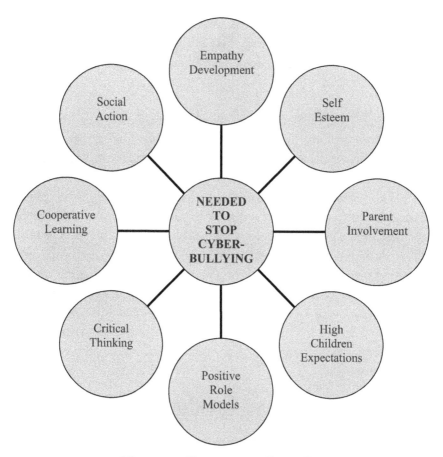

THINGS PARENTS CAN DO

Trusting, curious, and anxious to explore this Internet world and the relationships it brings, children need parental and teacher supervision and common-sense advice on how to be sure that their experiences in cyberspace are happy, healthy, and productive. Parents or teachers cannot watch their children every minute, but they do need to use strategies to help them benefit from the Internet and avoid its risks. Teachers and parents must constantly be on the alert for fighting injustice and cruelty at every turn. Teachers are important, but parents have the most power and leverage to guide their children's activities in cyberspace. It is important parents and teachers become aware of what your child sees and hears on the Internet, who they meet, and what they share about themselves.

Allowing kids to go online without supervision or ground rules is like allowing them to explore Harlem's New York City or the Watts area in Los Angeles by themselves. The Internet, like a city, offers an enormous array of entertainment and educational resources but also presents many risks. Your child needs help navigating this world.

There are steps that a parent can take to help the child. Take steps to instruct children about both the benefits and dangers of cyberspace and for them to learn to become "street smart" in order to better safeguard themselves in any potentially dangerous situation. Although you can take these steps to shield your children from such inappropriate material, it is almost impossible to completely avoid all such material. No option is going to guarantee that your child will be kept away from one hundred percent of the risks of the Internet. But you can still greatly minimize the chances that your child will be victimized by teaching them to follow basic safety rules, classroom rules and home management rules which the adult has demanded. Children need to be taught good "netiquette" which means to avoid being inconsiderate, mean, or rude. It is a teacher and parent obligation to teach children what is acceptable and safe and what isn't. It is to teach children what they need to navigate the darker side of the Web safely and effectively.

8 STEPS FOR A PARENT TO FIGHT CYBERBULLYING
1.
CONTACT THE POLICE
If you are receiving threats of violence, are being made to feel unsafe, or believe a law has been broken-call the police. better safe than sorry!
2.
IT CAN BE BREAKING THE RULES
Various services we use online each have their own
additional rules and regulations. Most companies providing
Web-hosting, email, and internet access have terms of use
that extend beyond what is or what is not allowed by law. Many
Web hosting providers are more restrictive than free speech laws.

3.
WHO IS RESPONSIBLE FOR THIS?

Find bullying content on a website with it's own domain, such as "meankids.org." You can use the service of WHOIS.net to lookup information on where a website is hosted. Here you can get the name of the hosting provider, and you can visit their site to find their terms of service and contact information to report any abuse of their service.

4.
WHO ARE THE PEOPLE IN YOUR NEIGHBORHOOD?

You can find information on URL, but you can also lookup where an IP address is originating. An IP address is like a digital fingerprint- It is traceable back to a specific computer. Be sure to include both the IP address and time the comment was posted.

5.
BULLYING BLOG BUSTER

Most bloggers terms of service state:" Member agrees not to transmit through the Service any unlawful, harassing, libelous, abusive, threatening, or harmful material of any kind or nature." They may terminate their password and blog site. Use the Blogger Problem Reporting Form.

6.
YOU DON'T HAVE MAIL

Contact the email service provider and have their account suspended. Free email services usually include Terms of Service. If you receive email from a gmail account, report it to them. Other free email providers like Yahoo! And Hotmail have similar policies.

7.
STREETPROOF YOUR BLOG

Install such software as Akismet, Spam Karma 2, and the bad behavior plugins. These help block comment spam from your site. They will also block users trying to use an open proxy to leave comments on your site from an untraceable IP address. traceable IP addresses mean you will be able to report abusive comments to their hosting provider and the authorities.

8.
INSTALL IDENTICONS OR MONSTER ID PLUGINS
These plugins can be used to display a custom image based
on the IP address of the person leaving a comment. If a regular
commenter suddenly has an unusual identicon, you might
want to double check the source of their IP address. It might
indicate someone is impersonating another user.

One possible advantage for victims, the school, and a grieving family of
cyberbullying over traditional bullying is that they may sometimes be
able to avoid it simply by avoiding the site/chat room in question. Email
addresses and phone numbers can be changed. Most email accounts now
offer services that will automatically filter out messages from certain senders before they even reach the inbox, and phones offer similar caller ID
functions. Unfortunately, this obviously does not protect against all forms
of cyberbullying. Publishing of defamatory material about a person on the
Internet is extremely difficult to prevent and once it is posted, millions of
people can potentially download it before it is removed.

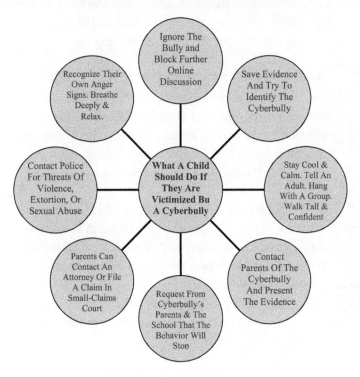

THINGS A VICTIM CAN DO

By exploring the Internet with children, teachers and parents greatly expand its capacity as an educational tool. By providing guidance and discussion along the way, you increase your children's online skills and confidence along with their ability to avoid risks. And you might be surprised by what kids teach you at the same time. Kids and adults can learn from each other.

There are *sixteen suggestions* to help keep your child safe online:

1. BECOME COMPUTER LITERATE.

Our youth are just more aware of technology than adults are. Educators and parents may not understand or engage in cyberspace the way children can, but kids are not developmentally ready to consistently make good decisions about how they use it. As adults, our area of expertise is in human relations, behavior, and effective problem-solving. This is the insight our children and teens need from us. Become computer literate yourself. Educate yourself about the dangers (identify theft, illegal purchases, hacking, cyberstalkers, scam artists, phishers, viruses, worms) because ignoring these computer crimes unfortunately won't make them go away. (Vuko, 2004) Perhaps, enroll yourself in a course to bring yourself up to speed on computer use. Learn the cyber vocabulary. Learn how to block objectionable material. Get to know the sources your child uses. Find out what types of information it offers and whether there are ways for parents to block out these objectionable materials.

Become aware of the Internet "lingo." Peruse the information in Appendix D. Know the Internet definitions. View a commonly used acronym used by kids in instant messenger (IM) and chat rooms. Print the list of commonly used acronyms in instant messenger and chat rooms from the National Center for Missing and Exploited Children. In the home, post this on your refrigerator or at school and the home by the computer. Learn the codes some children use to let others know that a parent is watching. Know their online lingo. (P911) is parent and teacher alert. (CRBT) crying real big tears. (DIKU) do I know you? (EMA) what is your email address? (G2G) got to go. (H&K) hug and kisses. (ILU) I love you. (IPN) I'm posting naked. (JTLYK) just to let you know. (KOL) kiss on lips. (LD) later dude. (PAW) parents are watching. (PIR) parent in room. (SN) screen name? (TAW) teachers are watching. (WU) what's up? (YBS) you'll be sorry. (National Center for Missing and Exploited Children, 2004).

If you do not know how to log on to the computer, ask your child to show you. Have your child show you what they do online and become familiar with all the activities that are available online. Find out if your child has a free web-based email account, such as those offered by Hotmail and Yahoo and learn their user names and passwords. Google your child. Search full name, email address, screen name-use quotation marks for an exact search- for example "Jane Smith."

2. AGREE ON THE RULES.

Facebook, MySpace, online communication, text messaging and instant messaging are all integral parts of the social world of young people and to tell them to turn off the computer is not the answer. Quality rules need to be established. Rules without relationship equals rebellion. Kids need a reason to follow an adult's rules, not additional rules. Bullying starts and ends with good supervision. You can't watch your kids every minute, but you do need to use strategies to help them benefit from the Internet and avoid its risks. Set up reasonable, clear, simple, easy-to-read rules for Internet use. Discuss these rules and then post them on or near the monitor.

<u>**Within these rules state the following**</u>:
- o What web sites are okay for the child to visit?
- o Who can the child talk to?
- o When and how long can they be online?
- o Where can they use a computer?
- o Whom to go to if they encounter problems online?

Monitor compliance with these rules, especially when it comes to the amount of time your child spends on the computer. Parents are encouraged to keep an eye on the photos, journal entries and messages on their children's My Space, Facebook, etc. Personal computers and online services should not be used as electronic babysitters. Remember that as long as the child lives in home or is in a teacher's classroom, they must obey the adult's rules. Some teenagers will not like this, but keeping them safe is your main concern. Follow the rules you set as well as those set by your Internet service provider.

Place your child under a contract. Make it so they are subject to very specific language, spelled out in their own handwriting. This allows them to join online Web sites. In return for the privilege of playing they must observe a strict set of rules-and harsh penalties should they violate any of them.

Basically parents and teachers do not like a child's attitude when they have to give up playing the free version to go run errands, eat dinner or get ready for bed.
They will know where parents and teachers stand on the Web sites. A handful of written sentences can change their behavior more powerfully than any of the dozens of threats parents can conjure up at the spur of the moment. Teachers and parents end up concocting consequences in the heat of the moment that both you and your child know won't come to pass. It makes a mockery of the punishment. The good thing about a contract is that it has all been thought out beforehand and it is all on paper and everyone agrees to it and knows what is expected. The most important part, though, is that you follow through on the punishments.

A model **contract** with any child simply states: 1) When mom or dad (teacher) says get off the computer, you have to get off. And you can't act out in frustration at having to get off. 2). You can only play on weekends, weekdays when there's no homework or when mom or dad (teacher) gives you permission to play. 3) Playing time is limited to two hours on weekends and one hour on weekdays. And the penalty for noncompliance: "Violate any of the rules and you lose access to the paid or free version of the Web site for one year." The contract gives the child control over their own destiny. And in doing so, it also moves them in the direction adults want them to go.

Keep your home computer in a busy area of your house. Avoid isolation. Locate the computer in a central location in the home. Never allow it to move into your child's bedroom. Keep it in the common area where you can watch and monitor your child. Make it clear: it's not that you don't trust your child; it's that there is a whole lot not to trust online and it often comes "wrapped in candy." Adopt a no-nonsense parental style. Demand that your child be the same person online that he is in real life. Convince your child that if they would not generally say something to another individual, they should not send it. If your child has inappropriate items on their computer, give them twenty-four hours to clean it up. Then let them know you expect to see everything!

3. COMMUNICATE.

Communicate. Communicate. Change is not an overnight process. It happens over time. Use technology as an opportunity to reinforce your family or school room values. Adults can change the parent-child-teacher relationship and improve the quality of life for everyone. It is unique. Communication is so very, very important. It is a good idea to talk with your kids about your concerns, take advantage of resources to protect them from potential dangers, and keep a close eye on their activities. Children are particularly at risk whenever they go online unsupervised. Unknowing and pampered kids visualize parents and teachers as sordid and dangerous. When doing so children are likely to participate in disturbing online discussions.

This is a great opportunity to learn about your kids. By exploring the Internet with your kids, you greatly expand its capacity as an educational tool. By providing guidance and discussion along the way, you increase kids' online skills and confidence along with their ability to avoid risks. Keep an open line of communication between you and your child. Consistent talking to your child is a major key to helping them stay safe online. Discuss cyberbullying with your children and ask if they have ever experienced it? Tell them that you will not blame them if they are being bullied.

Teach your child good communication and social skills. This will go a long way toward his or her success in school. Talk with your child. From the time children learn to talk, parents, but also teachers, can have a running conversation with them about how their day went. This makes it natural to continue the custom after the child starts into the cyberworld. Get to know their classmates and friends.

➢ Talk openly and honestly about the dangers of the Internet. The Emmy Award-winning "Connect with Kids" series features real kids, true stories, experts and educators. It is a way to help parents, teachers, and kids start a conversation about tough topics kids face every day. Take your child seriously if they report an uncomfortable online exchange. Talk also about the potential risks involved with email accounts. Teach your child to not open spam or emails from people they do not know in person. Report any evidence of sexual or other exploitation to CyberTipline at www.cybertipline.com or 1-800-843-5678.

➢ Ask your child about their online activities. Tell them to show you these activities. Ask your child about the people they are communicating with online.

➢ Help them feel comfortable about coming to you if something makes them feel uncomfortable or scared. Show concern, listen compassionately, and remain calm if your child shares a distressing incident which they have encountered while online. Try to not judge your child or threaten to take away their Internet privileges.

➢ Keep telling children that they are not just typing into a computer like a typewriter. They are literally sharing themselves with the world.

➢ Ask your kids to help you at first. An adult will be surprised by what their children can teach them at the same time.

➢ Take your child to the www.netsmartz.org where you can download activity sheets and watch online videos. The "Real Stories" section has the most impact, especially a video called *"You Can't Take It Back,"* which plays on children's empathy that they can all relate to. It is narrated by a teenage boy who rated his female classmates on a "Hot or Not" site created by one of his friends. This gives the parent an opportunity to open quality discussions with your child.

➢ Make Internet use a family or classroom activity while encouraging critical thinking. By setting aside time to go online with your kids you not only become aware of what they do online, you reinforce positive Internet skills. Helping your child with a research project is a great opportunity for them to learn about and distinguish which sites provide reliable information, are simply someone's opinion, and are to be avoided entirely.

4.FILTER AND MONITOR CONTENT.

Consider rating, blocking, monitoring and filtering applications for your computer. Software and services are available to help adults block sites they consider inappropriate. Some services rate web sites for content. Some programs prevent users from entering information such as names and addresses. Others keep kids away from chatrooms or restrict their ability to read email. Monitoring programs allow you to see where kids go online. Use software to filter the content and to monitor who and what reaches your kids while online. To see the Internet Filter Review of the top ten software applications, parents are urged to go to:_http://www.internet-filter-review.toptenreviews.com

Consider installing adult control filter software and/or tracking programs (Spector Pro, eBlaster, Spector CNE, etc.). This quality addition will cost you about one hundred dollars. You can also use McAfee Parental Controls which filters both IM and Chat rooms. Once your child becomes a "client" on a file sharing site, their activities and preferences are tracked and often sold to other vendors. The parent and teacher can find free downloads at "k9webprotection.com" and "safefamilies.org".

5.CHILDREN'S COMPUTER IDENTITY.

Help your kids keep their identity private. They should be taught to never share personal information about themselves, family, or friends. It is a good idea to create a pseudonym or a screen name for your child to protect their real identity. Encourage your child to use a gender-neutral screen name or nickname. Make certain the name doesn't include information revealing their identity or location. If a site or services ask the child to post a "profile" with their age, sex, hobbies, and interests, they should resist unless gaining approval from the parent. While these profiles help kids "connect" and share common interests, potential exploiters can and do use these profiles to search for victims. Kids sometimes will compete to see who has the greatest number of contacts and will add new members to their lists even if they don't know them in person.

Teach the child to check with you before giving out personal information. Have them look for privacy rights when they enter web site that asks for information about them. Many positive kids' sites now insist on an adult's approval before they gather information from a child. Yet, a caution. Some still openly admit they will use the information anyway they please. Help your child create a strong password. This type of password can protect your child's personal information online. The FTC recommends the child never give their password to anyone, even someone claiming to be from your online service provider. Your account could be hijacked and you can find unexpected charges on your bill.

To make a strong *password* for your child:

➢ Use a combination of capital (UPPER CASE) and lower case letters, symbols, and numbers. Most passwords have to be case-sensitive, which means upper case and lower case letters matter. Choose gender-neutral screennames or nicknames-such as their initials or a word. Make sure the name doesn't include information revealing their privacy settings on social networking sites to restrict access to their "spaces" or blogs to only people they know in person.

➢ Urge kids to restrict access to their profiles so only those on their contact lists are able to view them. Explain to them unrestricted posting of profiles places their personal information in a public forum and could put them at risk from those who wish to take advantage of such information.

➢ Make sure the password is at least eight characters. The longer they are, the harder they are to guess.

➢ Be sure to use a set of numbers and letters, instead of a

complete word. Yet, make certain it is something the child can remember.

➤ Have your child change his/her password often. Once a month is a good habit.

➤ Use different passwords for different accounts.

➤ Explain to your child to don't just say "Yes" when they are asked if they want to save their password to a computer, unless they are the only person who uses that computer.

➤ Do not keep your passwords on your desktop. Do not write passwords on the computer or tape them to the computer.

➤ Instruct your child to never give their password to anyone other than their parents.

➤ Remind your child to use the privacy settings on social-networking sites to restrict access to their "spaces" or blogs to only people they know in person. Visit social networking sites with your child and exchange ideas about what the parent thinks is safe and unsafe. People are not always who they seem to be in cyberspace. Parents should also be very careful about giving out your credit card number. The same applies to your Social Security number, phone number, or home address.

6. EMAIL & CHATS.

Share an email account and chat account with your child so you can monitor messages. Make certain you know their screen names and passwords. If your child has a new friend, insist on being introduced online to that friend. Regularly go over their instant messenger "buddy list" with them. Ask who these individuals are? When Mat Florian, a junior at Sherwood High in Montgomery County Maryland, signed onto his Facebook account recently to check the status of his four hundred plus friends, he had a friend request. It was from his dad. More and more moms and dads are signing onto Facebook to keep up with their offspring. They are also friending their children's friends. Some take the requests in stride. Others are less sanguine.

Bookmark your child's favorite sites for easy access. Spend time online together to teach your child appropriate online behavior. Keep track of any files your child downloads to the computer.

Set up strict chat room rules and regulations. Generally, if your child is going to get into trouble online, chances are that it will be something that happens in a chat room. The perpetrator will find someone vulnerable. They are skilled in what they do in manipulating children. They know their likes and dislikes and know which buttons to push. And they are patient. It sometimes takes months. He invites them into a private area of the chat room to get better acquainted. His first tactic is to create a comfort level, typically posing as a young person about the age of the intended victim. He may even send your child a doctored photo of himself. Next comes private chat via an instant message service followed by email, phone conversations and, finally face-to-face meeting. Children who are relatively quiet in online chats are especially targeted. The perpetrator may use different tactics. One is to say that his father will pick you up so the victim feels safe getting into the adult's car.

As a parent and teacher, *you can help by:*

- Helping your child realize that when they enter a chat room, others can know who they are and even email them once they have started chatting. Therefore, encourage your child to always use a nickname. The nickname should not be sexually suggestive and does not give away their real name.

- Remind your child that whatever they say in a chat room or instant messaging session is live. They cannot take it back or delete it later. Once online, chat as well as other web postings become public information. Many web sites are "cached" by search engines, and photos and text can be retrieved long after the site has been deleted. Children have been punished by their families; denied entry into schools; and even not hired because of dangerous, demeaning, or harmful information found on their personal sites or blogs.

- Your child should not say anything they wouldn't want their peers or the general public to know. This definitely includes their name, address, phone number or other personal information. Tell your child to never reveal their location or when and where they plan to hang out.

- Forbid your child from entering private rooms. Block them with safety features provided by your Internet service provider or with special filtering software. By posting the child's message to chat rooms, it reveals your child's email address to others.

- You child must never agree to meet anyone from a chat room in person. Many pedophiles pose as teenagers in chat rooms. Here they can instantly get your child's phone number. If you happen to agree that there can be a meeting, accompany your child to a public spot. If the topic turns to sex, instruct your child to merely sign out.

- Tell your child to never respond to a threatening email or message. If someone says or does something creepy, block them and do not respond. Never respond to messages or bulletin board items that are suggestive, obscene, belligerent, threatening, or make them feel uncomfortable. Encourage your child to tell you if they encounter such messages.

Childnet operates an excellent web site that provides adults with advice on chat rooms. www.chatdanger.com.

7.PHONES BILLS.

Parents need to monitor credit cards and phone bills for unfamiliar account charges. Be on the lookout for unknown telephone numbers on your bill or your child's cellular telephone bill and unexplained gifts your child has received.

8.USING ISP PROVIDER.

Forward copies of obscene or threatening messages your child receives to your Internet service provider. If your child receives an email containing threats or material making them feel scared, uncomfortable, or confused, report it to your ISP. Your ISPs address is usually found on the service's homepage. Find out what, if any, online protection is offered by your child's school, after school center, friends' homes, or any place where your child could use a computer without your supervision.

Parents and educators can check with your online service for ways to reduce unsolicited commercial email. Help your child learn to recognize junk email and to delete it immediately. Don't even read it first. Never download an email attachment from an unknown source. Opening this file could expose your computer system to a serious virus. A "spam" filter limits unsolicited email including mail promoting sexually explicit material. Some service providers include filters as part of their service, but if not there is software you can purchase.

9.CyberTipline.

Call the National Center for Missing and Exploited Children (800-843-5678) or visit the CyberTipline online if you become aware of the transmission, use, or viewing of child pornography online. Contact your local law enforcement agency or the FBI if your child has received child pornography via the Internet.

Encourage your child to join such organizations as I Safe and take the lead as I-Members. This empowers children to help educate their peers about online dangers. Help students get involved and take action.

10.Inappropriate Material.

Explain to your child that everything they read online may not be true. Any offer that's "too good to be true" probably is. If they see something bad teach them to quickly hit the "back" button on the browser.

Children often think email is private. This is not completely true. Tell your child to not put anything into an electronic message that they wouldn't want to see posted on the neighborhood bulletin board.

Never open an email message or spam from someone you don't know in person. Remind them not to respond to any online communication in a sexually provocative way. If in doubt about it, ask your parents or another adult.

11. CELL PHONES.

The sheer number of children who have cell phones makes them important on several levels. Naturally, they can be a valuable educational tool if used correctly. On the other hand, they can be a horrible tool in the hands of a cyberbully. Even students who do not have a computer often have a cell phone. Be smart when using the cell phone. All the same tips apply with phones as with computers. Except phones are with the child wherever they are, often away from home and their usual parental support systems. Children need to be careful who they give their number to and how they use GPS and other technologies that can pinpoint their physical location.

12. WEBCAMS & PHOTOS.

Your child should use webcams or post photos online only with your knowledge and supervision. Ask your child to remember that they may be embarrassed if their friends or other members of their family saw pictures of them online. If the answer is yes, they need to stop! In addition, remind that the camera has a large field of vision. Turn the camera off when not in use. Never post photos of others on your site without permission from their own parents. Once images are posted they relinquish control of them and can never get them back. Caution kids about posting identity-revealing or sexually provocative photos. Do not allow them to post photos of others even their friends- without permission from their friends' parents. Remind them once such images are posted they relinquish control of them and can never get them back.

13. PLAGIARISM.

Teachers and parents need to set the ethics standard. If an adult wants to prove their child plagiarized the Internet to do their work, there is actually a site called "turnitin.com" where parents and schools have registered so that kids have to turn their work in. Then a search program looks for similarities in sentences and compares what's on the Internet and determines if it's original or not. Teachers and parents should be aware there is a Website called "*Sparknotes*." Even a child who never reads books may read the whole book in a matter of pages. One read "*Romeo and Juliet*" in five minutes. There are also places like "Obscure Journals" and "The Straight A Club" where kids can get pre-written term papers. If you are looking for a good place for kids to use in learning how to use the Internet legally and ethically, here's one: US Department of Justice's "Cyberethics for Kids" page: http://www.cybercrime.gov/rules/kidinternet.htm". Another is an adult's FBI source for Internet safety: http://www.fbi.gov/publications/ pguide/pguidee.htm" It is recommended that you also use Google (search agent) a search for "safe surfing for kids" then decide if this is what you could use. (Vuko, 2004). Teachers worried about plagiarism can turn to "Turniton.com" which searches key words and phrases for plagiarism.

14.Sexual Exploitation.

Do not keep sexual exploitation to yourself! You are not alone! Tell an adult you know and trust. It is very hard to solve such problems on your own. Report emails with evidence of online sexual exploitation, such as child pornography, to the CyberTipline at www.cybertipline.com or telephone at 1-800-843-5678. This agency will refer your report to the appropriate law-enforcement agency. This organization accepts information about possession, manufacture, and distributions of child pornography; online enticement of children for sexual acts; child victims of prostitution; child sex tourism; child sexual molestation not in the family; unsolicited obscene material sent to the child; and misleading domain names.

Trust your instincts. If it doesn't look or feel right, it probably isn't. Trust your instincts. While surfing the Internet, if you find something that you don't like, makes you feel uncomfortable or scares you. Turn off the computer and tell an adult.

15.Replying to Cyberbullies.

Don't reply to messages from cyberbullies! Even though you may really want to, this is exactly what cyberbullies want. They want to know that they've got you worried and upset. They are trying to mess with your mind and control you, to put fear into you. Don't give them that pleasure.

Never send a message to others when you are angry. Wait until you have had time to calm down and think. Do your best to make sure that your messages are calmly and factually written. You will usually regret sending a "Flame"(angry) to someone else. Once you have sent such a message, it is very difficult to undo the damage that "flames" do. Encourage your kids not to write ALL IN CAPITALS. This is considered yelling on the Internet and is very rude. It may encourage others to "flame" them (sending of repeated, aggressive messages).

16. SAVING INFORMATION..

Do not erase or delete messages from cyberbullies. You don't have to read it, but keep it. It is your evidence. Unfortunately you may get similar messages again, perhaps from other accounts. Take a "screenshot". It is like a photograph of your screen when something is wrong. Press the "Print-Scn/SysRq" key on your keyboard. The image is now saved in temporary memory. Open a new word document, right click your mouse and select "Paste" to insert the screenshot. Make a note of the date, location, email address, name (nickname or real name) etc. The screenshot can be accepted into any program that accepts images. On any email address (the full header shows every stage of an email journey), date and time received, copies of any relevant emails with full email headers. The police and your ISP and your telephone company can use these messages to help you. You might notice certain words or phrases that are also used by people you know. These messages may reveal certain clues as to who is doing this to you, but do not try and solve this on your own. Get help!

In saving email, the more you save, the easier it will be to track down the people bothering you. Save the following from email: email address, date and time received, copies of any relevant emails with full email headers. People are not anonymous online, and with the right information, they can be traced by the Police and dealt with. If you receive email from cyberbullies, you can report it to your ISP with the full headers displayed. The full header shows every stage of an emails journey. Forwarding email with the full header displayed will let the support team track down where it came from.

Save the following from email:
    . Email address
    . Date and time received
    . Copies of any relevant emails with full email headers.

Save the following from groups or communities:
. URL of offending MSN Group site
. Nickname of offending person
. Email address of offending person
. Date you saw it happen

Save the following from Profiles you see on the web:
. URL of Profile
. Nickname of offending person
. Email address of offending person
. Date you viewed this Profile

Save the following from Chatrooms:
. Date and time of chat
. Name and URL of chat room you were in
. Nickname of offending person
. Email address of offending person
. Screenshot of chatroom.

Regular bullying as well as cyberbullying starts and ends with good supervision. Research substantiates the need to adopt a zero-tolerance policy, walk the corridors to discover the existence of bullying, and identify and document high-risk behavior. At school and at home there must be someone whom the bullying can be reported, limit the amount of abusive language to be tolerated, and have specific written policies and procedures in place. Parents and teaching employees need to be educated through seminars and workshops. There should be added a section on civility on the district's performance review form. (White, 2006)

PART IV
Laws, Confrontations, and Developments

Chapter 11:
Important Internet
Safety Laws Enacted

Student violence is escalating. If one were to track bullying by paying attention to recent television programming, you would find an obvious increase in violence. Children become less sensitive to the pain and suffering of others. It is time that the power of parental and educational justice and freedom meet hatred and bigotry head on. A couple of recent university classes I was teaching at National University researched violence on children's television shows. Each student was to watch two programs on the elementary children's programming for a total of sixty minutes. In the first class, the members averaged 20 violent acts per hour. In the second class, one year later, the class members averaged 31 violent acts per hour. This type of violence produces a lack of feeling and respect for other children they are playing with.

In the world of cyberspace, children have a swagger that indicates they believe there are no laws. Unfortunately, most cyberbullies easily escape punishment and repercussions because adults do not realize what is happening to the victim. Since cyberbullying is so new, school and law enforcement officials are still ferreting out the legal technicalities. Yet, rest assured, a school and school district are responsible if the bullying or cyberbullying is happening at school. No child deserves to be bullied. No child should bully another. Bullying is never okay! Many nations are picking up the challenge of stopping cyberbullying. In Canada they have a national initiative against bullying called "Walkaway" and "Wordshurt."

Congress is very concerned and has launched hearings to address cyberbullying. The Internet Service Providers have laws they should obey. The problem is that these laws are often broadly written. The documents the user typically agrees to without reading, ostensibly allows your ISP to watch how you use the Internet, read your email or keep you from visiting sites it deems inappropriate. Some reserve the right to block traffic and, for any reason, cut off a service that many users now find essential.

The Associated Press reviewed the "Acceptable Use Policies" and "Terms of Service" of the nation's ten largest ISPs. But the provisions are rarely enforced, except against obvious miscreants like spammers. AT&T, for instance, has a stated right to block any activity that causes the company "to be viewed unfavorably by others." Most companies reserve the right to change the contracts at any time, without any notice except an update on the Web site. Verizon used to say it would notify subscribers of changes by email, but the current contract just leaves this as an option for the company. The main purpose of ISP contracts isn't to circumscribe the service for all subscribers, but rather to provide legal cover for the company if it cuts off a user who is abusing the system.

Under mounting pressure from law enforcement and parents, MySpace agreed to take steps to protect youngsters from online sexual predators and cyberbullies, including searching for ways to verify users' ages. They will create a task force of industry professionals to improve the safety of users, and other social-networking sites will be invited to participate. Now members must be fourteen years of age, but main users must be 18 years and older now and provide their full name. If the user cannot verify this information they are prevented from viewing the personal information on another's profile. Users will now have the option of making their profiles private. The problem is that they can still lie about their ages. MySpace is also working to improve the way advertisements are targeted to its users. This will regulate the maturity level of some of the ads run on the site.

Facebook is trying to follow suit. This site has grown exponentially in recent years with teenagers making up a large part of their membership. Facebook told the press that they want to keep a trusted environment. They have installed spam and abuse detection systems in order to make it more difficult for spammers, or worse, to game the system. They now have protections for minors. They are automatically moving complaints about nudity or pornography, and harassing or unwelcome contact to the top of their queue for Customer Support to address within twenty-four hours. They are limiting certain search functionality as it applies to minors. They are making sure that minors know explicitly when they are in contact with someone who is an adult.

Sometimes people think they have a lifetime contract with Facebook, but this isn't so. Some users have discovered that it is nearly impossible to remove them entirely from Facebook. While the Web site offers users the option to deactivate their accounts, Facebook servers keep copies of the information in those accounts indefinitely. They save your information without telling you in a really clear way. It means that users cannot disappear from the site without leaving footprints. Facebook Web site does not inform users that they must delete information from their account in order to close it fully. Only people who contact Facebook's customer service department are informed that they must delete line by line all of the profile information, messages and group memberships.

These things makes it very hard for schools in which your children attend. Parents need to help their school district set a whirlwind tone when dealing with cyberbullies. If your child attends a school with a working anti-bullying, no-nonsense policy, you are in luck. But if the principal or teacher says "we do not have any bullying problems at this school," he is indeed playing ostrich. Help the principal become a leader in stopping bullying and cyberbullying. The principal must become the first point of contact. Help him or her develop a procedure that allows any community member the ability to report their concerns about a child who exhibits early warning signs of being a bully or a victim.

Parents need to ask when their school administrator can legally respond to cyberbullying and disciplining the student. The First Amendment places restrictions on school officials when responding with formal disciplinary actions in situations involving online speech by students. The basic legal standard is that school officials can place educationally based restrictions on student speech that appears to be sponsored by the school or that is necessary to maintain an appropriate school climate.

However, the situation is very complicated for all campus online speech or speech via personal digital devices used on campus. The court system has ruled that the speech must have caused or threatened to cause a substantial and material threat of disruption on campus or interference with the rights of students to be secure. Still, how this is to be viewed is still as mystery. There needs to be a school "nexus" to document the harm that has been caused or is likely to be caused. The administration must demonstrate that harmful material was posted, sent or displayed to other students through district internet system or on campus. If school nexus cannot be found, it is safest to support the victim in finding ways to resolve the situation.

Many school districts actually have policies in place directing the school administrator to respond quickly and responsibly to any parent complaint about harassment. The Hope Union School District maintains that their "school is committed to creating a school environment that is free from bullying and harassment. The school administrator will respond quickly and decisively to reported incidents of bullying."

Some school districts have come down hard, using provisions like North Carolina's_cyberstalking law to charge students criminally for electronically communicated threats, racial slurs, and, in one case, spurious accusations of pedophilia. The legal precedence of these cases is unclear, but many experts believe they are a violation of the **First Amendment** protection of parody. Judicial decisions in New York and Vermont based on the First Amendment show that the courts are reluctant to intervene.

In our battle to deliver justice in our youthful society, parents run up against one of our greatest amendments: **Amendment One.** This involves our precious right to free speech. Unfortunately, the courts have so declared that it also guarantees the sanctity of the cyberbully in our schools. At times it becomes the classic confrontation between good and evil.

In our schools, **Amendment One** places restrictions on school administrators when they try to respond to formal disciplinary actions when dealing with a cyber world of revenge and bitterness. Because of the basic newness of cyberbullying, case law is very limited. The power of justice and freedom meet hatred and bigotry head on.

The courts assist the school administration whenever there is a violation of computer usage. There are legal standards to hang their shingles on. Most activities can be regulated when sponsored by the school if we proceed cautiously and meet the intent of the law. If we can prove that the situation makes it necessary to maintain the appropriate school climate, adults can prevail. A school nexus may be found by demonstrating that harmful material was posted, sent or displayed to other students through the district Internet or on campus. Principals have found, however, that if a nexus cannot be found, it is safest to support the victim in finding ways to resolve the situation.

But use of the Internet at home is a totally different matter. Courts are much more reluctant to silence either students or adults. But addressing the issue as one found in criminal law, proving a student is a cyberbully can lead to arrest and prosecution. Yet, one hastens to add that this can happen only if the bully makes threats of violence to other students or adults or their property. If there are acts of coercion (trying to force someone to do something he doesn't want to), there are grounds for litigation. Making obscene or harassing telephone calls (including text messaging), harassment or stalking, hate or bias crimes, or pornography are all indications the bully has major problems. The law can be on your side. Even though it is always wise to seek the services of your attorney. Depending on the facts, the following actions might be possible for a parent who is protecting their child:

*Defamation. If another child, or any individual, publishes a false statement about your child or adult that damages his or her reputation, it has a good chance of succeeding in our legal system.

*Invasion of privacy/public disclosure. If your child has a private fact, and the cyberbully publicly discloses this information, your attorney may have considerable strength in presenting your case. The more this information is inflammatory or offensive to a reasonable person will generate legal acceptance.

Invasion of personal privacy/false light. If you can prove that the cyberbully has publicly disclosed information that places your child or adult in a false light, it can be litigated.

Intentional infliction of emotional distress. As assumed, the cyberbully most often wants to seriously hurt his or her victim. If these actions can be seen as outrageous and intolerable, and have caused extreme distress, then you have another potential legal persuasion. If these can be proven, the perpetrator can be fined or sent to prison for up to six months.

A child can link into another blog giving their readers a chance to share their thoughts. The number of personal blogs has quadrupled in five years according to Pew. During emotionally charged times, some children go to the Web. It is a blank slate to unload and call the frustrations and emotions of a personal crisis. The bloggers who are doing the best are injecting their personal lives.

In our democracy, teachers welcome and encourage parents to become involved in the formal education of their children in public schools. Parents have the right and responsibility to be included in the educational process and to have access to the system on behalf of their children. (Chapter 864. California Statutes of 1998.) Parents have the right and are entitled to the assurance of a safe and supportive learning environment for their child. Parents have the right to receive written notification of school rules, attendance polices, discipline codes and procedures for school visitations. (Education Codes Sections 51100 through 51102).

The Internet age continues to raise new questions about when off-campus behavior comes under the authority of public schools. Of course, students have been subject to punishment for off-campus behavior since the mid-19th century, when the Vermont Supreme Court upheld the discipline of a boy who was overheard using disrespectful language as he passed by his schoolmaster's house.

In a decision late last month, a federal appeals court ruled that a student's off-campus blog remarks created a "foreseeable risk of substantial disruption" at her high school, and thus she was not entitled to a preliminary injunction reversing her discipline. The lawsuit was filed on behalf of Avery Doninger, a senior at Lewis S. Mills High School in Burlington, Connecticut. It was alleged that she was barred from serving as senior class secretary and from speaking at her graduation this spring because of derogatory comments she wrote about school officials on the blogging site (livejournal.com). She wrote on the blog: "jamfest is cancelled due to douche bags in central office," and that readers should contact the superintendent "to piss her off more." In its May 29 decision, a three judge panel of the U.S. Court of Appeals for the 2nd Circuit, in New York City, unanimously ruled for school officials. "The blog posting directly pertained to events at LMHS, and Avery's intent in writing it was specifically to encourage her fellow students to read and respond," the appeals court said. The ruling was a decided victory for school authorities.

Teachers and parents need to work with student bystanders as well. These might be called the "silent majority." Either in collaboration with the schools, or with a group of parents, work with those students who are neither bullies nor victims. Worry about the unwritten honor code that silences and makes children reluctant to do the right thing. Part of the problem is that some adults believe in this code also because of their own experiences as students. Help the schools rewrite the script of "snitching" to "reporting."

According to Denver Psychologist and bully experts, Carla Garrity, you can outnumber the bullies if you teach the silent majority to stand up. If you can mobilize the masses to take action against the bully, you will significantly reduce the bullying. In so doing, stop the bystander's fear of retaliation. Find a way for children to report crime-related behavior that will not expose them to retaliation. Emphasize strength in numbers.

Towards the end of my public school administration, I was hired for a large high school basically to help stop the problems the district was having with diversity, bullying, and gangs. Bullying and cyberbullying were rampant. Teachers and parents were turning their heads when children were victimized both on campus and online. Utilizing the strength of the silent majority, I found that many students really wanted their school to be much better. Some eighty-five percent of the students were in this category. The school had large numbers of Hispanic, Hmong, African American and White children.

We began an organization of the silent majority which we called "*The Ambassadors.*" Giving these students special recognition and special training the number grew from some twenty students to well over one hundred fifty. The school began to change. Parents and educators began to communicate the expectation to take action. Many did not know what to do. They were taught skills and strategies to take a stand against bullying and other forms of violence. We began to attack the bullies both onsite and online. The school and community organizations acknowledged and rewarded caring behaviors of their classmates. Understandably, this organization received state and national recognition.

(Lindhurst HighAmbassadors became a standard
for stopping student violence and bullying.)

Court cases and anti-bullying legislation continue to shape the legal landscape related to bullying. Action against school bullies is needed; however, the proper course of action is not clear to the courts nor the legislators. As school districts and administrators wrestle with the question of how far they should go to prevent and prohibit bullying behaviors, they should also be prepared for the legal challenges that cases of bullying and harassment may bring and make efforts to minimize the risk.

There is legislation a parent and teacher can turn to for assistance in controlling bullying. The Protection from Harassment Act (CIPA), the Malicious Communications Act of 1988, and Section 43 of the Telecommunications Act may be used to combat cyberbullying. People may be fined or sent to prison for up to six months.

The federal law, the Children's Online Privacy Protection Act (COPPA), has been created to help protect children while they are using the Internet. It is designed to keep anyone from obtaining your child's personal information without an adult knowing about it and agreeing to it first. The act requires websites to explain their privacy policies on the site and get parental consent before collecting or using a child's personal information, such as a name, address, phone number, or social security number. The law also prohibits a site from requiring a child to provide more personal information than necessary to play a game or contest. Parents should be aware, however, that despite this law, your child's best online protection is you!

The **National Center for Missing and Exploited Children** (NCMEC) has a parent-teacher friendly website at www.cybertipline.com. Click on "Don't Believe the Type." This is part of a public service campaign specifically designed to help children recognize the dangers of the Internet, situations to avoid and how to "surf " safer. *"Help Delete Online Predators"* is a document that provides information to educators and parents about online sexual exploitation. It includes real-life stores about online exploitation, tips for talking with kids and a list of commonly-used chat abbreviations.

Concerned educators must also combat a few parents who are over protective of their children. If this parent feels any of their rights or their children's rights are being violated, they turn immediately to legal action or the ACLU. At Lindon High School (California) a student's cell phone was confiscated. In schools across the country cell phones go on and cell phones get confiscated, often on a daily basis. Students understand they may lose their beloved phone for the rest of the school day. Justin Tomek lost such a phone but when he went to pick it up at the end of the day he found that teachers were still going through his files. Students believe their text messages, photos and other information to be private communication. For teenagers, such protections are of deep value. Like diaries and letters in the days of old, today's student cell phones carry thoughts, conversations and images involving best friends, family members and romantic interests. They may be snippets of sentences, but they can be as personal and private as any eloquent journal entry.

After this threat from the ACLU, the school board abidingly revised its policy saying the previous policy may be a violation of the Fourth Amendment and the California Constitution's provisions providing privacy for people of all ages. Now teachers may only read text messages or look at photos on student cell phones if they believe such a search would show a school rule or law was violated. Acting like a whipped pup, the superintendent said "we worked it out pretty quickly."

Cell phone policies vary from district to district. Schools typically ban their use during classes. Some include lunch and passing periods. These policies keep school officials busy. Teachers are taking cell phones on a daily basis. There are good reasons to ban cell phones during classes, including the potential for students to cheat on tests by taking pictures on camera phones and sharing the images. Disruptions are another worry.

Oftentimes kids feel there are no laws to dictate what they do online. The real cyberbully is often under the mistaken impression that they cannot be traced. But cyber "footprints" do exist, especially if the culprit sets up a web site that had to be paid for by a credit card. At this point, the teacher or parent need only type in the name of the web page on www. whois.com and they can find out who paid for the offending page. There actually is an IP (Internet Protocol Address) which can be traced to all electronic communication from computers or mobile phones. Behavior words are downloadable, printable and sometimes punishable by law. Your child needs to hear this message. It is very easy now to track the sender of a message. There are all sorts of codes that are on regular email, and all emails have their own number. While there is no "silver bullet" to prevent cyberbullying, students need to know that bullying will not be tolerated in any form.

The Electronic Privacy Information center in Washington, D.C. maintains that free speech protects most of what is done online. Most ISPs have policies telling people not to post offensive material, but that warning is often ignored. Unless an actual crime has taken place and the culprit can be identified, law enforcement is all too often unable to arrest anyone. For the most part, cyberbullying is wrapped up in the old "he said-she said" rumor mill variety.

Schools and libraries are required by the Child Internet Protection Act (CIPA) to filter content that is accessible via the Internet. In addition, CIPA requires schools to monitor the online activities of minors and to have a policy in place that addresses the safety and security of minors when online. But as much as we try, the reality is some are not filtered. Internet filters will become increasingly hard pressed to restrict such content.

So far, courts are reluctant to intervene whenever a child airs dirty laundry on the Web. Adults get caught up in this message as well, but even this affects children. Marriages fall apart, but now either spouse can put out a vindictive video on YouTube saying almost anything they want. In this era when more than one in ten adult Internet users in the United States have blogs, according to the Pew Internet and American Life Project, many people are using the Web to tell their side of the story so everyone can read and hear about it. One person's truth can be another's lie. The confessions can stretch toward eternity in a steady stream of enraged or despondent postings.

Many Internet Service Providers provide parent-teacher control options to block certain material from coming into your child's computer. There is also software that can block your child's access to certain sites based on a "bad site" that your IPS creates. Check with your service provider to see if they offer age-appropriate adult controls. If not, consider using a software program that blocks chat areas, newsgroups and web sites. You might find a directory and other good information for blocking inappropriate sites for children at Kids.getnetwise.org/tools/

Filtering programs can block sites from coming in and restrict your child's personal information from being sent online. You can also find programs to monitor and track your child's online activity. The following are client software products the teacher and parent can install on the family or individual school computer. If the educator or parent has the latest operating systems on Mac and Windows PCs, you can simply configure and use OS-level parental controls that are pretty feature-rich.

- Net Nanny 5.6
- Bsafe Online
- Safe Eyes
- Webroot Child Safe

A number of national companies have an assortment of software designed specifically to help parents control their child's online activity. **One** such company is "SpectorSoft" Corporation from Vero Beach Florida. There are three major developments which can automatically record everything your child does on the Internet. One: Spector Pro. This will record every exact detail of a child's PC and Internet activity. It is easy to use. It will record emails, chats, IMs, keystrokes typed, files transferred, screen and web sites. It also provides screen snapshots, Internet access blocking, chat blocking, and danger alerts. It allows the parent or teacher to know everything your kids are posting about themselves on MySpace and everything their friends are posting about them. You can also add online search recording so the teacher or parent can know everything the child is searching for on Google, Yahoo, AOL, and MSN.

Two: eBlaster. You will install eBlaster on the computer you wish to monitor and start automatically receiving exact copies of every email sent and received on that PC. You will receive complete transcripts of all chat conversations and instant messages that take place on the monitored PC. It also allows the adult to block access to web sites and specific Chat/IM profiles. If your child sends an email when you are at work and your child is at home, within seconds the parent or teacher receives a copy of that email sent to your email address. Once it is responded to, you receive a copy of what the other person has emailed. You will be able to see which music, photos, video, software and more is happening. You will receive via email a detailed Activity Report as frequently as you feel a need.

Three: Spector 360. This is built for the parent or educator who doesn't have time to look at every web page each child views, every email they send, every instant message or every keystroke they type. This program will analyze the data and then show the adult the worst offenders so you know which child to zero in on with the detailed investigative features. Immediate email alerts notify you whenever certain words (and phrases) you specify are typed by the child or are contained in an email, chat, instant message or a web site. (SpectorSoft, 2008).

An important reminder, however, is that these run only on the computers they are installed on. Your child's access to any other net-connected computer or device (including those at a friend's home, and increasingly, cell phones) can be unfiltered. Which means it is also good for kids, teachers, and parents to work together on testing and using the filters between kids' ears: critical thinking and media literacy.

Many sites use "cookies" that track specific information about the user, such as name, email address, and shopping preferences. Cookies can be disabled. Ask your Internet service provider for more information. Also the latest versions of both Microsoft Windows (Vista) and Apple's OSX have parental control tools that can limit what your child can do online.

Once the parent or teacher suspects any child is being bullied online, copy everything! Save all emails or instant message conversations. The parents of those who are bullying may be liable for emotional damages on you're your. If the cyberbully's parents know what is going on (or have received a complaint) they have what is called in legal circles as "knowledge and notice" of harmful activity. If the parents are paying for their telephone bill and Internet charges into their home- they are legally responsible for the acts of their children while on the computer. Parents can be sued for damages.

Any cyberbullying should be reported immediately WiredSafety.org. Teachers and parents are encouraged to check out "Keeping Kids Safe on the Internet" or call for a free copy by calling 800-843-5678. Credit rights and other consumer protection laws apply to the Internet transactions. If you have a problem call law enforcement agencies.

CHAPTER 12:
WHAT A PARENT MIGHT DO IF THE SCHOOL DOESN'T RESPOND

As parents begin to appreciate the influence these cyber networks are having in the world of children, they must come to realize that schools have a major role to play in educating them about safely and appropriately using such sites. The rules for school administrators dealing with cyberbullying are "murky" but school leaders need to discuss strategies for handling situations connected to social networking sites. The key is that each school needs to have a discussion and come up with a policy, and then that policy has to be made clear to teachers, parents and students. Then the policy has to be followed.

With the advent and rapid growth of social networking sites like MySpace and Facebook, an increasingly significant portion of school-age socializing takes place online. The results is that school leaders are being forced to deal with a host of unsettled and even unsavory issues-such as when to monitor students' online activities and how to deal with the very real results of online socialization that spills into school hallways.

Does the school reach out to that wacky part of a child's life which occurs on Friday night that was documented in cellphones? One group of some six to eight boys might bring together all their computers on a Friday night. They set up camp in one of their friend's home basement and begin to perform negatively online against others. Is this to be the role of schools? Another group of middle school students might meet at the community center where YouTube videos are on one screen and on the other were sexual heartthrobs to take action with. Is this the role of the schools?

Students engage in public actions or behaviors which they do not want their parents, nor principals, to know about. However, even though most school principals do not spend their days trolling such sites for evidence of students' unseemly actions, they are faced with deciding when to follow up on tips or rumors. An example was the response of Principal Conn McCartan of Minnesota's Eden Prairie High School. He was mailed a computer disk containing photos of students drinking alcohol on a student trip. The photos had been posted on the social networking Web site Facebook. McCartan did not ignore the rule breaking even though most of the students were members of athletic teams and clubs. Importantly, he had previously alerted parents to the need that they monitor these social networking sites their children were using.

Every item of academic achievement will go nowhere without safe hallways, classrooms, and computer and technological systems. Teachers should encourage parents to be involved as early as possible in the school year. The school really needs involved parents. Get positively involved. Ruffle some feathers if necessary. Don't merely fret and worry. Worry does not empty tomorrow of its sorrow. It empties today of its strength. This type of parental worrying is like a rocking chair; it keeps you busy, but gets you nowhere. Volunteer in helping with the school's anti-bullying program. Parental involvement can really help change student attitudes. Get copies of your school's anti-bullying policies and tips. It is best to request this information from the school authorities in person.

It is recommended that schools attack the issue of cyberbullying head on. Each school must incorporate into its computer instruction classes clear rules governing the use of technology and warnings for potential offenders. Schools can assist parents by emphasizing to each and every student that whenever they access the Internet they generate an electronic fingerprint called an IP (Internet Protocol Address). This is a string of four numbers punctuated by three periods. With this authorities can use the number to trace all electronic communication from computers or mobile phones. Behaviors and words are downloadable, printable and sometimes punishable by law. Students need to hear this message, starting in the upper elementary school.

Parents and teachers should not over-react when the child is being bullied or cyberbullied at school. Ask yourself if this is serious enough to meet with the principal, teacher and parent? Should you meet with the police? When a parent meets with school leaders, they must make certain they know the parent is very serious about their assistance in eliminating the bully. Do not exaggerate. Be honest and stick to the facts as you know them. It is possible your child may not have told your all the facts. Be prepared to consider other information and other people's points of view. Remember, this may be the first time the educator has heard about this bullying episode. The school also has confidentiality rules which might prevent the educator from telling you about somebody else's child. When the meeting is over, arrange to contact the school again so that you can discuss the result of any proposed action.

To keep students "cyberspace-safe" schools should:

1. Print computer rules in student handbooks
2. Send a copy of computer rules home to parents
3. Post rules on your school's Web site
4. Post rules in every classroom
5. In the rules, place information about whom to contact if a student feels violated
6. Have students, parents and staff sign a document indicating they have read and understand these rules
7. Quickly follow up on all alleged incidents to prevent them from snowballing
8. Have firm sanctions in place for violators
9. Do not tolerate in cyberspace behaviors that you would not tolerate in your own homes.

A junior high school's cyberbullying policy might look like the following:

VERNAL JUNIOR HIGH SCHOOL CYBERSPACE POLICY

- All forms of harassment in cyberspace are unacceptable
- Neither the school's network nor the broader Internet (whether accessed on campus or off campus, either during or after school hours) may be used for the purpose of harassment.
- Cyberbullying includes, but is not limited to the following misuses of technology: harassing, teasing, intimidating, threatening, or terrorizing another person by sending or posting inappropriate and hurtful email messages, instant messages, text messages, digital pictures or images, or Web site postings (including blogs).
- Each person logging on or posting must use their own legal name.
- Sanctions may include, but are not limited to, the loss of computer privileges, detention, suspension, separation or expulsion from school.
- Any student who uses any form of harassment in cyberspace will be reported directly to the police department for possible further prosecution.

Your school and community can utilize a number of resources for promoting online citizenship. These include:

- Safeguarding the Wired Schoolhouse (www.safewiredschools.org)
- I-SAFE (www.isafe.org)
- Parents Guide to the Internet (www.ed.gov/pubs/parents/internet)
- Search Engines.com (www.searchengines.com/kids)
- CyberSmart!Education Company (www.cybersmart.org)
- NetSmartz (www.netsmartz.org)
- Surfswell Island (www.disney.go.com/surfswell)

The *Kidscape Web site* lists the top ten frustrations of parents of bullied children:

TOP TEN FRUSTRATIONS OF PARENTS WHEN DEALING WITH SCHOOL BULLYING

1. No response to letters or phone calls.
2. Being told their child is: fussing, over-sensitive, needs to "laugh it off"

3. Promising verbally to do things which do not happen
4. No blame approach
5. Asking repeatedly for the school's Anti-Bullying Policy
6. Being told that the bullying has been dealt with internally and given no details
7. No consequences for the bullies-"They've been spoken to"
8. Their children having to move classes or offered lunch in the library or with a counselor while the bully goes free
9. Family divorce has caused the bullying
10. Being told "we do not have bullying in this classroom or school"

When Hugh O'Neill learned from his eight year old son that he was being seriously bullied, he did what most fathers often say, "Fight back!" But displaying the manly art of pugilism on the back yard lawn demonstrated that his son was more lover than fighter. The exasperated father began consulting every textbook on the subject of bullying. He talked to psychotherapist pals and learned the troubling facts about bullies. He found out that kid-on-kid intimidation has spiked dramatically in recent years. He also found that bullying has of late received both a techno jolt and a feminist boost. The techno jolt of male and female cyberbullies made the situation even worse.

His son became more and more eager to stay home from school for any reason, including vague, symptomless illnesses. His research found that bullies were regularly taunting his child. Hugh found the secret to beginning to talk about the issue was to reveal some personal real-life bullying (or even made up) of how he was bullied. He halfheartedly also began to teach his son to act less like a prey, taught him to walk tall and look people in the eye and speak in a confident voice. But still his son kept coming home with having been victimized. He decided that he owed his son more than this as his parent. Right thinking parents everywhere have an obligation to all kids to insist on a school culture of decency and respect. He felt he owed his son more than diction tips as defense against a future felon.

Hugh's plan called for making the principal of the school his partner. He called the principal and demanded that in the upcoming meeting there be in attendance the assistant principal, teacher, and the counselor. He refused to accept inevitable bureaucratic delays. In the meeting, he got straight to the point. He would not accept administrative technicalities and maneuverings. Tony Soprano Jr. was bullying his boy.

He kept the discussion from becoming an investigation into the validity of Hugh's report. This was not a symposium on if his son had been bullied but a meeting about how to put a stop to it. He was not asking for sanctions against the other kid-just a street-clear order. He had to deflect the teacherly tendency to describe all conflicts as "misunderstandings." There is reluctance among educators to label one kid the bad guy and the other the victim. He met some resistance so he shifted in a more formal mode. He uttered the magic words; "my son's civil rights" are being violated. The school had a duty to protect his child. He followed up in a letter to the "bad seed's parents." Then he followed with a letter to the assembled educators. The paper trail was complete. His point was simple: You cannot control someone else's kid, but his parents can. If they worry that you are a nut who will set legal precedent by seizing their lakefront cottage as damages, so much the better. Bottom line was once some other adults had reasons to care about Hugh's boy's problem, the problem disappeared. "They just needed some skin in the game." (O'Neil, 2008).

CHAPTER 13:
IMPORTANT RECENT DEVELOPMENTS

Currently, thirty-two states have enacted anti-bullying laws and eight others are actively pursing anti-bullying legislation. In March 2007, the Advertising Council in the United States, in partnership with the National Crime Prevention Council, U.S. Department of Justice and Crime Prevention Coalition of America joined to announce the launch of a new public service advertising campaign designed to educate preteens and teens about how they can play a role in ending cyberbullying.

Childnet International launched advice and guidance for United Kingdom schools on preventing and responding to cyberbullying in September 2007. The guidance approaches cyberbullying as a whole school-community issue within the context of digital literacy. In January 2008, the Boy Scouts of America's 2008 edition of The Boy Scout Handbook addresses how to deal with online bullying. A new First Class rank requirement adds: "Describe the three things you should avoid doing related to use of the Internet. Describe a cyberbully and how you should respond to one."

In January 2008 KTTV Fox 11 News based in Los Angeles put out a report about organized cyberbullying on sites like Stickam by people who call themselves "brothias."

Northern California's KTVX Channel 10 ABC is concerned about the amount of cyberbullying appearing in their news-coverage area. Recently, under the leadership of anchors Sharon Ito and Jennifer Smith the television channel conducted a special Internet/television session to discuss the dangers of bullying both on the playground and online. Today's youth are facing a difficult dilemma which pits our children who have grown up immersed in technology against an adult generation that is less facile with the tools of the trade. These children have been born into a world filled with gadgets and online patterns. To them it is a way of life. Years of computer use has created children who think differently from parents and other adults. Interesting comments and factual observations surfaced. One authority indicated that the pattern of behavior can begin as early as age two. Environmental factors which lead to its development include too little supervision, anger and hostility in the home, and constant negative feedback. There is a need to not allow children and adults alike the statement when they are accused of being bullies:" We were just having fun!" There is a desperate need to watch our children's language filled with violent metaphors and correct them. Finally, no metal detector on earth can stop people from bringing fear, prejudice and conflict to the school.

The National Crime Prevention Council suggests that bullying is simply the most important issue in today's schools. There must be a "Zero Tolerance" policy established in our homes, schools, and communities. They recommend that parents encourage their schools to offer training in anger management, stress relief, and mediation. Parents and educators need to work on creating a safe corridor for children's travel from home to school. Hot spots need to be investigated. Finally, adults should treat each other with respect, courtesy and thoughtfulness in order that children can follow their example.

NetSmartz has developed Internet safety presentations for use with parents, teachers and children of all ages. This presentation can educate teachers, parents, and communities with slides detailing online risks, statistics, resources and tips for keeping children safe online. Adults can download the monthly newsletter of the NetSmartz safety presentations at BNet@vvy. In addition, NetSmartz411 is a parent's and teacher's premier, online resource for learning about Internet safety, computers and the web. A parent's or educator's questions are answered by professionals who know a lot about Internet safety. Other information can be viewed at http://www.netsmartz.org/educators.html.

To paraphrase Edmund Burke, *"All that is necessary for the triumph of evil is that good men (and women) do nothing."* Parents are the child's most important teacher. To stop bullying and cyberbullying by your children, discipline at home should be fair, consistent, age-appropriate and respectful. "If not you, who?" Never doubt that a small group of committed parents can make significant change. In fact, it is the only thing that ever has.

Work with your school. Question your child's school and teachers as to what- if anything-they are doing in cyberethics. This has national standards that are required to be taught, just like standards in reading and math. Make certain the district is teaching teachers cyberethics themselves because a lot of these problems are new to adults. Help make cyberbullying a part of your school's honor code. Conduct a student, staff, and parent assessment.

Create a parental committee at school to help implement an anti-bullying policy. Encourage the board of education to effectively train all employees. Help the principal institute a program in every teacher's classroom. Print computer rules in student handbooks. Place these rules on the school's website. Post the rules in every classroom and include one for each parent's refrigerator.

Provide all parents and teachers specific information who they can contact whenever their child has become a victim. Demand firm sanctions to be in place in your school and encourage through the PTA/PTO, booster clubs, or other parental groups the same thing at home. In the school and at home, rewrite the script from "snitching" to "reporting". Normalize the parent and victim's fears and worries. Help eliminate the fear of retaliation. Include a step-by-step way for children to report bullying and any crime-related information which will not expose them to retaliation. Parents need to help teachers in signing anti-bullying pledges with their colleagues and by their students. Parents and teachers can join other concerned parents in the school neighborhood in signing similar pledges.

Chapter 14:
Parental-School Leader
Confrontation: The Last Straw

The people who are in charge of facilitating schools' transition to the digital global economy- superintendents and principals-are typically the least knowledgeable about cyberspace. Many school administrators say, "I don't do technology, and that's why I hire somebody." Most technology experts say superintendents, in general, are sorely lacking in both the basics of using technology and its applications in the classroom and throughout the district. A technology survey of one hundred twenty-five superintendents and administrators in five Southern states by Robert J. Hancock of Southeastern Louisiana University, found that school leaders are lacking in technology training. More than ninety-six percent of those surveyed said they were unaware of national, state, or local technology standards and eighty-eight percent said they had not attended a technology-training session for administrators in the past three years. (Davis, 2008).

Teachers and parents suffering from their children's broken hearts and broken dreams do not have to march down the street with banners to demand social justice for their children. Courage is speaking out when you want to be silent. Parents and teachers alike have complained to myself that they have taken their complaint to a school principal about their child's victimization. Each point out that the principal listened attentively and apparently passed the word on to some teachers, but no amount of adult supervision could prevent the arrows from piercing their child's heart on the playground, in physical education class, or in the school bathrooms, away from the watchful eyes of the school employees. Their child cried out in vain that the only safe haven for them was in the home and the church.

Some parents complain that oftentimes teachers appear to be listening but do not always act. In these meetings, a parent can quickly know if there will not be positive results. Generally, the parent can start to feel this type of negative impact from the educator's own statements; i.e., "boys will be boys," "let them figure it out by themselves," "they do not have enough manpower nor finances to worry about just one child," "it's part of growing up." At times they will act when a parent complains, but not when a child goes to them for help. With this projected attitude the parent must enter a mission to save their child.

Passing the buck has always been the problem with some school administrators. Sadly, there are times when parents must act on behalf of their child when school staffs do not act. Too often teachers and staff may understand the problems of bullying but are afraid to contradict their principal. Arguing with this principal is sudden death. It is perceived as rocking the boat. For a parent, and even for the school itself, this brings about confusion, stagnation, poor morale, and corruption. It also causes frustrated parents.

Educators need to realize that parents of children who are being bullied do have options. They have a very important voice. They need not sit in silence when they know their child is near vomiting from stress before leaving for school each morning.

In reviewing heated comments from individuals addressed to *"Dear Abby"* in 2001, one parent said: *"Dear Abby: I have zero tolerance for bullying. As a mother, foster mother and grandmother, when it happened in my family,* a call to the principal describing the problem usually ended the problem. I always explained, both to the principal and the parent, that if the problem wasn't taken care of, I would press civil charges." Abby wrote back:" "Dear Carol: Good for you. Making sure the school principal is aware of the problem is a must. Also taking the time to document each incident is helpful should legal action be necessary."

Another parent wrote: "Dear Abby: I am writing about the letters you have printed about bullying. If an adult attacks an adult, the victim can call the police. If an adult attacks a child, the child can call the police. But if a child attacks or bullies another child, no adult will step in. The adults stand back and say things like, "They'll work it out," or "It's part of growing up," or "The bully must come from a broken home." All violence is wrong. Kids will not work it out. Talking to bullies doesn't deter them any more than talking to fish stops them from swimming. Child psychologists need to remember that bullies de it because they enjoy it. Bullies bully because society allows them to." "Dear Veteran: I agree that bullying must not be tolerated and must be dealt with on a proactive basis."

Finally a third parent wrote in: "Dear Abby: I grew up in one of the most affluent cities in the country. While I was bright, I was a loner. I was teased, taunted and physically bullied. Had I been wired just a little differently, I could have caused a bloodbath at my high school. Instead, I turned all my anger inward and became bulimic and suicidal. My parents and the twelve-step program of Overeaters Anonymous saved my life at age sixteen. During those years, my high school saw two suicides and several suicide attempts, all from bright but alienated students. While administrators offered counseling, they never addressed the core issues of bullying, teasing and labeling. Since high school, I have become a much happier person. I have traveled in thirty countries, met and spoken with world leaders, enjoyed financial prosperity, friendship and love. Please let your teachers know that the various twelve- step programs can be lifesaving resources not only for adults, but also for young people. Former Outcast." "Dear Former Outcast: Your letter illustrates that while the teen years may feel like a life sentence for some, there really is an end in sight. I'm pleased to spread your message."

If the school does not respond, parents are encouraged to arrange a meeting with the principal, assistant principal, teacher and possibly the counselor. Come armed with the particulars relative to your child's situation with bullies. Get the story of the bullying as correct as possible from your child. Listen to your child with your heart and you mind. Help your child know they have done the right thing to bring it to your attention. Even ask your child what they think is the best action to take. Let your child know you will be on their side until you find a solution.

Do provide the school an opportunity to help correct the problem over a reasonable amount of time. A reasonable amount of time might be one week. If you do this, request a daily update. Tell the administrators you will be happy to discuss your child's problems when they have resolved the bullying issue. During this time frame especially, do not let anyone try to put the blame of bullying on your child, a victim of the bully. The blame is always on the bully and the reason for bullying is that adults allow it to happen. Remind your school that every day your child is being bullied is like an eternity to him and your child wants the bullying to stop. Demand that your child be protected as well as the entire issue effectively addressed.

After communicating with this cadre of educators, write a recap of what was said. Fax or email a copy to the principal. Let the administrator know that you are doing this so that there is a clear understanding about your desire to solve the bullying issue.

STEP-BY-STEP APPROACH FOR THE PARENT TO USE AND THE EDUCATOR TO BE AWARE

It is now time to play hardball. Let's review what parents can do now that they are aware the problem and it is simply not going away?

1.BE CERTAIN OF THE STORY.
Get the story of the bullying as correct as possible from your child. Ask for their cooperation if they must also make some changes. Begin to document everything in writing.

2.THOUGHT PROCESSES.

Be positive in your thought processes about approaching the teacher or principal. The school authorities may really have no clue that your child is being bullied. Give them a reasonable amount to time (three days to one week) to work out the problems. Request a daily update from your school.

3.LETTER TO TEACHER.

Parents are encouraged to write a letter to a teacher who has witnessed bullying in his or her classroom or at school. They should keep a copy. Unfortunately, for a variety of reasons, some teachers are highly resistant to change. They may be suspicious of authority. They are politically conservative. This type of teacher is not an easy person to lead, govern, congeal, motivate, or cajole. This teacher is, however, easily insulted, provoked, intimidated, or angered. Thankfully, only a few teachers are just awful adults. For these meetings, parents should start to tape record statements and have witnesses sign documents about bullying events. They will take pictures of injuries, save all written notes and write down any information they feel is important. If the parent is dealing with a phone bully, they should not throw written notes away. These may be used to identify a bullying pattern or possible identify handwriting. If the child has bullying telephone conversations, try to get the bully on your answering machine or on tape. Make it a habit not to answer the telephone right away. Wait for the answering machine to pick up a message. Get caller ID and take a picture of the number that the call is coming form. This will document the phone number, date the call came in and time of day. Taping someone's conversation without his or her consent cannot be used in court but using a recorded message left on a message machine can. Parents should have the child record in a notebook everything the bully said. Written notes can be used in court. Call the telephone company and get their advice on threatening calls. If the phone company feels the parent has a basis they can trace and record threatening calls for you.

4.LETTER TO PRINCIPAL.

Write a letter to the principal after each incident. Keep a copy. Try to control your anger and your "poison pen" document. Some will get angry right back. Administrators will be more willing to help your child if you, as a parent, act and write statements about your child's bullying situation in a mature and diplomatic way. For over ninety percent of school principals, school administration is a dynamic, complex and demanding occupation which they handle extremely well. They truly care about the safety of each and every child. However, there are some principals who care little about the services their school provides. They are more interested in their self-interest than the safety of the students its services are aimed at. Generally, this is the type of principal who has worked himself up via the legend of the chairs. He or she really wants to ascend to the throne of the superintendency. He does not want to rock the ship for his board of education. In your school, if the principal is a warden, you will have a prison. If the principal is a despot, you will have a police state. If the principal is loveable and fun, but has no expectations, you will have a beach party. If the principal is a wimp, afraid to take necessary action against violence, you will have chaos. Following your meeting with the principal, write a recap of what was said. Fax a copy to the principal and ask him or her to correct or change anything that is incorrect or any misunderstanding.

5.LETTER TO SCHOOL BOARD.
Write letters to School Board Members separately after each incident. Keep a copy. The primary responsibility of the board member is to ensure that every situation in the district becomes a learning situation to the greatest extent possible. However, there are a few board members who think they occupy the position of the "All-Mighty." There is always a lot of jockeying; little feints here and there, shadow boxing. They use the "sandwich technique" when speaking to upset parents. They begin by saying a few nice words, then slip in a knife and twist it a little, then say a few more nice words before sending the parents on their way.

6.LETTERS TO SUPERINTENDENT.
Write a letter to the Superintendent after each incident. Keep a copy. Superintendents operate at the will of the board of education. They are not elected by parents. You, however, elect the board members. The superintendent is called upon to juggle different interest and conflicts among subgroups. This can be professionally dangerous. Few superintendents last long when a group of parents, a staff, or board members become upset. This is an educational fact of life. Unfortunately, many superintendents "kowtow" to the strongest board member fulfilling a self-fulfilling prophecy. "If that is what they expect me to do, then I'll become that."

7.ATTEND SCHOOL BOARD MEETING.

Go to the school board meeting and speak out. Bring along a host of other concerned parents. It is not just your child that you are thinking about, but all the children who are being bullied. Find other parents to join you. At the board meeting, they will try to confound you with such issues as bad morale at the school, teachers will not be willing to do that, we have tried everything. Morale is a state of mind. It refers to the zeal people have for their work. When people do not like your actions, they threaten you with lower morale.

8.LETTERS TO STATE REPRESENTATIVES.

After you have checked to see if your state has an anti-bullying statute, write multiple letters to your State Representatives (The State Senate and House Education Committee). Tell them what is happening in your school and how your administrators are handling your child's case. Write a letter to each member of the Education Committee separately after each incident.

9.LETTER TO THE NEWSPAPER.

Write a "Letter to the Editor" of your local newspaper. Do not embarrass your child with details, but write instead about your school's lack of response for bullied students in general. Once you have written the letter, personally visit the newspaper editor to explain your concerns in detail.

10.USE MULTI-MEDIA.

Consider going to the television stations. Bullying can be very dangerous and taxpayers have a right to know what is going on in their local schools. Voters also have a right to know what their candidates for the school board believe and if they will support and vote for good common sense anti-bullying policies. There is strength in numbers. Try to find out the names of other families within your child's school who are experiencing similar harassment issues.

11.CPS AUTHORITIES.

Consider getting your Child Welfare Authorities involved. They may help if there is enough documentation. Help them understand that your child's civil rights are being violated.

12.CONTACT AN ATTORNEY.

If you are not satisfied with the responses, call and hire a respected attorney. Your attorney will undoubtedly tell you to document everything.

School administrators are constantly being charged to document, document, document. You must do the same! Try to visualize this as your attorney would. Tape record statements, type them up and have witnesses sign the statements. Take pictures of injuries, buildings, and people. Get the dates, time, locations and names of those who were involved, but also those in the school and school district you have talked to. Write down any information that you feel important for reference later, especially any comments made by the principal, superintendent, board member, or teachers.

In her article *"Stop Bullying Now"* Julie Clark suggests documenting everything recording the names of the children and adults involved. List the time and location of each event." Generally, experts agree that it is better for the parent of the victim to avoid face-to-face confrontations with the parents of the bully. Arguments between parents usually make matters worse. Speaking to the bully may exasperate the situation because it sends a signal to the bully that your child is a weakling. Your child should not have to tolerate bullying at school any more than adults would tolerate such situations at work. Ask your attorney to get a restraining order for the safety of your child. There are also assault and battery laws that pertain to juvenile offenders.

13. POLICE DEPARTMENT.

Contact your police department. Swift action is needed. For major harassment situations such as physical or sexual assault, call the police immediately. Age is not an issue. Do not wait. If your issue generally involves online bullying (cyberbullying), save everything. Save all emails or instant message conversations. Computer specialists can track down Internet provider addresses of offending Web sites. Some police departments have hired this type of specialist. If your son or daughter is getting threatening email, your local police department may be able to help or lead you to a private investigator with computer skills. If the emails are terrorist-type threats, report this immediately to the F.B.I.

Even with following the advice above, a parent may still run into monumental roadblocks. One such individual was the parent of David Knight. To summarize, David's life at school was near hell. He was teased, taunted and punched for years. But the final blow was the humiliation he suffered every time he logged onto the Internet. Someone had set up an abusive website about him that made his life unbearable. He went to the website and sure enough there was his photo saying "Welcome to the website that makes fun of Dave Knight." There were pages of hateful comments directed at him and everyone in his family. Whoever created the website asked others to join in, posting lewd, sexual comments and smearing David's reputation. He was even accused of being a pedophile. He was accused of using the date rape drug on little boys.

Rather than a mere few people, like thirty in the school cafeteria, the site was ups there for six billion people to see. Along with this came nasty emails. One said, "David, you're gay, don't ever talk again, no one likes you, you are immature and dirty, go wash your face." Anyone with a computer could see it. And he couldn't get away from it. It never went away just because he came home from school. He found that the Internet is a new play ground and there are no off hours. It made him feel even more trapped. He felt so trapped he decided to leave school and finish his final year of studies at home.

David's mother said that one of the most frustrating aspects of the whole affair was that the bullies who went after her son hid behind the anonymity of the Internet. She cried out that it is a cowardly form of bullying. It is like being stabbed in the back by somebody and you have no way of ever finding out who they are, or defending yourself against the words they say. It is more damaging than face-to-face confrontations. She continued explaining that David began withdrawing completely, isolating himself from everyone. Most adults do not understand how damaging cyber abuse is. These are deep emotional wounds.

The parents tried everything to get the carnage to stop. First they went to the police to investigate. The police complained their hands were tied. They went to the school but they, too, said their hands were tied also. They wanted clear evidence that the material was being sent from a school computer. Then the parents appealed to Yahoo because they learned that Yahoo has policies telling users not to post offensive material. They found out, in reality, most of the time people can say whatever they want.

So they turned to the Association of Internet Providers (ISPs) who told the parents they were not censors. Eventually, the parents did get Yahoo to take down the website about David. But it wasn't easy. It took seven months of messaging, phone calls, and finally the threat of a lawsuit got them to act. David is now trying to recover.

CHAPTER 15:
SUMMARY

The past informs the present but it does not have to predict the future. The strength of the human spirit is tested when children begin their adventure of entering school based on the concepts and training derived from the home. Parents are the biggest single influence on a child's attitudes and behaviors, but a teacher comes in a close second. Parents' words and actions at home and teacher's words in the classroom will be imitated by children in other settings. Parents and teachers need to teach children good cyber citizenship and how to use technology responsibly. A child's freedom and self esteem is hammered out on the anvil of caring, discussion and debate, If teachers and parents see cruelty or wrong, that they have the power to stop, and do nothing, they make themselves sharers in the guilt.

According to University of Georgia Professor Arthur Horne, children raised in a home where family members use "put-downs," sarcasm, and criticism, or where they are subjected to repeated frustration or rejection or where they are witnesses to the abuse of another family member come to believe that world is hostile and see striking back as their only means of survival." Parents and educators must simply discipline their children whenever bullying occurs. Parents of victims, and concerned teachers, must apply all necessary pressure possible to eradicate the problem. Although teens push for independence, parents should remain active and involved in their lives. In our modern technological society, this means being directly involved with the Internet and all its' services. Being a positive role model means teaching children respect and proper behavior. Together, the schools and parents must remain a strong united force by anchoring the values that guide children's actions and decision making.

Modern technology has made it possible for bullies to exert power by using cyberspace. These cyberbullies slither like snakes in the weeds, ready to strike. They deliver hurtful images or messages, threats, and obscenities easily and effortlessly and at the same time gain the attention of a huge bystander audience. With the anonymous quality of the Internet, cyberbullies can perpetrate acts of bullying online that they would never consider doing in person.

Awareness and education are the keys to the prevention of cyberbullying! Spend some time on the www.cyberbullying.org Web site learning what you can do about cyberbullying. Parents and teachers must strive to develop a child's confidence and independence to ensure the child's success throughout life. These qualities will also protect the child against being victimized at school. All educators and parents must take the blinders off. They must take responsibility for what their children do in school. The stress involved with bullying and cyberbullying takes a huge toll on family life and personal happiness. It robs families of pleasant times and turns the entire household upside-down. Peaceful harmony is replaced with anger, stress, fear and other negative emotions.

It is often a very hurtful, difficult and time-consuming challenge to deal with the effects of cyberbullying after it has occurred. It can take a lot of time and effort to get Internet Service Providers (ISPs) and Mobile Telecommunications Service Providers (the phone companies who sell you your cell phone and pagers) to respond and deal with your complaints about being cyberbullied.

Schools cannot ignore the child's first teachers- parents. Good schools understand that parent involvement is not an event. It is a process. Parents must become actively involved in their schools. Parents have the right to communicate with individual teachers and the principal about their child's progress at school and their safety as well.

Adults need to encourage children to avoid bad situations both at school and online.

AVOID BAD SITUATIONS

Let us conclude by reviewing a poem written by Laura, a former victim: It is called:

I AM

I am the person you bullied at school
I am the person who didn't know how to be cool
I am the person that you alienated
I am the person you ridiculed and hated

I am the person who sat on her own
I am the person who walked home alone
I am the person you scared every day
I am the person who had nothing to say.

I am the person with hurt in her eyes
I am the person you never saw cry
I am the person living alone with her fears
I am the person destroyed by her peers.

I am the person who drowned in your scorn
I am the person who wished she hadn't been born
I am the person you destroyed for "fun"
I am the person, but not the only one.

I am the person whose name, you don't know
I am the person who just can't let go
I am the person who had feelings too
And I was a person, just like you!

To walk safely in the woods at night we need a light so we do not trip over tree roots or fall into holes. In our technological society, our children also walk through the dark forest of evil at times. But concerned parents and teachers can be their light to show the way ahead so their children do not stumble as they walk. If teachers and parents do not help the children being bullied, then we are validating the actions of the bully. This cannot happen! Never doubt that a group of committed and united parents and teachers can make significant change. In fact, it is the only thing that ever has. When the dignity and safety of an individual is assaulted, the dignity and fabric of our schools and families as a whole is diminished.

Parents and educators alike must become more noble. Stand on the wall and tell the bullied to not worry. If you are strong, you can do their battle for them. Stand firm and broadcast out: "Not on my watch" will you bully this person. This is where it can change. Right here, right now! To paraphrase the words of John F. Kennedy, "the elimination of bullying and cyberbullying will not be finished in the first one hundred days, nor will it be finished in the first one thousand days, nor in the life of adults living today, nor even perhaps in our lifetime on this planet. But let us begin!" If not, let this massacre be on your shoulders until the day you die!"

References

- Aratani, Lori. (2008, March 12). To Facebook generation, Having parents online is out of line. *Washington Post.*
- Belsey, Bill. (2004). *Always on! Always alert.* Bullying.org .Canada. Retrieved from www.cyberbullying.ca.
- Berson, I. R., Berson, M. J. & Ferron, J.M. (2002). Emerging risks of violence in the digital age: Lessons for educators from an online study of adolescent girls in the United States. *Journal of School Violence,* 1(2), 51-71.
- Brennan. Walter (2005). "Tackle the 'Vampire'Bullies," *Occupational Health,* Volume 57, Number 6, (June, 2005)
- Brunner, Judy M. & Lewis, Dennis K. (2005). *School house bullies.: Preventive strategies for professional educators.* (Motion Picture DVD). United States. Corwin Press.
- California Statutes. Chapter 864. 1998. Education Code Sections 51100-51102.
- Chandler, Michael Alison. (2008, Jan. 24)). Facebook Free-for-All Started with call to official's home." *Washington Post.*

- *Columbia Tribune. Online.*(2008, May 13). Legislators approve law banning cyber bullying." Retrieved http://www. columbiatribune.com/2008/May/2008051News018.asp
- Coloroso, Barbara. (2003). *The bully, the bullied, and the bystander.* New York: Harper Resource Books
- Cox, Lauren. (2008, April 17). Peanut butter deadly taunts. *ABC News.*
- Cristie, Janet. Social worker. Boca Raton, Florida.
- Crosbie, Sarah.(2003, March 29). When Bullying Reaches Into Cyberspace. *The Kingston Whig-Standard.* Retrieved http://www. cyberbullying.ca/whig_standard.
- CyberSmart!Education Company.(2008) Retrieved www. cybersmart.org.
- Davis, Michelle R.(2008). *The knowledge gap.* Digital Directions.
- Dobson, James. (2005). *When your child is bullied: statistics on bullying.* Colorado Springs: Focus on the Family. Retrieved www. bullyonline.org/schoolbully/school.htm
- Dr. Phil Show.(2005, April 6) *Dealing with bullies.* Retrieved www.drphil.com/advice/bully/parents.html.
- Dupont, Rene (Producer), & Clark, Bob (Director). (1983). *A christmas story.* (Motion Picture). United States: Metro-Goldwyn-Mayer. MOTION PICTURE
- Federal Bureau of Investigation. *A parent's guide to Internet safety.* Cyber Division. http://www.fbi.gov/publications/pguide/ pguidee.htm
- Floyd, N.M. (1985). Pick on somebody your own size! Controlling victimization. *The Pointer.* 29(2), 9-17.
- Focus on the Family. Dr. James C. Dobson. *Wounded Hearts.* Frank Peretti, 2004.
- Frontline. (Jan. 22, 2008). "Growing Up Online." PBS Station. McArthur Foundation and Park Foundation. www.pbs.org.
- Georges, Thomas M. (2003). *Digital Soul.*Westview Press.
- Goldbloom, Richard ((2005, June 11). Primer on school bullying: If the school says "we don't have that problem here," don't believe it. *Reader's Digest.* Retrieved www.readersdigest.ca/ mag/2001/10/bullying.html.

- Harold, Erika. (2003).Preventing youth violence and bullying: Respect yourself, protect yourself. *Platform statement of Miss America* Retrieved www.gravityteen.com/abstinence/queen_eharold1.cfm
- Healey, Melissa. (2008, April 27). Guest Editorial. *Los Angeles Times*.
- Heimowitz, Debbie. (2007). *Adina's deck*. (Motion Picture DVD), United States. Stanford University. Retrieved http://www.adinasdeck.com/
- Hinduja, S. & Patchin, J. (2007). Cyberbullying: An Exploratory Analysis of Factors Related to Offending and Victimization. *Deviant Behavior*, 29(2), 1-29.
- Investigative Reports.(2000). *Bullied to death*. (Motion Picture DVD). United States. A & E Television Network..
- I Safe America. (2008). Community Outreach Initiative. Retrieved www.isafe.org.
- Keith, S. & Martin, M.E. (2005). Cyber-bullying: Creating a Culture of Respect in a Cyber World. Reclaiming Children & Youth, 13(4), 224-228.
- *Kidscape*. (2005, April 25). Top ten frustrations of parents of bullied children. Retrieved www.kidscape.org.uk/parents/top10frustrations.html>
- Kowalski, R. et. Al (August 2005). Electronic Bullying Among School-Aged Children and Youth. Poster presented at the annual meeting of the American Psychological Association. Washington, DC.
- Kursham, Neil. "Raising your child to be a mensch"
- Lewin, Adrienne. (2005, March 12). School bullies take teasing online. *ABC News Original Report*.
- NASSP. (2008, Spring). "A Legal Memorandum" (Vol. 8, no. 2). "Eliminate Bullying-A Legal Imperative."
- *National Center for Missing and Exploited Children*. (2004). Protect Your Child's Online Life. Retrieved www.cybertipline.com.
- *National Center for Safe Schools* (NRCSS (1999, Winter)). Recognizing and preventing bullying. Fact Sheet # 4. Retrieved www.safetyzone.org/publications/fact4_index.html

- *National Education Association.* (2003, March). National bullying awareness campaign. Parents role in bullying prevention and intervention.
- Netday Survey. (2005, March) *NetSmartz.* Retrieved http:// www.netsmartz.org/news/sep03-01.htm.
- Loftus, Christine (2008, May) Tips to help when your child is bullied online. Retrieved www.netsmartz.org.
- Olweus D. (1978). *Aggression in the schools. Bullies and whipping boys.* Washington, D.C. Hemisphere.
- Olweus, D. (1983). *Bullying at school-what we know and what we can do.* Cambridge, MA: Blackwell Publishers. Retrieved www. safeyouth.org/scripts/faq/bullying.asp>
- O'Neil, Hugh. (2008, February). "A Father Beats Back His Son's Tormentor For Good." *Best Life.*
- Parents Guide to the Internet. Retrieved www.ed.gov/pubs/ parentinternet
- Pepler, D., Jiang, D. Craig, W. and Connolly, J. (2008). Developing trajectories of bullying and associated factors." *Child Development,* Vol. 79, Issue 2.
- Peretti, F. (2000). No more bullies: for those who wound or are wounded. Nashville: W. Publishing Group.
- Peterson, Karen. (2002, February 6). Kids spread hateful rumors online. *USA Today.* Retrieved http://www.usatoday.com/ tech/2001-04-30-web-bully.htm.
- Richie, David. (2008, April 22). Internet threat alleged. *Sacramento Bee.*
- Rigby, K. (2002). *New perspectives on bullying.* London: Jessica Kingsley Publications.
- *Sacramento Bee.* (2008, Feb. 27). Editorial. 2008.
- Saltinski, Ronald. (2008). *Artificial Intelligence and the Future of Learning.* National University Spring Symposium. San Diego, California.
- *National Education Association.* (2003). Parents role in bullying prevention and intervention. Retrieved www.nea.org/schoolsafety/ bullyingparentsrole.html

- *NEA Today.* (1999, September). Easing the strain of students' stress. Department: Health. NEA Washington, DC. www.nea. org/neatoday/9909/health.html
- Scott, Darrell. (2008). *Columbine high school: The point."* Testimony at the United States House Judiciary Committee.
- Sorrentino, Johanna. (2008). Teen bullying in the news: What you need to know. *Education.com Inc.*
- SpectorSoft.com. Online. Vero Beach, Florida. Retrieved Http:// www.spectorsoft.com/
- Stanfield, James. (1995). *Be cool.* Santa Barbara: James Stanfield Company, Inc.
- Steinhauser, Jennifer.(2008, May 13). Cyber-bully case in L.A. indicts a Missouri mom. *New York Times.*
- STOPcyberbullying.org.(2008) Policy Statement. Retrieved www.stopcyberbullying.org?kids/are_you_a_cyberbully.html.
- Swartz, Jon. (2005, March 6). Schoolyard bullies get nastier online. *USA Today.* Retrieved www.usatoday.com/tech/ news/2005-03-06-cover-cyberbullies_x.htm
- *U.S. Department of Education.* (2003, July 19)Rates of Computer and Internet Use by Children in Nursery School and Students in Kindergarten thorough Twelfth Grade. In Issue Brief, October 2005, page 1, NCEAS 2005. June 15, 2006 .*The Children's Online Privacy Protection Act (COPPA). Child Internet Protection Act (CIPA) Bullying prevention in the School: Research-based strategies for educators.* Retrieved Office of Safe and Drug-Free Schools. www.thechallenge.org/10-y11no3/y11n3-bullying-prev.htm
- * *U.S. Department of Education.*(2002) National Center for Education Statistics, The continuation of Education 2002, NCES 2002-025. Washington, DC. U.S. Government Printing Office. Retrieved. Http://nces.ed.gov/
- *U.S. Department of Homeland Security.* US-CERT.(2008, May).. National Cyber Alert System. Cyber Security Tip ST06-005. Retrieved http://www.us-cert.gov/cas/tips/ST06-005.html
- *U.S. Department of Justice.*(2000, October). Indicators of school crime and safety. Retrieved www.ojp.usdoj.gov/bjs/pub/pdf/ iscs00ex.pdf

- *U.S. Secret Service.* (2001, March 21). The final report and findings of the state school initiative implications for the prevention of school attacks in the United States. Washington, D.C.
- Vuko, Evelyn, and Radnofsky, Mary. (2004, May 28). "Teacher says: Teaching cyber ethics." *Washgintonpost*.com.
- Weizenbaum, Joseph. (1984). *Computer power and human reason.* Penguin Books.
- White, Gayle Webb. (2006). *Bullying: Added cost of doing business.*" Southern Arkansas University.
- Wiener, Jocelyn. (2008, May 18). Underage prostitutes marketed on Internet. *The Sacramento Bee.*
- *Wikepedia.* (2008, March 14). Definition of Wikepedia, Wikis, Blogs, Podcasts, IM, .IMVU, YouTube, Facebook Retrieved http://en.wikipedia.org/wiki/Wikipedia/Cyber-bullying/.
- Willard, J. (2006). Stop bullying now Retrieved http://stopbullyingnow.hrsa.gov/adult/indexAdult. asp?Area=cyberbullying
- WiredSafety.org.(2008). Keeping kids safe on the internet. Retrieved
- Wolak, Janis, Mitchel, Kimberly, and Finkelhor, David.(2006). *Online victimization of youth: five years later.* Alexandria, Virginia. National Center for Missing and Exploited Children. Retrieved http://www.unh.edu/ccrc
- Ybarra, M. L., & Mitchell, K. J. (2004). Youth engaging in online harassment: Associations with caregiver-child relationships, Internet use, and personal characteristics. *Journal of Adolescence,* 27, 319-336.

APPENDIX A

HOW TO REPORT CYBERBULLYING EMAIL:.
* Using MSN Hotmail:
    * Sign in to MSN Hotmail
    * Click Options (right hand side, next to help)
    * Click mail on the left hand column
    * Click Mail Display Settings
    * Under Message Headers, select Full
* Using MSN Premium or MSN Plus
    * Right click on the mail
    * On your keyboard, press the Alt and the Return keys
    * Click Message Source. The message opens in a new window with all the header information visible
    * Copy all the text and paste it into a new message.
* Using Outlook Express or Outlook
    * Right click on the unopened mail, and click Options
    * Under Internet headers, copy the full content of the header
    * Open the email in question and forward a complete copy of the message, inserting the full message header that you copied.

* Using a Yahoo Account
  * Open the Yahoo account
  * Click on Options
  * Select mail viewing preferences
  * By default, these will be set to briefs
  * To view the full headers, click All
* Reporting chatroom cyberbullying
  * Highlight the chatter's name
  * Use the ignore button to stop all conversation with that person
  * Take a screenshot of the abuse
  * Note the time, date and chatroom name
  * Report to the chatroom moderator and service operator
  * Speak to your parent

It isn't your fault that there are some very strange people in the world. Don't be ashamed to tell somebody about any disturbing, threatening, weird or frightening behavior you encounter in chat. People are not anonymous online, and with the right information saved, they can be traced by the Police and dealt with.

What to do if someone has stolen your account.
If somebody has stolen or "hacked" your account and changed all the login details, you will need to get in touch with a support team to get it back. It is not possible to have your password reset if you supply incorrect information.

You may need to delete your current email accounts, cell phone/pager accounts and set up new ones. If you have persistent cyberbullying problems, it is recommended that you do this as soon as possible, unless you are working with the police and your Telecommunications Provider to keep the account active to try and catch the cyberbully.

How Do I Take a Screenshot of Offensive Content?

A screenshot is like a photograph of your screen. It captures everything that you can see on your screen at the press of a key and is useful for recording details you might want to report.

1. Have the information you wish to record open on your screen and press the PrintScn/SysRq key on your keyboard. The image is now save in a temporary memory.
2. Open a new Word document, right click your mouse and select Paste to insert the screenshot.
3. Make a note of the date, location, email address, name (nickname or real name) and any other information that you think might be useful and then Save the file.

- The screenshot can be inserted into any program that accepts images.

How Do I Save An Address in Groups?

If someone or something makes you feel uncomfortable it is important to tell someone you trust who can help you to report your experience to the right people. If you encounter potentially illegal or offensive content in MSN Groups or have seen a Group that you believe should be placed behind an adult advisory notice, save the URL and contact the service provider immediately.

a. With the offending Group open, right click your mouse over the address bar in your browser and select Copy.
b. Click here to Contact Us.
c. Under the section Enter the Web address of the Group, right click your mouse in the box and paste the URL. Please ensure that all other information on the form is completed before sending it to the service provider.

How Do I see a Person's Passport ID in Groups?

Groups' members are known by their Nicknames, but each of them has a Passport ID that is associated with this Nickname. Passport IDs can be hidden from other members while using MSN Groups. If you need to report anybody, service providers can take action if they have their nicknames but they can act even faster if they also know their Passport ID.

1. Open the message's posted by the user you wish to report and click on their nickname.
2. On the Member Information screen copy the Group Name, Nickname, the time they joined and any recent messages that have been posted.
3. Click here to Contact Us to report the member, placing all of

the above information in the form provided.
- To hide or unhide your email address from the rest of the Group click Manager Tools or Member Tools on the far left and then Check Your Email Settings. IN the page that opens remove the tick from the box under Email.

How Do I Save An Address in the Member Directory?

If someone or something makes you feel uncomfortable it is important to tell someone you trust who can help you to report your experience to the right people. To report potentially illegal or offensive content in the Member Directory, or to report a profile, save the address (URL) and contact the service provider immediately.

1. With the offending Group open, right click your mouse over the address bar in your browser and select Copy.
2. Click her to Contact Us.
3. Under the section Enter the Web address of the public profile, right click your mouse in the box and paste the URL. Please ensure that all other information on the form is completed before sending it to us.

How Do I Report Cyberbullying from a Hotmail Account?

You can report cyberbullying messages direct from your email inbox and every report you make will actually improve the intelligent filters that protect your account.

1. Sing in to Hotmail and click on the Mail tab to open the inbox.
2. Select an email you suspect to be an abusive message. Tip- a question mark is placed on all email from unknown senders.
3. Click the Junk option and select from either Report or Report and Block sender, and then simply follow the directions given.

- If you need to report an email to an authority or organization, then include the full header so that action can be taken. Under Message Headers select Full and then click OK. You will now be able to forward mail with full headers displayed.

Appendix B

My Children's Computer Safety Rules Pledge

A Pledge Between Parents and Children

I agree that I will not:
1. Give out personal information such as my address, telephone number, work address/telephone number, or the name and location of my school without my parents' permission.
2. Never agree to get together with someone I "Meet" online without first checking with my parents. If my parents agree to the meeting, I will be sure that it is in a public place and bring my mother or father along.
3. Never send a person my picture or anything else without first checking with my parents.
4. Respond to any messages that are mean or in any way make me feel uncomfortable. It is not my fault if I get a message like that. If I do I will tell my parents right away so that they can contact the service provider.

5. Give out my Internet password to anyone (even my best friends) other than my parents.

I agree that I will:

6. Tell my parents right away if I come across any information that makes me feel uncomfortable.

7. Talk with my parents so that we can set up rules for going online. We will decide upon the time of day that I can be online, the length of time I can be online and appropriate areas for me to visit. I will not access other areas or break these rules without their permission.

8. Check with my parents before downloading or installing software or doing anything that could possibly hurt our computer or jeopardize my family's privacy.

9. Be a good online citizen and not do anything that hurts other people or is against the law.

10. Help my parents understand how to have fun and learn things online and teach them things about the Internet, computers and other technology.

    Child's Signature   Date   Parent's Signature

Appendix C

Are You a Cyberbully?

The following questionnaire can help parents determine if their child is or will be a cyberbully. The questionnaire was launched by STOPcyberbullying.org.

Often people who are victims are also bullies. Before you feel too bad for yourself take the quiz below to find if you, too, are part of the cyberbullying problem? Rate yourself on the following point scale according to if, and how many times, you have done the below activities. Give yourself 0 points if you've never done it. 1 point if you have done it one or two times, 2 points if you have done it three to five times, and 3 points if you have done it more than five times.

Have You Ever...
___Signed on with someone else's screen name to gather info?
___Sent an e-mail or online greeting card from someone's account?
___Impersonated someone over IM or online?
___Teased or frightened someone over IM?

____Not told someone who you really are online, telling them to "guess"?

____Forwarded a private IM conversation or e-mail without the permission of the other person?

____Changed your profile or away message designed to embarrass or frighten someone?

____Posted pictures or information about someone on a Web site without their consent?

____Created an Internet poll, either over IM or on a Web site, about someone without their consent?

____Used information found online to follow, tease, embarrass or harass someone in person?

____Sent rude or scary things to someone, even if you were just joking?

____Used bad language online?

____Signed someone else up for something online without their permission?

____Used an IM or e-mail address that looked like someone else's?

____Used someone else-s password for any reason without their permission?

____Hacked into some0one else's computer or sent a virus or Trojan horse to them?

____Insulted someone in an interactive game room?

____Posted rude things or lies about someone online?

____Voted at an online bashing poll or posted to a guestbook saying rude or mean things?

Now Calculate Your Total Score:

0 – 5 Points: Cyber Saint

Congratulations! You are a cyber saint! Your online behavior is exemplary! Keep up the good work!

6-10 Points: Cyber Risky

Well, you are not perfect, but few people are. Chances are you have not done anything terrible and were just having fun, but try not to repeat you behaviors, since they are all offenses. Keep in mind the pain that your fun might be causing others!

11-18 Points: Cyber Sinner

Your online behavior needs to be improved! You have done way too many cyber no-no's! Keep in mind that these practices are dangerous, wrong, and punishable and try to clean up that cyber record!

More than 18 Points: Cyber Bully

Put on the brakes and turn that PC/MAC/text-messaging device around! You are headed in a very bad direction. You qualify, without doubt, as a cyberbully. You need to sing off and think about where that little mouse of yours has been clicking before serious trouble results for you and/or your victim(s), if it hasn't happened already!

Appendix D

Talking the Talk.

A quick introduction to knowing what people are saying to each other in cyberspace.

Sure you might be able to "walk the walk" with your fancy new cell phone, pager or PDA, but can you "Talk the (cyber) talk? There now exists a very new and different way of communicating online. In some ways, it seems like a new language. What follows is an ever-growing list of letters, numbers and symbols (emoticons) that are used by the online world to communicate with each other.

* IM-ing   Using Internet Messaging
* SMS   The Short Message Service (SMS) is the ability to send and receive text messages to and from mobile telephones. The text can comprise of words or numbers or an alphanumeric combination. SMS was created when it was incorporated into the Global System for Mobiles (GSM) digital mobile phone standard. A single short message can be up to 160 characters of text in length using default GSM alphabet coding, and 70 characters when UCS2 international character coding is used.

* EMS   Enhanced Messaging Service (text messaging with more bells and whistles)
* MMS   Multimedia Messaging Service (MMS) is the ability to send messages comprising a combination of text, sounds, images and video to MMS capable handsets.
* PDAs   PDA stand for Personal Digital Assistants. Yu might recognize these better if we used names like Palm Pilot, RIM Blackberry, Handspring Visor/Treo, Sony Clie, iPaq, Pocket PC, etc. Most of these are not only personal information organizers, they can now connect to the Internet receive and send email and browse the World Wide Web.
* SPOT   Smart Personal Object Technology. It uses FM radio networks to deliver a slow but steady stream of data to devices like wristwatches and fridge magnets, sending information such as sports scores, weather reports and stock quotes, or even short text messages.

OTHER ACRONYMS:

2L8	Too late	2U2	To you too
4GM	Forgive me	AAYF	As always your friend
AFK	Away from keyboard	ASAP	As soon as possible
ASL	Age, sex, location?	B4N	Bye for now
BAC	Back at computer	BD	Big Deal
BG	Boyfriend	CYA	See ya
F2F	Face to face	FOCL	Falling off chair laughing
FY1	For your information	G2G	Got to go
GBH	Great big hug	GAS	Greetings & salutations
GF	Girlfriend	GR8	Great
H&K	Hugs & kisses	IDNDT	I did not do that
IMHO	In my humble opinion	INRS	It's not rocket science
K	OK	MYOB	Mind your own business
MMA	Meet me at…	POS	Parent over shoulder
RFC	Request for comment	SWAK	Sealed with a kiss
THX	Thanks	U2	You too
UR	Your	WH	Welcome back or write back

W8Am	Wait a minute	XOXOXO	Hugs and kisses
>U!	Screw you!	?	Huh?
?4U	Question for you	LOL	Laughing Out Loud
BRB	Be right back	MUSM	Miss you so much
A/S/L	Age, sex, location	BF	Boyfriend
TAW	Teachers are watching	SN	Screen name?
POS	Parent over shoulder	WTGP	Want to go private
143	I love you	LMIRL	Let's meet in real life
747	Let's fly	AFKI	Away from keyboard
B4N	By for now	CP	Chat post
CYO	See you online	DQMOT	Don't quote me on this
GAL	Get a life	EMA	What is your email address?
IMC	In my opinion	IANAL	I am not a lawyer, but..
IPN	I'm posting naked	KOC	Kiss on cheek
P911	My parents are coming	SAW	Siblings are watching
YBS	You'll be sorry	SNERT	Snot nosed egotistical rude teenager

EMOTICONS:

Emoticons are facial expressions made by a certain series of keystrokes. Most often producing an image of a face sideways.

#-)	Wiped out, partied all night		
#:-o	Shocked	%-(	Confused
%-6	Brain-dead	%-\	Hung over
>>:-<<	Furious	>-	Female
>:-<	Angry, Mad	:-(	Unsmiling blockhead
:-I	Indifferent, bored	(:&	Angry
*-)	Shot to death	:.(	Crying
:'-(	Shedding a tear	☹	Having a hard time
8-#	Death	: ( )	Loudmouth. Talks all the time
^5	High five	}{	Face to face
-:-(	Flame message		

APPENDIX E

RECOMMENDED RESOURCES

- National Clearinghouse on Child Abuse and Neglect Information
  Nccanch.acf.hhs.gov
  330 C. Street, SW
  Washington, DC 20447-0001   1-800-394-3366

- Federal Bureau of Investigation. Cyber Division
  Innocent Images National Initiative
  11700 Beltsville Drive
  Calverton, Maryland 20705
  www.fbi.gov

- National Center for Victims of Crime
  www.ncvc.org
  2000 M Street, NW, suite 480
  Washington, DC 20036-3307   1-800-FYI-CALL

- Childhelp USA
  www.childhelpusa.org
  15757 North 78th Street
  Scottsdale, Arizona 85260-1629   480-922-8212

- NetSmartz Workshops
  www.NetSmasrtz.org

  1-800-843-5678

  * Federal Trade Commission
    www.ftc.gov/infosecurity

- National Center for Missing & Exploited Children
  699 Prince Street
  Alexandria, Virginia 22314-3175   1-800-843-5678
  www.missingkids.com

- United States Department of Education
  www.ed.gov/technology/safety.html

- Childnet. London, United Kingdom.
  www.chatdanger.com

- Safety Publications:
- The Bernestain Bears in Cyberspace
- Child Safety on the Information Highway   800-843-5678
- Internet and Computer Ethics for Kids. Winn Schwartau. Seminole, Florida.
- A Parents' Guide to the Internet and How to Protect Your Children in Cyberspace. Pary Aftab. SC Press, Inc. New York.
- The Parents' Guide to the Information Superhighway: Rules & Tools
- Teen Safety on the Information Highway. Larry Magid.

- Other Web Sites:
  * Play it Cyber Safe   www.playitcybersafe.com
  * The Children's   www.childrenspartnership.org
    Partnership

* CyberNetiquete Comix	Disney.go.com/cybersafety/index.html
* CyberSmart!	www.cybersmart.org
* CyberTipline	www.cybertipline.com
* Federal Trade Commission	www.ftc.gov/infosecurity
* GetNetWise	www.getnetwise.com
* Internet Crimes Against Children Task Forces (ICAC)	www.icactraining.org
* Internet Content Rating Association (ICRA)	www.icra.org
* Internet Keep Safe Coalition	www.ikeepsafe.org
* SafeKids.com	www.safekids.com
* Stay Safe Online	msn.staysafeonline.com/play.html
* Surf Swell Island	Disney.go.com/surfswell/index.html
* Virtual Global Task Force	www.virtualglobaltaskforce.com
* Wiredkids.org	www.wiredkids.org

- Videos for parents and their children:
- Let's Get Real. Chasnoff and Cohen. Women's Educational Media. San Francisco. (Real interviews with real kids grades 7 to 12).
- Set Straight on Bullies. Ferguson and Stephens. Westlake Village. National School Safety Center.
- Bully Dance. Perlman and Page. Oley. Bullfrog films. (Good for students whose first language is not English.)
- Gum in my Hair. Twisted Scholar. Seattle. (For middle schoolers. Great kid music.)
- Don't Laugh at Me: Creating Ridicule Free Classroom. Yarrow and Roerden. Video and Compact Disk. Operation Respect Inc. (Complete curriculum includes guidebook and videos. Two different grade levels: 2-5 and 6-8).

Appendix F

Parent Questionaire

My child is:_____   Male   Female   Grade Level:_____

1a. In the past my child has observed other students being bullied at school.

   Agree   Unsure   Disagree

1b. In the past my child has observed others students being cyberbullied.

   Agree   Unsure   Disagree

2a. My child has reported to me that he or she has been the victim of bullying at school.

   Agree   Unsure   Disagree

2b. My child has reported to me that he or she has been the victim of cyberbullying at school.

   Agree   Unsure   Disagree

2a. My child has reported to teachers or other school staff that he or she has been the victim of bullying at school.

   Agree   Unsure   Disagree

2b. My child has reported to teachers or other school staff that he or she has been the victim of cyberbullying at school.

Agree   Unsure   Disagree

3a. My child has a clear understanding of school policies, practices and procedures related to bullying behaviors.

Agree   Unsure   Disagree

3b. My child has a clear understanding of school policies, practices, and procedures related to cyberbullying behaviors.

Agree   Unsure   Disagree

4a. As a parent, I have a clear understanding of the school's policies, practices, and procedures related to issues of harassment and bullying.

Agree   Unsure   Disagree

4b. As a parent, I have a clear understanding of the school's policies, practices, and procedures related to issues of cyberbullying at school and at home.

Agree   Unsure   Disagree

5a. As a parent, I believe the school has taken appropriate measures to reduce and/or eliminate bullying.

Agree   Unsure   Disagree

5b. As a parent, I believe the school has taken appropriate measures to reduce and/or eliminate cyberbullying.

Agree   Unsure   Disagree

6a. I have little or no anxiety about my child's safety related to bullying when sending him or her to school.

Agree   Unsure   Disagree

6b. I have little or no anxiety about my child's safety related to cyberbullying when sending him or her to school.

Agree   Unsure   Disagree

7a. I believe that the school staff has taken appropriate prevention and intervention steps related to bullying for all students.

Agree   Unsure   Disagree

7b. I believe that the school staff has taken appropriate prevention and intervention steps related to cyberbullying for all students.

Agree   Unsure   Disagree

8a. My child has stayed home at least one school day during the past 12 months due to the fear of being bullied at school.

Agree Unsure Disagree

8b. My child has stayed home at least one school day during the past 12 months because of being threatened or harassed online.

Agree Unsure Disagree

9a. My child has reported that he or she has repeatedly been called derogatory names at school.

Agree Unsure Disagree

9b. My child has reported that he or she has repeatedly been called derogatory names or was flamed on the Internet.

Agree Unsure Disagree

10a. My child has reported that he or she has been repeatedly threatened or physical hit while at school.

Agree Unsure Disagree

10b. My child has reported that he or she has been repeatedly threatened or harassed on the Internet either at school or at home.

Agree Unsure Disagree

11a. My child has reported being repeatedly humiliated by others while at school.

Agree Unsure Disagree

11b. My child has reported being repeatedly humiliated or ostracized while online which carried over into his or her school days.

Agree Unsure Disagree

My child has indicated that he or she has been bullied at school or at home in the following locations. (Circle all that apply.)

Common areas	Hallways	On the Internet at school
Restrooms	Playground	On the Internet at home
Classroom	Phys. Educ. Class	On the Internet at friends
School bus	Locker room	On his/her cell phone
Cafeteria	Extracurricular Program	Other:_____